# Fakes, Frauds
# &
# Other Malarkey

**Also by Kathryn Lindskoog**

*Creative Writing for People Who Can't Not Write*
*How To Grow a Young Reader*
*The C. S. Lewis Hoax*
*Around the Year with C. S. Lewis and His Friends*
*A Child's Garden of Christian Verses*
*The Gift of Dreams*
*Loving Touches*
*Up from Eden*
*The Lion of Judah in Never-Never Land*

# Fakes, Frauds
# &
# Other Malarkey

## 301 Amazing Stories
## &
## How Not To Be Fooled

### Kathryn Lindskoog

## Illustrations by
## Patrick Wynne

## ZondervanPublishingHouse
*Grand Rapids, Michigan*

*A Division of HarperCollinsPublishers*

Fakes, Frauds & Other Malarkey
Copyright © 1993 by Kathryn Lindskoog

Requests for information should be addressed to:
Zondervan Publishing House Grand Rapids, Michigan 49530

Library of Congress Cataloging-in-Publication-Data

Lindskoog, Kathryn Ann.
    Fakes, frauds, & other malarkey : 301 amazing stories & how not to be fooled
/ Kathryn Lindskoog.
        p.   cm.
    ISBN 0-310-57731-4
    1. Imposters and imposture. 2. Swindlers and swindling. 3. Fraud. 4. Decep-
tion. I. Title. II. Title: Fakes, frauds and other malarkey.
    HV6751.l56   1993
    364.1′63—dc20                                                    92-43941
                                                                        CIP

*Cover design by Anne Huizenga*

*Printed in the United States of America*

93 94 95 96 97 98 / ❖ DH / 10 9 8 7 6 5 4 3 2 1

*To the memory of C. S. Lewis,*
*undeceived and undeceiver*

# CONTENTS

**Acknowledgments 9**

**PART I:**
**PLAY—THE PERSISTENT URGE**

**Chapter 1 / Childhood's Surprise Delights 13**
Now You See It, Now You Don't 14
Innocent Impostures 16
Short Sheets and Tall Tales 20

**Chapter 2 / Spunky Spoofs and**
**Precocious Pranksters 27**
Jokes Practical and Impractical 28
Entertaining Possibilities 41
Truth or Consequences 50

**PART II:**
**PRETENSE—THE SKY'S THE LIMIT**

**Chapter 3 / Acceptable Rates of Inflation 57**
Cutting Corners to Make Points 58
Black and White and Read All Over 69
Forging Ahead with History 81

**Chapter 4 / Wowing an Audience 97**
Tale Spinners as Winners 98
Beguiled and Beguilers 111
Crooked Bylines 121

**PART III:**
**POWER-PLAY—**
**YOUR MONEY OR YOUR MIND**

**Chapter 5 / Flummoxed by Flim-flam Artists   143**
Delicious Deceptions   144
Winking at Hoodwinkers   159
Cheating in the School of Life   174

**Chapter 6 / Swindlers, Hoaxers,**
**Shams and Scams   187**
Steal My Wallet, Not My Heart   188
The Garden of Eden All Over Again   201
Holy Hoaxes   214

**PART IV:**
**THE SLIPPERY SLOPE—**
**FRAUD SQUADS IN ACTION**

**Chapter 7 / Doing Battle with Deception   229**
Countering Counterfeiters   230
Misconstruing the Simple Truth   239
Courting Disillusionment   248

**Chapter 8 / Damned, Duped, or Delivered?   255**
Hard-hearted Cynics Who Devalue Love   256
Soft-headed Suckers Who Devalue Truth   263
Soft-hearted, Hard-headed Lovers of Truth   268

**Hoaxer's Epilogue   275**

**Appendix:  Biblical Wisdom about Deception   279**

**Recommended Reading   283**

*The figure of Fraud came close and pulled his head and body, but not his tail, onto the ledge.*

*His face was the face of an honest man, absolutely benign in appearance; but the rest of him was a serpent.*

Dante Alighieri, *The Inferno*, Canto 17

# ACKNOWLEDGMENTS

I owe immense thanks to my friend Ranelda Hunsicker, whose words, ideas, and research helped to make this book possible. Special thanks also to Don and Sharon Cregier, who have repeatedly sent books and articles from their home in Prince Edward Island. Thanks to George Gorniak, who sent a book and articles from England. Thanks to my husband, John, and other friends and relatives who contributed material, both intentionally and unintentionally. And thanks to Patrick Wynne, my illustrator, who always sees what I mean.

Thanks also to the many authors whose works of all kinds have enriched my understanding of the nature and scope of deception. My chance purchase in about 1985 of Curtis D. McDougall's wonderful old book *Hoaxes* was my first windfall. Other favorites are *The Pleasures of Deception* by Norman Moss. *People of the Lie* by M. Scott Peck . . . *The Scholar Adventurers* by Richard D. Altick . . . *The Hermit of Peking* by Hugh Trevor-Roper . . . *How to Lie with Statistics* by Darrell Huff . . . *One Fairy Story Too Many* by John Ellis . . . *A Gathering of Saints* by Robert Lindsey. . . . I can only urge readers to browse in the annotated list at the back of this book.

Finally, I thank my editor, Bob Hudson, who has provided a wealth of materials, enthusiasm, and scholarly support. I wish that all authors could be blessed with such an editor.

—Kathryn Lindskoog

# PART I:
## PLAY—THE PERSISTENT URGE

# CHAPTER 1
# CHILDHOOD'S SURPRISE DELIGHTS

*Illusion is the first of all pleasures.*

—Voltaire

Childhood is a time of delicious delusion, when the boundaries between appearance, reality, and make-believe aren't always clear. Memory takes a quick romp through the world of peekaboo and pretend, tooth fairies and tall tales. All our roots are there. The fruits that come later, of course, may be either good or evil.

# NOW YOU SEE IT, NOW YOU DON'T

*The child, whose credulous first hours burn at the heart of living . . .*

—David McCord

A baby is born believing. The hazy new world appears and disappears and appears again, over and over. Faces come and go, warm milk comes and goes, great hands come and go and come again. We all bobbed along for weeks on an ocean of shifting comforts and hurts, lights and shadows. Warm and cool, wet and dry, full and empty. A baby believes without reservation the felt facts of the moment.

Gradually we started noticing details, and then we got curious. We discovered the pleasure of exploration and surprise, and some of our surprises became wonderful games. One of the earliest of these games was shaking the rattle. The wonder of cause-and-effect gradually grew in our brains. We were busy taking in the world, learning enough so that we could start to be taken in by the world's illusions, for good and for ill. The more we know, the more ways we can be fooled.

Peekaboo is the first and sweetest game of trickery. It is an early form of hide-and-seek. A big person ceases to exist, then magically bursts forth again, exclaiming, "Peekaboo!" The effect is stunning to babies, who never tire of this wonderful trick. Eventually they are apt to figure out how to work it themselves by hiding their faces. Later, they make toys disappear a million times by dropping them on the floor and demanding them back again.

A favorite peekaboo trick for toddlers is the nose-stealing game. Grandpa pulls off the little nose with a light tweak, shows the toddler the tip of his thumb projecting between the second and third finger of his fist, then puts the nose back on again. "Do it again!" the toddler usually insists, relishing the drama and its happy ending. We are born believing, and we love to learn about disbelief in these happy ways.

Playful deception sharpens perception. Children gradually get wiser. "Simon says," the childhood trickery game, increases alertness. The leader calls out an order to each player in turn, such as "Simon says, 'Take four giant steps forward,'" "Simon says, 'Take ten baby steps forward,'" or "Take three scissor steps forward." The trick is that it's against the rules to take any steps at all unless the leader begins with "Simon says," and the leader slyly leaves it out much of the time. The young players have to learn to be on guard, which isn't always easy—as countless adult investors realize, after losing all their savings.

Most people love to let their guard down, whether they realize it or not, for that is part of being a healthy human. Hearts are made to trust with, as lovers know. But crooks know it also. When trust gets mushy, it turns into gullibility. Eve found that out early on, the hard way. (Genesis 3 tells how Eve, the first woman, trusted the cunning serpent in the Garden of Eden and thus brought sin and death to the human race.)

Eve's children no doubt played "Let's pretend," because children have never had a better game. Pretending, like trusting, is exactly what young children should do. But this gift of creative make-believe can turn into lying. The purpose of make-believe is to teach and delight, but the purpose of a lie is to deceive.

Everything human is apt to go awry, including creative make-believe. That's the human condition, ever since Eve's big mistake.

# INNOCENT IMPOSTURES

*A little credulity helps one along through life very smoothly.*
—Elizabeth Gaskell

Is there always an "ill" in "illusion"? Perhaps some illusions are good because they make life healthier and happier.

Gift-givers are often benevolently tricky, resorting to elaborate schemes to conceal their plans and stash away secrets. Gifts can be wrapped in ways that disguise the contents, and the element of surprise is sometimes enjoyed more than the gift itself. The tricked and the trickster enjoy the final culmination of the trick together, which is the easiest way to tell that a trick was a good idea.

Deception adds zest to benevolence. It is such fun to try to do good without getting caught that certain organizations capitalize on this and institutionalize it. They assign everyone a temporary "secret pal" to mystify with friendly gifts and messages.

There is another kind of kindhearted deception. Most people believe in protecting the very young and the very old from too much bad news. All good parents want to provide a sense of security for their little children. During the Second World War, Norman Rockwell painted a picture of a weary father holding a newspaper with terrible headlines, looking tenderly at his two children nestled snugly in bed. He withholds frightening information from them and pretends for their sake that the world is better and safer than it really is. (Children often return the favor as they grow up, and pretend for their parents that their behavior away from home is better and safer than it really is.)

Parents tend to "kiss a hurt to make it well," knowing that this tried-and-true folk medicine will probably ease the pain, or at least the crying. That kind of kiss is a bit like the magic feather that Walt Disney gave to Dumbo the baby elephant, enabling him to fly so long as he thought it would work. There is benevolent deception in magic feathers, sugar-pill therapy, and, as in the following story, stone-soup nutrition.

According to the old story, a hungry traveler convinced a stingy but gullible woman that he could make them a pot of soup from nothing but his magic stone. As the water boiled in her pot, he suggested that a bone would make the soup heartier, and so she found a soup bone for him. Later he mentioned that an onion and some seasoning would improve the soup's bland flavor, although it wasn't needed. She grudgingly agreed. A carrot and a potato would add to the texture, he said, and she produced them both. Then they both enjoyed their magic soup. There is nothing more practical than stone-soup pragmatism. The magic ingredient in many endeavors is expectation aroused by marvelous claims.

### Holiday Hocus-Pocus

Our culture furnishes children with many special-occasion fables and fantasies with marvelous claims. Every year many children blow out the candles on a birthday cake and make a wish, assured that it is supposed to come true. If they have access to pennies and wishing wells, they make wishes there. And if they are lucky enough to know traditional rhymes, they chant to the first evening star:

> *Star light, star bright,*
> *First star I see tonight—*
> *Wish I may, wish I might*
> *Have the wish I wish tonight.*

Although some parents disapprove of the deception, every year in many homes with young children, Santa Claus brings gifts, the Easter bunny brings baskets of candy eggs, and the tooth fairy brings coins. In a few families the stork brings a new baby, Jack Frost brings winter ice, and the Great Pumpkin of Peanuts fame brings Halloween excitement.

With or without the Great Pumpkin, and with or without full approval, Halloween is the great American festival of pranks, pretending, and nostalgia. At Halloween time in 1990, ninety-two-year-old George Osterman went to a celebration of the one-hundredth birthday of the tiny El Toro Grammar School he had attended as a child. Now the school was refurbished and set in a historical park.

17

Osterman cast his mind back eighty years and said, "I remember around Halloween when we found a wagon on top of the school." He pointed to the roof. "[The wagon] was completely assembled. Somebody took it apart and built it back up top." The sense of wonder inspired by that magnificent stunt had lasted a long lifetime.

At the 1990 celebration, Cub Scouts and Brownies wore bonnets and kerchiefs and answered to names of students who attended the school almost a century ago—names like Obie Pettit, Gertrude Pesterfield, and Ella Scott. Today's children sat at old-fashioned desks and pretended to be doing lessons on slates with chalk. No doubt the real Obie Pettit, Gertrude Pesterfield, and Ella Scott had also sat there at times imagining that they were someone else. Some things never change.

One year a very little girl named Jennifer had a splendid time trick-or-treating. When she awakened early the next morning, that's all she could think of. So she dressed up in her disguise again, located her sack, slipped out the door, and started back around the neighborhood ringing doorbells to rouse the neighbors, announcing "Trick or treat!"

My son Jon did the opposite as a preschooler. Every year he would put on his tiger costume with his grandmother's help and go around to her neighbors on the day before Halloween, announcing "Treat or trick!" and giving each neighbor a chocolate cupcake with a candy pumpkin on top. He loved to fool them by doing it early and backwards that way. During the rest of the year, Jon often pretended that he was a Boy Scout and I was a roaring tiger that pounced on him at his camp in my bedroom. Without fail, his giggling would turn to panic and he would cry out for me to be a lady again.

### Getting Carried Away

In or out of Halloween, children tend to get carried away by pretending. My son Peter loved to pretend that he was a cook. One day he mixed samples of several ingredients from my cupboard in a glass measuring cup: vinegar, flour, pepper, salt, sugar, Tabasco sauce, baking soda, and paprika. It foamed a little. "Ah!" he announced triumphantly, holding it aloft, "this is delicious!" And before he realized what he was doing, he took a huge swig of it. His face turned red and his eyes watered. "It isn't delicious," he whispered hoarsely.

It's not surprising that young children become briefly confused about what's what; there are adults on the loose who believe that soap opera characters are real. Worse yet, there are adults who spend their lives pretending to be someone they are not. (Read about imposters in Chapter 4.)

One day a preschooler named Greg disappeared in a large Santa Ana department store and couldn't be found. I knew his mother. After searching in vain, she recruited store personnel to help. They mounted an alert and repeatedly announced over the loudspeaker that a three-year-old boy named Greg was lost and should be brought to the office. They sometimes added a request for the parents of another boy named Steve to come to the office to pick him up. After half an hour, Greg's mother was beside herself with fear. She went to the office to make a telephone call, and there was Greg, perched on a chair and perfectly happy. "I'm named Steve today," he explained.

At times like that, frazzled parents resort to threats, both realistic and fantastic. Some families invoke various bogeymen all year to encourage good behavior, and some storytellers invoke them for pleasure. James Whitcomb Riley invented the original Orphan Annie, a household helper who delighted children with scary stories after supper. Here is one of the beloved stories in today's English:

*And one time a little girl would always laugh and grin*
*And make fun of everyone, her relatives and kin;*
*And once when there was company, and old folks were there,*
*She mocked them and she shocked them and she said she didn't care!*
*And as she kicked her heels, and turned to run and hide,*
*There were two big Black Things a-standing by her side.*
*They snatched her through the ceiling 'fore she knew what she's about!*
*And the Goblins will get you*
   *If you*
     *Don't*
       *Watch*
         *Out!*

**19**

# SHORT SHEETS AND TALL TALES

*Jest, and youthful jollity.*

—John Milton

Most people like to flirt with fake fear; that is why Steven King novels sell by the millions. The favorite horror hoax of children takes place in a dark room where a trusted storyteller coaxes them into handling vile materials: they touch a tangle of worms, hold two eyeballs, and dip their fingers into a bowl of fresh blood. When the lights go on, the worms were spaghetti, the eyeballs were grapes, and the blood was warm water. Imagination did the rest.

The best day for people of any age to trick and be tricked is April Fool's Day, when we celebrate being bamboozled by harmless hoaxes. As Mark Twain said, "April 1 is the day on which we are reminded of what we are on the other 364."

## Formal April Fooling

In March 1860, many of the most important people in London received formal invitations that read, "Tower of London. Admit Bearer and Friend to view the annual Ceremony of Washing the White Lions on Sunday, April 1. Admittance Only at White Gate." Many carriages arrived, but there is no White Gate at the Tower of London, and there has never been a Ceremony of Washing of White Lions.

Over a century later, on April 1, 1966, BBC television's well-known commentator Richard Dimbleby presented a documentary about spaghetti farming on the Swiss-Italian border. British viewers watched Swiss farmers pulling strands of spaghetti out of the trees and laying them out to dry in the sun. Dimbleby explained that it took many years of patient labor for plant breeders to produce perfectly uniform spaghetti, all the same length. Another improvement has been elimination of the spaghetti weevil. Dimbleby concluded, "brought from garden to table at the very peak of condition . . . there's nothing like real, home-grown spaghetti."

Four years later, on the Huntley-Brinkley program on NBC, John Chancellor reported on the 1970 pickle crop, featuring a fine dill pickle tree at a place called the Dimbleby Pickle Farm. One year after that, a doctor on BBC Radio warned that people with red hair can catch Dutch Elm Disease.

In 1985 George Plimpton published an article in the April 1 issue of *Sports Illustrated* about a phenomenal new baseball player trying out for the New York Mets. "Sidd" (Siddhartha) Finch was a young Englishman who had studied mind control in a Tibetan monastery and developed the ability to throw a baseball 168 miles per hour with perfect accuracy. Sidd had attended Harvard briefly, played the French horn, and pitched with one foot bare for balance.

Plimpton's opening lines were, "He's a pitcher, part yogi and part recluse. Impressively liberated from our opulent lifestyle, Sidd's deciding about yoga—and his future in baseball." Readers who checked the first letters of these words found this hidden message: "Happy April Fool's Day: ah, fib." Nearly two thousand readers wrote in about the joke, many of them delighted to have been tricked. But about forty were so upset that they wrote in to cancel their subscriptions.

On April 1 in 1990, England's *News of the World* announced a $14 billion blunder: The French and English halves of the tunnel under the English Channel would not meet in the middle after all. According to the story, the French had used the metric system and the British had not, and so the two halves were going to miss each other by fourteen feet. There should be a journalism award for the most successful public April Fool spoof every decade.

## Family April Foolery

Private family jokes tend to be cherished year after year, generation after generation. On the morning of April 1, 1901, a certain Magnolia Le Guin wrote in her diary, "I'm suffering with neuralgia and baby is cross—teething—but if I can I want to make some cotton biscuits and some kind of a pie (an April fool pie) to have outside covered with wheat-dough, and cook them, to fool Askew, Fred and some of the rest of the family . . . I went to Jackson last Friday and had 8 or 9 teeth pulled by Dr. Cantrell, so since then I am not well. One broken . . ." She was sick, but not too sick for April Foolery.

21

Magnolia's cotton biscuits almost surely had a big wad of cotton in the middle. Some mothers cook a pancake with a circle of cloth hidden inside. There is an easy recipe for fake poached egg on toast that makes a perfect April Fool breakfast. The cook must toast slices of ordinary pound cake instead of bread; the cake stays intact and looks much like real toast. On each piece of toast the cook spreads a circle of whipped cream the size of a poached egg. In the center of the white, the cook places a canned apricot half, cut side down. The result is extremely convincing on the breakfast table, and amazed families usually gobble it down happily because it tastes good.

No one knows what Magnolia Le Guin baked in her playful pie, but April 1 is an ideal day for mock apple pie. To make it, the cook spreads 56 soda cracker squares in a large pie pan; brings to a boil $1\frac{1}{2}$ cups water, $1\frac{1}{2}$ cups sugar, juice of a half lemon, and 1 teaspoon cream of tartar; then pours the hot liquid over the crackers and sprinkles a little cinnamon on top. The slushy "pie" is baked in the oven at 450 degrees for 20 minutes, and is best served á la mode. It passes for a so-so (not excellent) real fruit pie, crust and all.

One of the most traditional April Fool's tricks is for a child to tie a strong thread around a billfold and place it where people walk, then to hide nearby with the thread in hand; when someone reaches to pick up the billfold, it whisks away. Another favorite old trick is calling a friend or relative on the phone and urging her to rush outside to see some nonexistent weather or a marvel in the sky.

A new twist on an old trick involves a new do-it-yourself test for household radon gas. The trickster stands on a stepladder and holds a plastic bowl with some water in it up against the ceiling. Then he mentions that he can finish the test faster with just a little help. He gets his victim to stand close and lift up a broom or a tennis racket handle, with which he gently presses the bowl against the ceiling. Then he climbs down and removes the ladder, leaving the victim stranded with a bowl of water over his head. "April Fool!"

## Shenanigans

Short-sheeting is a classic shenanigan all year long. The victim's bed is opened and remade, with the bottom sheet folded back up to serve also as the top sheet. When the victim clambers in, there is no space for his legs. In another bedtime trick, the victim's pajama legs are basted shut at the bottom so his feet can't get through. In all these tricks the victim is bewildered, to the immense delight of observers.

There used to be a category of home entertainment called parlor tricks. Some require props and others don't. For example, two people can demonstrate fake mind-reading talent. One of them is sent away while the group chooses a number between one and ten, and then she comes back in and tries to read the mind of her partner who knows the number. She stands behind him with her fingers on his temples and concentrates. In fact, the partner carefully clenches his jaws the correct number of times, and she can count the clenchings.

With the aid of a calculator, math magic is easy. Tell someone that you can find out his house number and age without his telling you what they are. Hand him a calculator and ask him to enter his house number and double it. Then have him add 5. Then have him multiply by 50. Then have him add his age. The total at this point will be an apparently meaningless number, as he can see. Now have him hand you the calculator, and you subtract 250 from whatever his total was. On the calculator you will see his house number followed by his age.

Next, tell someone that if he will choose any number from one to nine, you can not only guess what number he chose, but you can get the calculator to show you one hundred and eleven thousand, one hundred and eleven times his secret number. To do this, simply enter 15,873 on the calculator, then have him multiply it by his secret number. Say "Many people choose 7 because it is a favorite number," and ask him to multiply his answer by 7. Then look at the calculator. The new answer will be his original number six times is a row. (If his secret number was 4, your answer will be 444,444.)

There is a variation of the last calculator trick which is good for confusing people. Inform your friend that your calculator is trained to tell you six times in a row whatever number someone else has used for multiplying. To demonstrate, type as if at random 37,037. Then have your friend multiply that by any single number without telling you what it was. Next, have him multiply that total by 3. The calculator will state six times in a row whatever number your friend used. (If your friend used 8, the calculator will show 888,888.)

There is a wonderful old-fashioned addition trick that can be done without a calculator. The trickster claims that he can predict in advance the answer to a large addition problem in which someone else will make up half the five-digit numbers. The trickster writes down his prediction, folds it, and gives it to a witness. First the other person writes out on a piece of paper any five-digit number, such as 10,386. Under that the trickster writes a five-digit number. They repeat this three times each, and when they add up these numbers the total will be what the trickster predicted—299,997. (The trick is, whatever numbers the other person wrote down, the trickster always puts below each digit the number that would total nine, so that each pair of numbers equals 99,999, and three times 99,999 is 299,997.)

### Assorted Nincompoopery

Photo opportunities are also opportunities for trickery. The cheapest way to take lots of pictures at a social event is to have no film in the camera. (One filmless high school boy used to spend hours snapping photos at cheerleading practice and chatting with the girls, thus winning enviable dates.) Boys sometimes hold two fingers up behind the head of a person who is smiling into the camera. Another favorite boys' prank is appearing twice in one photo: when a camera pans slowly from one side of a group to the other for a formal photo, they pose on the first side; then they run like lightning around to the other side and end up on both sides of the picture, as if they were twins.

It is easy to take Polaroid portraits of two or more people with the same plain background, then cut all the pictures in half under the eyes and switch halves. The effect is stranger than a fun-house mirror, an uncanny distortion of reality.

One can create a trick movie of ordinary people by having them walk around backward before the camera. When the film is ready, it must be run backward so the people are seen walking forward. They will then be walking with puzzling posture and odd coordination. They can't walk forward that way in real life if they try, yet they do it on the screen.

At a beach, with or without a camera, one can pack a pair of jeans full of damp sand and stand them up with the legs in the air and a pair of shoes on top, soles skyward. This creates the appearance of someone standing upside-down in the sand. If there are two or three upside-down people together, wearing different sizes of jeans and shoes, so much the better.

## CHILDHOOD'S SURPRISE DELIGHTS

What is the sense of all this nincompoopery? It is born of the human need to play, and our love of surprises and mystification.

One afternoon recently my eighty-eight-year-old mother was walking home from a neighbor's house and noticed several young Mexican children playing blind man's bluff on the lawn next door. They didn't know much English, and she didn't know any Spanish, but this was no time for words anyway. She motioned for them to keep quiet, tip-toed into their midst, and knelt down near the blind-folded girl who was groping for her friends.

The girl came to my mother, felt her hair and shoulders, and tried to guess which of her playmates this could be. "No!" her friends squealed every time she guessed wrong. At last she gave up in bewilderment, took off her blindfold, and beheld a white-haired stranger. "Surprise!" my mother exclaimed in English, hauled herself up, and trotted on home immensely satisfied. Playing tricks is all in a day's work for people who are children at heart.

*The greatest pleasure I know is to do a good action by stealth,*
*and have it found out by accident.*

—Charles Lamb

# CHAPTER 2
# SPUNKY SPOOFS AND
# PRECOCIOUS PRANKSTERS

*Half the work that is done in this world is to make things appear what they are not.*

—E. R. Beadle

Playful deception spans childhood and the adult world as practical jokes, magic tricks, and other harmless spoofery. Vast quantities of human energy are invested in this happy flummadiddle. But sometimes play turns painful.

# JOKES PRACTICAL AND IMPRACTICAL

*The little foolery that wise men have makes a great show.*

—William Shakespeare

Few practical jokes are practical, but according to Lynchburg history professor Sheldon Vanauken, the Battle of Lynchburg, Virginia, was an exception. In June 1864, General David Hunter approached Lynchburg with plenty of Union troops and settled in for the night just west of the city. He fully expected to capture Lynchburg the next day from Confederate General Jubal Early and his too-few soldiers.

That night General Early ordered a switch engine and a few empty railroad cars to glide slowly out of the city, wait quietly, and then steam back at great speed with whistles blowing. A cheering crowd of Lynchburg citizens and soldiers greeted the empty train at the station, and a band played loud military music. Later, the scenario was repeated. According to one of General Hunter's officers, trains were heard coming and going all night, obviously bringing in huge numbers of fresh Confederate troops to defend the city.

General Early's troops skirmished confidently the next day; and because the city was full of their unseen reinforcements, General Hunter did not risk the major assault he had envisioned. He soon decided to retreat, and Lynchburg was saved by one of history's most simple and successful deceptions.

## Keeping People in the Dark

Unlike military subterfuge, the purpose of impractical practical jokes and magic tricks is simply to fool, surprise, and puzzle people. (At their worst they hurt people, and at their best they delight people.) Most of us have the urge to pull a silly prank sooner or later, and some of us indulge that urge frequently. What the prankster creates is unusual predicaments and confusion.

One night the friends of a Mr. O'Brien in London boarded up the outside of his bedroom window and recruited his servant to help with

28

the joke. When he rang for his servant in the morning, O'Brien was assured it was still night. (This was before people had bedroom clocks.) When he eventually opened the shutters, there was still no glimmer of light outside. He was finally driven out of his bedroom by sheer hunger, and learned that he had spent most of the day in bed.

It seems that for centuries victims of practical jokers have been walking around with notes on their backs that say "Kick me." They have been sent on wild goose chases to stores to buy everything from left-handed monkey wrenches to black whitewash, bottle-stretchers, striped ink, or bumble-bee feathers. Best of all, they have been taken on snipe hunts.

Snipe hunts exploit our sense of nighttime adventure, love of cuddly creatures, and gullibility. Snipe veterans excite snipe novices with elaborate descriptions of the furry little snipes that are quickly and easily captured at night. The group goes out to a dark but safe area like an orchard, and the hunt begins. The newcomers wait in a circle with flashlights and open sacks while the old timers go to flush out some snipes and chase them into the circle. In fact, the old timers tiptoe back to the car or the cabin to relax. They eventually burst into the snipeless circle and announce, "Now you've been on a snipe hunt!" This initiation has been going on for generations.

In the region of Reading, Pennsylvania, people traditionally hunt for eldedritches instead of snipes. Each novice is loaned an "eldedritch whistle," an "eldedritch bag," and an "eldedritch light." The whistle must be tooted frequently to lure the eldedritches to the circle, and the light must shine on the open end of the bag to guide the eldedritch in. One eldedritch hunt has been remembered for over fifty years around East Reading. It was a dark, foggy night when three tricksters took a couple of their buddies ten miles into the country. It turned out that the two tooting the whistles were really tricking their tricksters and managed to beat them back to the truck and drive home without them. The tricksters had to hike all the way back.

Ironically, once people know about snipe hunts, they tend to disbelieve in grunion hunts, which take place on certain nights at certain sea shores, with flashlights and sacks. Grunion hunts are real.

In the summer of 1990 engineer Colin Andrews directed a night watch called "Operation Blackbird" at the Vale of Peusy in Wiltshire in southern England, with engineers from four nations, BBC backing, and $1.8 million worth of special equipment. He and Patrick Delgado were riding high as experts on the mystery of the rings and circles that sometimes flatten grain. ("Crop circles" were recorded as far back as 1678 in England, and have been attributed at times to whirlwinds, magnetism, microbes, fairies, and spaceships.) On July 25 the engineers announced triumphantly that new designs had appeared overnight: "This is the breakthrough we have been waiting for. The circles formed by this phenomenon are the most beautiful and spectacular we have ever seen." A few hours later they admitted that they had been hoaxed by unknown pranksters in this one case.

In September 1991 two men named Doug Bower and David Chorley made a new crop circle for the tabloid *Today*. Circle expert Delgado was lured into declaring publicly that this one couldn't possibly be manmade; then he was informed of its origin. "I was taken for a ride like many other people," he admitted. Bower and Chorley said that they had been making dozens of circles in English fields since 1978 and were amazed at public gullibility. They made another to demonstrate for British television after their confession, but the desperately embarrassed Delgado protested that this one was "totally different from the real thing. This is a hoax, and it's easy for us to see that it is a hoax." His crop-circle career seemed to be fading fast.

### Sowing Confusion

Tall tales about nature have always abounded. On the rainy first day of spring in 1983, a man who called himself "Robert Parker of the Weather Service" called forty radio and television stations and newspapers to report that the National Weather Service had issued a New York area "typhoon watch." The news went out; but in fact there was no storm, and typhoons exist only in the Pacific Ocean.

In the late 1700s the British scholar and forger George Steevens was probably responsible for an article in the *London Magazine* about the poison tree in Java. "The effluvia of this noxious tree, which through a district of twelve or fourteen miles had killed all vegetation, and had spread the skeletons of men and animals, affording a scene of melancholy beyond what poets have described . . ." This fake report was supposedly from a certain Dutch travel writer. (Steevens was such a notorious liar that someone suggested, "Suppose we believe one half of what he tells us." Samuel Johnson replied, "Ay, but we don't know which half to believe.")

On one of the main trails in Georgia long ago someone painted on a large rock "Turn Me Over." When travelers struggled enough to do so, they found the words, "Now turn me back that I may fool another." The place got the name Talking Rock.

In about 1800 the fun-loving clergyman Sydney Smith once fastened oranges onto the shrubs along the driveway at his country estate in England. He also fastened antlers onto a couple of his donkeys to please a guest who said she wished he had some deer.

When famous nature artist James Audubon was visited by a French naturalist named Raffinesque in Kentucky in 1818, he told him all about the Devil Jack Diamond-Fish in the Ohio River, which grew to ten feet long and had stony, bullet-proof scales that were diamond-shaped. Raffinesque not only went for the story hook, line, and sinker, but he reported to his readers that he had seen Devil Jack Diamond-Fish for himself. This claim did not enhance his scientific reputation.

Next, Brian G. Hughes announced that he was sponsoring the great South American Reetsa Expedition, and his reports about that rare tropical beast were published in New York newspapers for months. This rather unpleasant box-manufacturer liked to spend his excess time and money on jokes. When a Reetsa was finally captured and brought to New York, thousands met the ship to see Hughes lead it ashore. It was an ordinary steer (Reetsa spelled backwards.)

One of Hughes' favorite tricks was going to a bar on a rainy day and leaving his good umbrella hanging near the door. Then he would sit in a corner and wait until someone made off with it. He would rush after the man in time to see him open it, causing a big sign on the umbrella to proclaim "This umbrella stolen from Brian G. Hughes."

One night Hughes left a kit of burglar tools and several empty picture frames on the steps of the Metropolitan Museum of Art. The next morning, staff members rushed about inside trying to find the location and identity of the stolen paintings.

Lavina Queen, a popular actress in those days, was summoned to the Waldorf-Astoria to receive an honor from the Prince of Amsdam, Cyprus, and Aragon. In a large room thick with incense, she was seated on a kind of throne, surrounded by her friends and the royal retinue. The dark, bearded prince, elegant in robe and jewels, brought her a golden star and a parchment on a velvet pillow. Speaking no English, he read the parchment in a strange language and pinned the star upon her breast, making her a Princess of the Order of St.

Catherine of Mount Sinai. Later she learned that the Prince was Brian Hughes in disguise. She scraped the gilt off the star of the Order of St. Catherine of Mount Sinai and discovered that it was an old Jersey City police badge.

## Artificial Aristocrats

The Prince of Amsdam, Cyprus, and Aragon was just one in a long line of aristocrats who were really imposters.

When the Sultan of Zanzibar was visiting London, Cambridge officials received notice that he wanted to visit them for a day. He and his elegantly robed retinue arrived by train, and dignitaries gave them a champagne reception and a tour of Cambridge. In fact, the men from Zanzibar were Horace de Vere Cole and other Cambridge students in makeup and rented costumes, and the real Sultan was still in London. The Cambridge officials were completely fooled.

Horace de Vere Cole was a wealthy dilettante who specialized in jokes. In 1910 he organized some London friends to play a trick on the British Royal Navy. Virginia Woolf and three men were disguised (in dark makeup, false beards, and rented costumes) as the Ethiopian emperor and three princes. Virginia's brother Adrian Stephen played the part of a German translator, and Horace Cole played the part of their escort from Britain's Foreign Office.

The bizarre group boarded a train at Paddington station, saying "chuck-a-choi" and demanding formal reception from the station-master there. A telegram to the admiral at Weymouth produced the attention they hoped for. They were welcomed with a (literal) red carpet, and a naval officer in full ceremonial garb escorted them in a special car to the harbor, where a launch bore them to the Dreadnaught to meet Home Fleet Admiral Sir William May. They inspected a marine guard and enjoyed a tour of the ship, during which they loudly exclaimed "bunga, bunga" in response to everything they looked at, including the light bulbs.

On the train back to London, Cole informed railroad personnel that the royal guests could be served food only by people wearing white kid gloves, and so at Reading a worker rushed out to buy gloves for the waiters. Cole eventually provided the full story and a photo to the press, keeping the names of the hoaxers secret as long as possible. The Navy was not amused, but the public was. For a time the popular exclamation used to express delight or surprise in England was "bunga, bunga," and Cole was dubbed "the prince of practical jokers."

The American imposter Stanley Weyman copied Cole's Dreadnaught hoax in 1915. He identified himself to the U.S. Navy as the Romanian consul-general and said that the Queen of Romania wanted him to pay his respects. Wearing a light-blue uniform with gold braid, he was taken in a launch to tour the *Wyoming,* which flew the Romanian flag in his honor. He inspected the guard of honor, was entertained by the officers, and invited them to a private dinner at the Hotel Astor, courtesy of the Romanian consulate. A detective happened to recognize Weyman's name on a Hotel Astor press release, and as a known imposter Weyman was arrested in the middle of his expensive dinner with the Navy officers. (That did not stop him. During his period as the State Department's bogus chief of protocol, he had his photo taken at the White House with Princess Fatima of Afghanistan and President Warren Harding. During another period he was personal physician to movie star Paula Negri.)

In 1947 the Crown Prince of Saudi Arabia was visiting Hollywood with his retinue. Practical joker Jim Moran studied the Prince and his group, then recruited three actors to help. On the evening when the real prince was departing, Moran made a reservation at Ciro's and arrived in costume and a limousine. In the course of the evening, while every eye was on him, he emptied a pouch of jewels on his table and sent what looked like a magnificent diamond over to the band leader. (It was really a superb amethyst which had cost him $30.) Later, as he walked across the empty dance floor on his way out the door, the Prince dropped his pouch, and jewels went bouncing in all directions. Barely pausing, the Prince impatiently signaled his companions to leave it all behind, and out they went. In an instant, some of the biggest names in Hollywood were scrambling on the floor to get at the jewels, which were all colored glass from the dime store.

### Sheer Silliness

When Moran drove alone cross country, he liked to break the boredom with a rubber face mask that looked like a grinning idiot. He wore it on the back of his head, and when people pulled close to pass him, he leaned his head out the window so that the idiot face grinned backward at them. That no doubt broke their boredom also. (It is said that in India Bengal tigers attack people from behind, and so the government issued face masks for people to wear on the back of their heads—which fooled the tigers and saved many lives.)

Dignity is the favorite target of pranksters. Horace de Vere Cole once attended the elaborate church wedding of a close friend of his and behaved himself perfectly. When the bride and groom stood on the church steps afterward, a gorgeous young woman screamed, ran to the groom, and embraced him—crying loudly for him to always remember their years together. She added that she would be waiting if he ever wanted to come back, then she fled. (She was, of course, an actress hired by Cole.)

The elegant St. Thomas Church on Fifth Avenue in New York has a couple of cynical details slipped anonymously into the carved decorations to mock the monied congregation. Over the bride's door there is a delicate dollar sign, and above the choir area there are three moneybags marked "J.P.M." (for millionaire J. Pierpont Morgan).

Somewhere in the Midwest there is a teetotaling Baptist church with the following verse inscribed on the cornerstone:

*When all the temple is prepared within,*
*Why nods the drowsy worshiper outside?*

These seemingly innocent lines from *The Rubaiyat of Omar Khayyam* refer to the joys of drinking wine in a tavern in the morning. How did such a motto find its way onto a Baptist church? A college literature student was courting a young woman in that church, and when he was asked to provide a good literary inscription for the cornerstone he made the most of his opportunity. The romance soon fell through, but thirty years later an aging California professor of literature was still enjoying his little joke. He told about it when I was his student.

Pranksters are sometimes inspired by people's reverential awe for British royalty. In 1953 Queen Elizabeth and Prince Philip accepted an invitation to dine with Mr. and Mrs. Douglas Fairbanks at their London home. On the big day, "the power company" called Fairbanks to announce that the electricity would go off in his house that evening while new cables were being laid in the neighborhood. He believed it and went into such a panic that he had to call a doctor.

The mischievous brother-in-law of Prime Minister Neville Chamberlain once noticed a crew of workmen with shovels and drills waiting for directions in the heart of London. No one knew who he was, but he looked and sounded impressive. He pretended to be in charge, ordered the work crew to follow him, recruited policemen to keep the crowds moving, and supervised the excavation of a chunk of Piccadilly. The next day mystified London authorities had to assign workers to get the hole filled and the pavement repaired.

## Famous Lives

Jokes endure when they are played on or by famous people. Benjamin Franklin entered an inn where a gang of men wouldn't make room for him by the fireplace. He ordered a large quantity of oysters and insisted that the landlord feed them to his horse. Everyone trooped out to the stable to see a horse eat oysters, then trooped back in again to report that the horse wouldn't eat them. Now Franklin had a seat by the fire and said he would eat the oysters himself.

Thomas Edison bragged about getting by with hardly any sleep, but in fact he often dozed off. Once he dozed off at the beginning of a meal with his workers, and they replaced the food on his plate with a few crumbs, as if he had eaten. When he awakened he saw that he had finished his meal and eagerly went back to work.

Franklin D. Roosevelt liked jokes, and he decided to test the claim that in reception lines no one listens to what anyone says. At a large White House party, he smiled and shook hands with every guest while murmuring, "I murdered my grandmother this morning." If the story is true, no one noticed what he said except one Wall Street banker who answered politely, "She certainly had it coming."

Lord Halifax, past British Ambassador to the United States, reportedly found himself traveling in a railroad compartment with two overly prim ladies. When the train plunged into the darkness of a tunnel, Lord Halifax noisily kissed his hand a few times. When the train pulled into his station later he arose to leave and said graciously, "To which of you charming ladies am I indebted for the delightful incident in the tunnel?" Then he left them there staring at each other.

Writers seem to be especially attracted to practical jokes. When Mark Twain and a friend were touring Italy, they entertained themselves by flummoxing unwanted tour guides. For example, when a guide showed them a letter in the handwriting of Christopher Columbus, they peered at it and asked who Mr. Columbus was. They said that they had just come from America, and they heard nothing about his discovering it. Was he dead? What did he die of? Were his parents living? "I have seen boys in America only fourteen years old that could write better than that."

Eugene Field was the editor of the *Denver Tribune* in the 1880s, when flamboyant British writer Oscar Wilde was touring the United States. Mr. Wilde was coming to Denver to lecture, and so Field gave out the wrong time for Wilde's arrival at the train depot and impersonated him there. Field wore golden curls and a monocle, with velvet knee-britches and silk stockings. He lolled effeminately on a cushion, smelling a sunflower and outraging the crowd. When the real Oscar Wilde arrived later, the excitement was over and he was practically ignored.

Once after writers James Whitcomb Riley and Bill Nye got on a train together, Nye announced with alarm that he only had one ticket for them instead of two. He urged Riley to crouch on the floor under a suitcase to hide from the conductor, who was coming to punch tickets. Then Nye handed the conductor two tickets, pointed to his friend on the floor, and explained, "He always travels that way."

A group of American writers used to meet for lunch at New York's Algonquin Hotel, and one of them, John Peter Toohey, often complained about the high prices there. One day the others had a special Algonquin menu printed for him with truly astronomical prices. Toohey took one look at the fake menu, threw it on the floor, and stomped out in a rage. Later he learned that he had been codswalloped. Another member of that circle was Alexander Woollcott. When one of his friends listed Woollcott as a reference for leasing an expensive apartment, Woollcott told the real estate company that he didn't expect them to rent to "such a notorious drunkard, bankrupt, and all-around moral leper."

American writer H. L. Mencken bought a stack of postcards showing the most extravagant castle in Europe and had them all printed to say "Mr. H. L. Mencken's Summer Estates on the Chesapeake." He also had stationery printed for a fictitious legal firm and used it to send letters to male friends notifying each that he was being sued by an ex-girlfriend for $100,000 for breach of promise.

In Columbus, Ohio, James Thurber's brother Roy got up at 3:00 A.M. one morning and barged into the room of Charles, his quiet, mildly nervous father. "Buck, your time has come!" Roy said ominously, as he shook his father awake. "Get up, Buck." Charles managed to escape and rouse the rest of the family. They found Roy in his bed fast asleep, and when they awakened him he explained that his father had come into his room earlier, ranting about someone named Buck getting into the house. The family believed Roy's story and thought that poor addled Charles had had a nightmare.

## The Art of Joking

In his book *The Compleat Practical Joker,* H. Alan Smith (who was a humorous writer, not a practical joker) has described hundreds of jokes, some recounted here. The single best jokester Smith told about was his artist friend Hugh Troy. When Hugh Troy was a student at Cornell, he reported track-and-field scores to newspapers. He thought about how sad it must be to be listed as coming in last. After a while, he started listing a student named Johnny Tsal who came in behind everyone else in every event, sparing others the embarrassment. (Spell Tsal backward.)

Once Troy managed to paint a professor's rubbers to look like bare feet. Then he covered them with lampblack so the professor wouldn't notice that anything had been done to them. The next time the professor walked in the rain, the lampblack washed off and he appeared to be walking on large bare feet.

When early transatlantic flights were big news, what appeared to be a plane wreck was discovered on a field at Cornell one morning. The wreckage was littered with choice cheeses from Holland and documents explaining that this had been a goodwill flight from Amsterdam, Holland, to Amsterdam, New York. Troy and his friends had created the wreckage from scratch, without using a plane.

When Troy was rudely ordered to paint some quick pictures at an outdoor high-society bash at an estate on Long Island, he painted signs instead of pictures and posted them at the gate, on a busy highway. They said "Picnic parties welcome," "Free merry-go-round for the children," and "Lemonade for all."

When Troy was in the Army in World War II he had to fill out bundles of reports on trivia to send to the Pentagon. Noticing ten strips of flypaper hanging on each side of the mess hall, he gave each of the twenty a code name and mimeographed an extremely complicated 24-hour report sheet with a sketch locating each strip. Every day he tallied the exact number of flies trapped and retained on each strip, and sent the report to Washington. After about a week, some fellow officers said they were in trouble with Washington for not sending in flypaper reports, so he gave them copies of his form and they began sending them in also.

A government folklorist came to Saipan in the South Pacific in World War II to gather native folktales. Hugh Troy knew our heritage of fine children's literature, and he knew a little boy named Emmanuel who spoke both English and Chamorro. So he concocted folktales from our stories and taught them to Emmanuel in English, but pretended that Emmanuel spoke only Chamorro. Day after day, with the folklorist watching, Emmanuel repeated Troy's stories to his grandfather in Chamorro as a military translator wrote them down. (The boy got five candy bars and five comic books later for every story.) The folklorist was thrilled to see how closely Saipan folklore resembles our own books like Mother Goose and Winnie the Pooh.

In 1952 Hugh Troy was still at it. He was disgusted about how many people use the ghost-writing industry instead of writing their own speeches, and so he ran a satirical ad in the *Washington Post*. "Too busy to paint? Call on THE GHOST ARTISTS. 1426 33rd St., N.W., Phone MI 2574. WE PAINT IT—YOU SIGN IT! Primitive (Grandma Moses Type), Impressionist, Modern, Cubist, Abstract, Sculpture also. WHY NOT GIVE AN EXHIBITION?" He was flooded with calls and mail from people in Washington, D.C., who hoped to pass themselves off as artists. The *London Times* devoted a half page to the gullibility of the American public, and *The New Yorker* commended him for his satire. But other artists started seriously advertising themselves as ghost artists once he gave them the idea. The joke was on him.

One of the most successful jokes of all time was a trick to promote a second-rate scenic painting. In 1917 a Brooklyn art dealer had bought many copies of "September Morn," featuring a modest nude, and they weren't selling. A friend emptied the dealer's display window, set up the picture, hired several dozen little boys to stare at it, and anonymously reported this immoral situation to the authorities.

The art dealer was arrested, the story made news, and the country went wild over "September Morn." Seven million copies sold. The original now hangs in the Art Institute of Chicago.

### Miscellaneous Pranks

In contrast to the few master-jokers with spectacular results, there are countless little jokes going on all the time in ordinary lives. A certain pilot on a commercial airline would sometimes stroll into the cabin during bumpy weather with a book under his arm clearly titled *How To Fly in Twenty Easy Lessons*.

The amazed purchaser of a new economy car believed that he was getting hundreds of miles to the gallon. In fact, his neighbors were secretly filling the gas tank for him every night.

Two people with good ears were going to meet for the first time. A mutual friend warned each of them in advance that the other was rather deaf but very sensitive about it, so it must never be mentioned. He advised them both that if the other person raised his voice, it was a sign that he needed to be spoken to a bit more loudly. As a result, the two ended up bellowing at each other.

Various bewildered people used to get Christmas cards from one family or another that they couldn't recall ever meeting. They racked their brains in vain. These people didn't know it, but they all had one friend in common, a man who would save the Christmas cards he received one year and send them out the next year. His trick required finding envelopes the right size and making sure he didn't send cards to people who knew the signers.

Someone placed an after-Christmas ad in the local paper saying, "Will pay good prices for used Christmas trees." He gave his victim's name, address, and phone number, and let nature take its course.

Another man prepared bookplates with his victim's name on them and pasted them into a few dozen worthless second-hand books. He added his victim's address and the promise of a reward if they were found and returned. Then he left them on benches and counters in his victim's neighborhood.

My first home was on a quiet little dead-end road in the country outside Novato in Marin County, California. One lazy Sunday afternoon my father, who was not a practical joker, made a sign that said

"Nudist colony to the right" and posted it at the intersection of the highway. He sat on his front porch all that afternoon and watched as people drove by, eagerly craning their necks, then drove back past again looking disappointed.

# ENTERTAINING POSSIBILITIES

> *Nothing is quite as funny as the unintended humor of reality.*
>
> —Steve Allen

On September 4, 1991, a young man was arrested in Detroit for driving without a license, and he felt so cooped up that he impetuously tried to escape. He climbed through an opening in the ceiling above a jailhouse sink and found himself in a tiny crawl space that led nowhere. When he tried to get back down head first, his pants hooked on some metalwork and dangled him from the hole, helplessly waving his arms. Fire fighters rescued him, but not without Associated Press somehow getting his picture and sending it to newspapers across the country.

Bloopers, blunders, and human bewilderment never lose their appeal. But because life's funny predicaments are usually private and fleeting, *Candid Camera* has engineered thousands of spoofs to produce that kind of humor for television audiences. In one of the sequences, the crew started a car rolling gently downhill, and the driver steered it into a service station. When she told the attendant there was something wrong with her car and asked him to check under her hood, he was dumbfounded: her car had no engine at all.

In the 1960s Norman Cousins used old *Candid Camera* programs and Vitamin C to help his body heal itself of a serious disease, popularizing the Biblical truth that a merry heart is like good medicine.

### Media Spoofs

Don Imus sometimes played practical jokes by telephone as part of his New York radio program. He once called a McDonald's at 8:30 A.M. and introduced himself as Sergeant Kirkland of the International Guard, who needed some lunches to go—in fact, 1200 hamburgers for a scheduled troop movement.

"Twelve—pardon me, sir?" the young assistant manager stammered. "Wait a minute, please." He reported the order to his boss. When his boss told Imus they didn't have that much food, Imus asked him to get it from other stores.

"This is the *government,* you know!"

"Yes, sir, I'll have to do that, sir," the manager agreed. Then the fun started. Imus said that on 300 he must hold the mustard but put on plenty of mayonnaise and lettuce and no onions. On 200—no, 201, he must hold the mayo and lettuce but lay on the mustard and make those medium-rare. On the first 300, 275 should be rare with onions and mustard and mayo and no lettuce—and don't butter the buns on half of those. (The victim was still faintly agreeing.) Butter on 134— make that butter on 135, but no mustard or lettuce and plenty of mayo. Then 250 just plain, but with lettuce on three of those, cooked medium-well with no butter on the bun. The order ran on and on, a masterpiece of high-speed double-talk.

Imus once received an announcement that he had won an award for being air personality of the year. When he arrived at the hotel in New Orleans where the radio conference was supposedly being held, all he found was a telegram reading "Gotcha!"

Ron Chapman, a disc jockey in Dallas, tried a simple radio spoof one day as an experiment. He said without any explanation, "Go to your checkbook, make out a check for $20. Make it payable to KVIL. Mail it to this address. Thank you." In three days, he claimed, he received 12,000 checks. To his amazement, in less than a week he had received almost one-quarter of a million dollars. (He invited all donors to reclaim their money, and he donated the rest to charity.) His experience was reported as true a few months later in the June 27, 1988, issue of *Forbes* magazine, in a warning article title "Are You a Born Sucker?"

Joseph Skaggs is a journalism professor who has specialized in hoaxing the media for twenty years. He does it for fun and to point out that (1) people who run the media are too lazy about checking their sources, and (2) the public is too gullible. Skaggs once appeared on *Good Morning America* as Joe Bones, founder of the Fat Squad, which physically restrains clients from eating. He has posed as Dr. Josef Gregor, an entomologist hawking pills made from cockroach extract; Dr. Richard Long, a marine biologist crusading to save the Geoduck clam from Japanese harvesters; Giuseppe Scaggoli, director of a celebrity sperm bank; and Jo-Jo, King of the New York Gypsies, who is angry about the name of the gypsy moth. He has also appeared as Joey Skaggs, an artist who produces underwater sculptures called "condominiums for fish." But when invited to appear on *Entertainment Tonight* to be interviewed as a media prankster, he fooled the media again. He sent an imposter there to play his part.

Most entertainment spoofs are brief, but Alan Abel's "heavily endowed" Society for Indecency to Naked Animals (SINA) lasted for six years. In 1966 he wrote a book, *The Great American Hoax*, telling how easy it was to hoax much of the United States and England about a crusade to defend morality by putting clothes on animals ("A nude horse is a rude horse"). His telephone number was MOrality 1-1963 and his swanky office address was on Fifth Avenue in New York City. On a door there he had a sign that said SINA NATIONAL HEADQUAR-TERS; G. Clifford Prout, Jr., President; Alan Abel, Vice-President. Abel could afford the rent, because all he rented was the outside of a door to a locked broom closet. His followers picketed the White House, and he was interviewed on major television shows.

People who are outraged by Abel's various organizations seem to enjoy thinking that they are real. He has posed on television interviews as the dean of "Omar's School for Beggars"; as the organizer of affluent women who join "Females for Felons" to supply heterosexual service to prison inmates; and as a cosmetic surgeon who specialized in plastic surgery to beautify dogs. In 1987 the *Daily News* announced, "A shadowy Iranian who claims to have made a $6 million commission in the Iran arms deal turned up here yesterday and repeated his promise to return the money to the United States government—after deducting $200,000 for dinosaur research." Abel twice helped his wife run for president disguised as Yetta Bronstein, a Bronx housewife with the motto "Put a mother in the White House."

At least half the information in Alan Abel's obituary was false, including the claim that he died. He says he pursues his media-hoax career to shake people up and add a little levity to life.

## Alarms and Diversions

Without Alan Abel to promote it, the American Society for the Conservation of Gravity seems to be sinking out of sight. It opposes all unnecessary jet flights, because of gravity depletion. "A single moon rocket launching uses more gravity in a few moments than the entire world used during all the eighteenth Century. The United States, with only 6 percent of the world's population, uses 59 percent of its gravity." Members of the society receive desk-top gravity status indicators that provide instant gravity checks in the immediate area. ASCG reportedly hopes to get the ton reduced to 500 pounds and is evaluating the relative merits of synthetic gravity, artificial gravity, or new gravity mines.

It is claimed that in the 1870s the whole boom town of Palisade, Nevada, known as one of the most violent towns west of Chicago, was in on a huge spoof. To build up its Wild West image, when a train pulled in the townspeople usually staged public shoot-outs or bank robberies. (Beef blood from the slaughterhouse added to the effect.) Everyone in town played a role at one time or another, and no one let out the truth. As a result, Palisade was becoming famous; but after the iron-ore rail to Eureka was abandoned in 1876, the town faded away. As long as the hoax lasted, however, there was not one real-life crime recorded in Palisade.

Jonathan and Darlene Edwards are to art what Palisade was to law and order; they slaughter music. Their career began in 1957 with "The Original Piano Artistry of Jonathan Edwards: Vocals by Darlene Edwards"—a popular album noted for its "carefree abandon." Since then they have averaged one amazing new album every five years. The album covers hint that the outrageously kitschy music is a joke, but there is no clue that Jonathan and Darlene Edwards are alter-egos of band leader Paul Weston and his vocalist wife Jo Stafford—superb musicians. Edwards fans love the charade. Although Paul Weston and Jo Stafford overflow with wit, Jonathan and Darlene have no sense of humor at all. They think their music is *très* beautiful.

The great Russian pianist Vladimir de Pachmann found at one concert that the piano stool was too low and couldn't be raised, so he called for a book to sit on. He tried the book, acted dissatisfied, and stood back up. At that point the audience was getting worried. Then he tore out a single page, threw the page away, sat back down, and went on with his performance.

When the British impresario Philip Lee first visited New York in the mid-1800s, he had been warned about the wild behavior of American authors but gathered that it was a joke. His actor friend E. A. Sothern assured him it was true and arranged a private dinner for Lee

44

with twelve writers and critics (who were really actors). During the dinner the men laid all kinds of weapons on the table, and then a fight broke out. The room was filled with shouts, shots, and struggle. Someone thrust a knife into Lee's hand, saying, "Defend yourself! This is butchery, sheer butchery." Sothern advised him, "Keep cool, and don't get shot." The performance ended when real police burst in because of all the commotion.

## Cambridge Codswallop

In 1948 Humphry Berkeley, a Pembroke College student at Cambridge University, was seized by a fit of spring frivolity and dreamed up a 300-year-old traditional English boarding school for boys, to join the ranks of other famous boys' schools like Eton, Marlborough, and Rugby. He invented a name and address that would strike everyone as vaguely familiar: he called it Selhurst School, Near Petworth, Sussex. He had letterhead stationery printed for Selhurst's imaginary principal, Headmaster H. Rochester Sneath. He gave Selhurst 175 pupils and a variety of problems and projects that required correspondence.

For example, on March 15, H. Rochester Sneath wrote a rather formal letter to the headmaster at Marlborough to find out "how you managed to engineer a visit recently from the King and Queen." Sneath wanted such a visit at Selhurst for its 300th anniversary. Marlborough's disconcerted headmaster replied that he had not "engineered" the royal visit; the King and Queen had come of their own accord. He signed the letter F. M. Heywood, revealing his name.

A week later, Sneath wrote a confidential letter of warning to Heywood about a French teacher (fictional, of course) named Agincourt who was applying for a job at Marlborough. Sneath explained that during the one semester when Agincourt had taught at Selhurst, five pupils dropped out. He was once seen climbing a tree naked at night, and on another occasion he threw a flower pot at the wife of the Chairman of the Board of Governors.

> Should you wish any further information, I should be glad to furnish it, for I would not wish another Headmaster to undergo the purgatory that I suffered that term.

I am staying for some days with my sister Mrs. Harvey-Kelly at Castle Brae, Chesterton, Cambridge, and I would be grateful if you would reply to this address.

The Cambridge address belonged to one of Berkeley's friends, and he used it for his spoof. As soon as Heywood replied stiffly that Agincourt had not applied for a job, Sneath wrote back to say that Agincourt had given up his academic career and was now a waiter in a Greek restaurant in Soho. "Incidentally, I dined with the Lord Chancellor last night and he spoke of you to me in the highest possible terms." Next, Sneath asked Heywood for the name of the private detective he normally used; and then he also asked Heywood to recommend a competent nursery maid. On April 4, Heywood replied in disgruntled bewilderment that he didn't employ a private detective, and he was not an agency for domestic servants.

Next, Sneath wrote an elaborate letter to famous playwright George Bernard Shaw, claiming that the late Mrs. Shaw was connected with Selhurst and inviting him to speak at Selhurst's 300th anniversary—on the set topic of "A Clarion Call to Youth." "Incidentally," wrote Sneath, "you may remember meeting me in Dublin some years ago." Shaw's secretary declined for him, and Shaw added a note: "Never heard of any such connection. Too old (91) anyhow."

Before and after April Fool's Day 1948, Sneath sent about thirty of these dignified but ridiculous—sometimes outrageous—letters to a variety of distinguished people who should have known that there was no Selhurst School. The tone of the letters was like something by the future Monty Python comedy team, but only two of the recipients caught on.

It was Sneath's April 13 letter to the *Daily Worker* that ended his amazing career; he made it clear that he was not a Communist but did want to institute the study of Russian at Selhurst and was blocked at every turn, even in obtaining textbooks. Among the responses was a long, detailed letter from the School of Slavonic and East European Studies at the University of London and an urgent one-sentence letter from an editor of the magazine *News Review,* requesting an interview. Sneath's imaginary secretary Penelope Pox-Rhyddene failed to deflect *News Review* with her explanation that Sneath was seriously ill and could only communicate by mail. A reporter found that the Selhurst telephone number was nonexistent, that there was no boarding school near the small town of Petworth, and that the National Union of Teachers had no record of Selhurst.

The reporter eventually went to Cambridge and located Humphry Berkeley, then exposed him in an April 29 article titled "Death of Rochester Sneath." The head of Pembroke College was forced to expel Berkeley for two years, after which he graduated in good standing. In later life Berkeley became a distinguished Member of Parliament, and in 1974 he published the entire hilarious story in a book titled *The Life and Death of Rochester Sneath*.

### Oxford Bosh

Once some Oxford students decided to make fun of Freudian psychology by staging a mock lecture. They rented an auditorium and sent out invitations from the imaginary Home Counties Psychological Federation for a lecture by Sigmund Freud's German friend and colleague Dr. Emil Busch. He was to speak on "Freud and the New Psychology." The lecture was free, and so the auditorium was packed.

According to Norman Moss in *The Pleasures of Deception,* Dr. Busch spoke with a thick German accent about the little-known influence of something called co-aesthesia. After the lecture he was asked, "Would you dissent from Freud in postulating that co-aesthesia is a more vital explanation of the subconscious than sex?"

He answered, "From Professor Freud, I would not dissent. He is my very good friend. But of him I feel sometimes that for the number of trees, the wood he does not see." Dr. Busch was, of course, an Oxford student in a false moustache, a fake accent, and the ability to keep a straight face. The unsuspecting audience applauded appreciatively at the end of the lecture, and the jokesters got their successful escapade written up in the paper.

Norman Moss has also told the story of Reginald Jones, a real physicist with the Clarendon Laboratory, who got the job of disrupting a distinguished scientific seminar at Oxford because Clarendon had been excluded. Jones telephoned the seminar chairman, passed himself off as a boiler-room mechanic, and warned that because of a pressure-block in the steam pipes and some other problems which he described, the radiators were apt to blow up. In response to this scientific nonsense, the scientists hastily closed their meeting and

47

evacuated the building—in spite of the fact that there is no such thing as a pressure block and the radiators couldn't blow up.

When Jones was a young physicist, he assured his colleague Gerald Touch that one can persuade a highly intelligent scholar to do preposterous things simply by talking to him on the telephone. He offered to demonstrate it that evening when Touch was visiting a distinguished Oxford professor.

That evening the host's telephone rang several times with no one on the line. (Jones made those calls and hung up.) At last Jones called and identified himself as a telephone engineer who had been notified that something was wrong with the scholar's phone. (At that point the victim assumed that his phone was out of order.) The engineer said that he wouldn't have a repairman available for a week, due to being short-staffed. (The victim assumed that he was in danger of being without a telephone for a week.) When the victim begged for faster repair, the engineer said that if the trouble turned out to be a leak to earth, he could fix the telephone from his office right away; but that would involve some testing by the owner. The poor man was eager to cooperate. After that, Jones led him to tap the telephone with a pen, take off his shoes and tap it again, stand on one foot and tap it, and so forth, while Gerald Touch watched in amazement.

Jones finally said, "I'm afraid I still can't tell. There's only one thing more to do—well, no, I think we'd better leave it until we can get our own man around." At that the scholar begged to try the next test. Jones gave in and told him to approximate the test they do with telephone equipment, by lowering his telephone into a bucket of water. The victim rushed off to get the bucket of water.

At this point Gerald Touch, who couldn't control his laughter, forcibly tried to rescue the telephone. His host hung on tight and told Jones, "I'm terribly sorry, but there's a young friend here who's trying to stop me. I think he's a bit drunk. He says it'll damage the telephone if I put it in the water."

Jones learned that the young friend was a physicist. "Physicists! They're the bane of our life here in Oxford. They always think they know about telephones, and they're always wrong." So it was that a fine scholar lowered his perfectly good telephone into a bucket of water.

Jones was a champion joker among British scientists; and when recruited to help to defend England, he successfully tricked the Nazis repeatedly in World War II by combining his expertise in physics with his hoaxing ability. Years later, he shared some of his techniques with the CIA. He once delivered a lecture at the Institute of Physics in London titled "The Theory of Practical Joking: Its Relevance to Physics," in which he said, "The object is to build up in the victim's mind a false world-picture which is temporarily consistent by any tests that he can apply to it, so that he ultimately takes action on it with confidence." As Norman Moss sums it up, "The victim of a hoax has been given manufactured evidence."

Sometimes the evidence is literally manufactured. Americans are said to buy almost 4 million dollars worth of practical joke materials every year. These include artificial spiders, webs, snakes, lizards, flies, pet poop, and severed arms. There are phony car phones that come with fake antennas. There are dribble glasses that leak on drinkers, and plastic ice cubes. There are stick-on glass cracks for windows and unattached faucets that mysteriously pour out real water. There are negotiable dollar bills with Santa Claus's portrait in place of George Washington's, and birthday candles that won't blow out. This is the wonderful world of masks, wigs, and false noses; vanishing ink and squirting cigars.

# TRUTH OR CONSEQUENCES

*Matilda told such dreadful lies*
*It made one Gasp and Stretch one's Eyes.*

—Hilaire Belloc

One of life's first safety rules is "Don't pull away someone's chair when he is sitting down." It is amazing how many children spontaneously invent this old prank, which seems to come naturally to human beings. Some pranks hurt innocent bystanders or downsitters, and others backfire on the pranksters themselves.

The accidents that happen to tricksters are basically the same as those that happen to other people at work or play, but accidents to tricksters have a special twist. For example, in 1956 India's most famous prestidigitator, a man named Sorcar, stunned BBC-TV audiences by sawing a woman in half and failing to revive her.

## Costly Illusions

Chung Ling Soo, "the Marvelous Chinese Conjurer," was famous for stopping bullets with a china plate. His wife Suee Seen would go down into the audience and have two people scratch their initials on a couple of lead bullets, which she carried back to the stage and secretly slipped to her husband. Those bullets were supposedly loaded into a pair of rifles, which assistants aimed at the magician. He wore magnificent Oriental robes and had his plate ready. When the rifles were fired at him, he pretended to catch the initialled bullets on his plate and then offered them to the audience for examination.

On March 18, 1923, in a London theater, Soo collapsed on stage with the two marked bullets still hidden in his hand and one plain bullet in his chest. He was at least the tenth illusionist to die from one variety of this trick or another. In his case, wear and tear on a special seal inside the altered rifle allowed it actually to fire a bullet instead of only sounding as if it did so. (It turns out that Chung Ling Soo was really named William Ellsworth Campbell Robinson.)

Of course, most stage magicians never get hurt and never hurt others; and they aim to deceive people, but not to rob them. In his book *The Psychology of Deception,* Joseph Jastrow notes that gaining the confidence of the person to be deceived is the first step in both magic tricks (sleight of hand) and criminal fraud. Expectation is the trickster's key tool. "First actually do that which you afterward wish the audience to believe that you continue to do." To convince an audience that you are throwing coins into a hat, begin by throwing a few in. Some magic experts add, "The more educated the audience, the more easily fooled."

By 1926 the British people had great confidence in news announcements on BBC Radio. On the evening of January 16, millions of listeners heard a speech from Edinburgh interrupted for news flashes from London, where an angry mob led by Mr. Popplebury was rioting in Trafalgar Square. Big Ben was knocked down and demolished. The minister of traffic, who tried to escape in disguise, was hanged from a lamp post. Listeners could hear the noise of the Savoy Hotel being blown up.

Telephone and telegraph lines were flooded with inquiries. When officials claimed that there was no riot, much of the public insisted, "We heard it on the radio." Finally the BBC had to explain its entire program in detail, including the clear announcement before the speech from Edinburgh that everything that followed would be a spoof. Most listeners had evidently forgotten that announcement as soon as the alarming news flashes began.

Americans made the same mistake twelve years later. On October 30, 1938, Orson Wells and the Mercury Theater players of the Columbia Broadcasting System presented their seventeenth weekly radio drama—an H. G. Wells story, *The War of the Worlds,* adapted to radio-news format. In the program, a farm in Grovers Mill, New Jersey, was invaded by rockets containing octopus-like Martians armed with tripod machines, heat-ray weapons, and black gas. A real radio announcer stated clearly at the beginning, middle, and end of the program that it was only a drama. Many listeners failed to notice that assurance, however, and the obvious fact that the live eye-witness accounts of the invasion were compressed from hours into minutes. In the fantasy, martial law prevailed immediately, and 7,000 ground soldiers were killed in Grovers Mill with no explanation of how they got there. Bombers were destroyed in flight before they would have had time to take off. Broadcasters, scientists, the Secretary of the Interior, ambulances, and troops were whisked here and there as if by magic. One fictitious radio reporter after another died on duty, but the program's up-to-the-minute news coverage continued anyway. In less than an hour New York City was an empty ghost town.

In the real world, thousands of New York and New Jersey residents fled their homes in panic. Hundreds of people had to go to hospitals to be treated for shock. Citizens with firearms rushed to the Princeton area to fight the invaders. Police in many cities were swamped with telephone inquiries. A Memphis newspaper rallied its staff to produce an extra edition about the invasion. Some church services were interrupted by the spreading alarm, and in many places people gathered hastily to pray for protection. Those who stayed by their radios, however, heard Orson Wells' cheerful conclusion: *The War of the Worlds* was a "holiday offering . . . —the Mercury Theater's version of dressing up in a sheet and jumping out of a bush and saying 'boo!' . . . tomorrow night . . . if your doorbell rings and nobody's there, that was no Martian. It's Halloween."

The entire program is commercially available in a "Golden Age Radio" series of cassette tapes. (Rights are owned by Metacom, Inc., of Plymouth, Minnesota.)

Ironically, recent accounts of the program mistakenly say it took place on Halloween rather than the night before; and some people assume that the program was an intentional deception. On October 4, 1991, at Blalack Junior High School in Carrollton, Texas, a weeping assistant principal made the following announcement over the public address system: "A historical event has taken place. The President of the United States has been assassinated." Students and teachers were stunned; some burst into tears. Four minutes later, the assistant principal returned to say that her previous announcement was only a trick to see how students would react to a tragedy. In a television interview later that day, Principal Lora Folsom explained that some students were learning about the 1938 *War of the Worlds* radio program, and she had wanted an announcement that would cause a similar kind of reaction.

"They were playing with our emotions, and they shouldn't have done that for any reason," an eighth-grader protested. "This has hurt a lot of people. What really makes me mad is how the assistant principal faked crying." Another student told the press the next day, "I was shocked. Once someone does that to you, it's hard to ever trust what they say."

## Counting the Cost

One of the byproducts of hoaxes is undermined trust; Samuel Johnson summed it up: "All imposture weakens confidence and chills benevolence." In a wise old cautionary tale, a young shepherd was supposed to cry "Wolf!" to summon help if he and the flock were attacked. He found that falsely crying "Wolf!" broke the monotony and got him attention, so he did it repeatedly. Then one day he was really attacked, and when he cried "Wolf!" no one came. That is a good story for school administrators as well as for children.

Radio hoaxes continue at such a rate that the Federal Communications Commission receives about a dozen reports a year. One of the most harmful was a bogus 1990 murder confession on KROQ in Los Angeles, arranged by playful announcers. The Sheriff's Department searched for the killer for ten months at a public cost of over $12,000.

In Evaline Ness's picture book *Sam, Bangs and Moonshine,* Samantha almost caused her best friend Thomas and her cat Bangs to drown in the sea because Thomas believed her tales about a mermaid. She was always telling tall tales, and her father had warned her in vain that "moonshine is flummadiddle, but real is the opposite." It took the near accident to teach her what he meant. "There's good moonshine and bad moonshine," her father explained after he saved Thomas and Bangs. "The important thing is to know the difference." He didn't explain, but the most obvious difference is that bad moonshine is unkind to other people.

Fanny Crosby, the well-known hymn writer, tripped herself up once with a bit of moonshine. One afternoon at the New York Institution for the Blind where she was the leading student, she was asked to show a visitor around. In one room he caught sight of a stack of her books *The Blind Girl and Other Poems.* "Oh, here is the Fanny Crosby book," he exclaimed. "You must know her, I suppose." Fanny merely nodded.

"Is she a likable girl?" he pressed. Fanny couldn't resist the chance for a little joke, and so she answered, "Far from it!" He said he was sorry to hear that, but wanted one of the books anyway. He gave her his card to pass on later to Fanny Crosby. After he left, Fanny learned to her dismay that this guest had been Johann Ludwig Tell-kampf, a prominent professor at Columbia College. She had thrown away his chance to enjoy meeting her and her chance to enjoy meeting him. She was still thinking about that mistake years later.

Tennessee's Stoney Jackson has recalled sadly his excitement as an impoverished Disciples of Christ minister who became a contestant on CBS's wildly popular *$64,000 Question* in 1956. He made himself an expert on "great love stories." After his first appearance he worried about the fact that the producer was secretly feeding him answers in advance, but people back home told him to shut up and not be an idiot. The thrill of being a national TV celebrity and a local hero numbed his strict conscience while he won $20,000 and paid off his debts.

When another contestant was unfairly dropped from *The $64,000 Challenge*, Jackson's conscience revived, and he tried to reveal the network hoax to *Time*, the *New York Times*, a major Tennessee paper, and his hometown paper; but none of them were interested. Another game-show contestant broke into print about the deception, however, and then the tide turned. The nation went into shock. Jackson plunged from local celebrity and popular speaker to *persona non grata*—not so much for faking as for whistle-blowing. He finally got to testify about the rigged game shows before a Congressional committee but was bitterly disappointed to find that the investigation itself appeared to be rigged—only a sham to placate the public and protect the powerful.

After the scandal, he hoped to write a book about America called *The Age of Hucksters and Suckers*. He didn't, but he still believes that the network betrayal of its devoted public in the 1950s produced a moral lassitude and cynicism that harms us to this day.

*Half the harm that is done in this world*
*Is due to people who want to feel important.*

—T. S. Eliot

# PART II:
## PRETENSE—THE SKY'S THE LIMIT

# CHAPTER 3
## ACCEPTABLE RATES OF INFLATION

*A pinch of probably is worth a pound of perhaps.*

—James Thurber

Many hoaxes are designed to deflate pomposity, expose gullibility, or prove the carelessness of experts. In contrast, journalists have often indulged in bunkum and ballyhoo for the sheer fun of it. For these and several other reasons, including pride, hoaxes have become part of our official history.

# CUTTING CORNERS TO MAKE POINTS

*A little inaccuracy sometimes saves tons of explanation.*

—H. H. Munro

In May 1991 a couple in the affluent Chicago suburb of Oak Park applied for a building permit to remove thirty-eight art-glass windows from their house and cover it all with aluminum siding. In twenty minutes they had their permit and were free to start knocking out windows. But instead of altering the house, they announced on radio and television that their house had been designed by Frank Lloyd Wright, and they had been granted a permit to ruin it.

This couple was part of a group struggling for a historic preservation ordinance to protect Oak Park's rare architectural heritage, and local officials had been wrongly insisting that all the architectural gems there were safe. "It was clearly a publicity stunt," one of the embarrassed officials grumbled to the press. Of course it was; it made news and proved a point.

## Spoofing Art Lovers

Many of Hugh Troy's practical jokes were designed to prove points also. When New York's Museum of Modern Art offered the first showing of Van Gogh's paintings on American soil, in 1935, Troy set out to show that most of the enthusiastic visitors were curious about Van Gogh's life, not his art. Troy mounted an unusual item in a blue velvet shadow box and labeled it professionally: "This is the ear which Vincent Van Gogh cut off and sent to his mistress, a French prostitute, Dec. 24, 1888." He slipped this exhibit into the display, and it stole the show; visitors flocked around to look at Van Gogh's ear more than his paintings. Artist Hugh Troy had modeled the mummified ear out of dried chipped beef.

Centuries earlier, Michelangelo spoofed art lovers by producing an ancient statue. He carved a Cupid, broke off one arm, and buried the rest of it. Later he arranged to have it discovered, and the Cardinal

58

of St. George purchased it. After the Cardinal had enjoyed his ancient treasure long enough, Michelangelo announced that he had made it, and gave the cardinal the missing arm. Which is more valuable: a damaged antique Cupid or a new Cupid that is whole? Michelangelo's prank illustrated the fact that people tend to place a high value on old art just because it is old.

William Ralph Inge, an Anglican writer, summed up chronological snobbery this way: "There are two kinds of fools: one says, 'This is old, therefore it is good'; the other says, 'This is new, therefore it is better.'"

Paul Jordan Smith, a Los Angeles scholar, tried a trick that was just the opposite of Michelangelo's. Because his wife's fine realistic paintings were dismissed as outdated, he threw together a garish modernist painting of a primitive woman waving a banana skin (his failed attempt at a starfish). A young art critic happened to see the painting without knowing its origin and pronounced it extremely interesting. Smith decided that critics liked anything unintelligible, and he knew they favored foreigners; and so he named the painting "Exaltation," had it handsomely framed, and entered it in an art show under a Slavic version of his own name—Pavel Jerdanowitch. He said the painting portrayed an island woman who had just killed a missionary and then defied local custom by eating a luscious banana.

"Exaltation" was a hit, and Jerdanowitch was soon contacted by art magazines in Paris. They asked for photos of his art, but since he had none he sent instead a biographical sketch and a brooding photo of himself with heavy make-up and a beard grown for the occasion. He said he was born in Moscow, grew up in Chicago, suffered from tuberculosis, and lived for a while in the South Seas. All this was repeated in *Livre d'Or*, a 1926 art book where he was praised as a pathfinder. That book devoted a full page to his second painting, "Aspiration," which hung in the Marshall Field galleries in Chicago and was featured in *Art News*. Smith called it the quintessence of a new Disumbrationist school, and people took him seriously. His next two paintings were exhibited in the Waldorf-Astoria. In 1927 Smith confessed in the *Los Angeles Times* that his paintings were a hoax to mock modernism; but the joke was on him, because in 1928 they were exhibited at Vose Galleries in Boston. The catalog there spoke in all seriousness to "those who realize that real art depicts not what we see but what we feel, hear, and smell; these soul revealing creations will be sources of ecstatic, moronic rapture."

In 1936 a portrait painter named Howitt-Lodge repeated Smith's trick by sneaking a mess of paint blobs, beads, a cigarette stub, hair, tinsel, and a sponge into the International Surrealist Exhibition in London under the title "Abstract Painting of a Woman" by D. S. Windle. When he announced the swindle, modernists answered that he might intend it as a hoax, but he was probably a surrealist at heart.

One of my own English instructors, Laurence Nelson, won a regional poetry contest to make the same point. When he accepted first prize for his profoundly modern symbolic poem, he explained to the assembled poetry connoisseurs that if they listed the first words of all the articles in the current *Readers Digest* in order, they would see where he got the poem they liked so well. Metaphorically speaking, his name was mud in Southern California poetry circles after that.

This kind of protest against modernism-run-amok has worked repeatedly. It fell flat in 1961, however, when BBC Radio presented twelve minutes of random noises as "Mobile for Tapes and Percussions," purportedly by Piotr Zak, a young Polish composer. The *Daily Express* declared afterward, "Not only did thousands of unsuspecting listeners accept this piece of nonsense with reverence and respect, but two of Britain's most pompous newspapers solemnly reviewed it. For years, people have been duped, often outrageously, by the growing cult of obscurantism." In fact, newspaper critics had listened carefully to the noise and had stated correctly that the composition was "nonmusical" and "an insult." Not every attack upon modernism is a smashing success like the Angry Penguins hoax.

## Poetic and Sexual License

In the early 1940s there was a trendy literary magazine in South Australia called *Angry Penguins*. One day in 1944 editor Max Harris received a letter from Ethel Malley of Sydney about her brother Ern Malley, who had died of a rare thyroid disease at the age of twenty-six. Malley was an uneducated young man who worked as a mechanic and sold insurance, and he had owned only one book, Thorstein Veblan's *Theory of the Leisure Class*. After his death his sister Ethel found his poems and wondered if they were of value. Max

Harris read them and said yes, they were valuable. He published them, declaring Ern Malley one of Australia's greatest writers.

Malley had explained about his poetry, "All must be synchronized, the jagged / Quartz of vision with the asphalt of human speech." He wrote of such things as the "umbelliferous dark" and "The black swan of trespass on alien waters."

Here is a typical passage of modern poetry by Ern Malley:

> *You have hawked in your throat and spat*
> *Outrage upon the velocipede of thriftless*
> *Mechanical men posting themselves that*
> *Built you a gibbet in the vile morass*
> *Which now you must dangle on, alas.*

Unfortunately for Max Harris, Ern and Ethel Malley never existed. As soon as Malley's poetry was published and praised, the true authors identified themselves—a couple of serious Australian poets who concocted the entire hoax in one afternoon to embarrass silly modernists.

Max Harris's next misfortune was that the South Australian police attacked the poems as indecent and launched an obscenity trial. Although there were no dirty words in the poems, there were some innuendoes. For example there was mention of people in a park at night; and as one policeman testified in court, "I have found that people who go into parks at night go there for immoral purposes." The public considered the trial absurd, but Harris was fined £5.

According to columnist Jack Anderson, Ern Malley has never been forgotten in Australia. In 1987, forty-three years after the poems first appeared, Allen & Unwin of Sydney reissued *The Poems of Ern Malley* with 101 pages of commentary.

It is too bad that Ern Malley did not live long enough to meet and marry Penelope Asche. When editor Mike McGrady of *Newsday* interviewed sex-novelist Harold Robbins and learned that he had been paid advances totaling two million dollars on the strength of one title alone—*The Adventurers* (a million dollars per word), he felt this called for satire. He invented a title and an author—*Naked Came the Stranger* by Penelope Asche.

Then McGrady recruited twenty-four journalists and explained his book plan: "There will be an unremitting emphasis on sex. Also, true excellence in writing will be blue-penciled into oblivion." He

61

gave the writers a rough outline about a sexy suburban housewife getting even with her unfaithful husband. Each writer was to write a chapter independently, including two sexual encounters—at least one of them bizarre. McGrady's job was to edit out anything intelligent or sophisticated, keep the story dirty enough, and unify details like the heroine's hair color.

McGrady submitted the completed manuscript to a major publisher, and it was published in 1970. McGrady's lively blonde sister-in-law played the part of author Penelope Asche on television interviews. She spouted clichés and insisted that 75 percent of suburban people live just like the people in her book. (As McGrady said, this book would have overstated the situation in Sodom.) After the book was well received, McGrady announced the big joke.

But people paid no attention to him and kept buying the book anyway. It sold 100,000 copies in hardback, more in paperback, and more in a British edition. Royalties piled up until each of the twenty-four authors received $5,000 for a single chapter. Bernard Geis offered the team a half million dollars for a sequel, but they declined; McGrady didn't want to deceive or demean readers any longer than necessary to make his point. He followed up with a funny book about the entire episode: *Stranger than Naked, or How To Write Dirty Books for Fun and Profit.*

## Inviting Rejection

In contrast to Penelope Asche, Doris Lessing is a superb British novelist with over twenty-five books to her credit, and she has reportedly been considered for a Nobel Prize in Literature. Her novel *Golden Notebook* has sold 900,000 copies in hardback, and her Children of Violence series sold almost a million. For years she planned a kindly hoax to dramatize how hard life is for serious writers whose names are unknown.

In 1983 she brought out *The Diary of a Good Neighbor* under the pen name Jane Somers. Because her agent kept her true identity secret, her usual British publisher turned the book down flat. Her U.S. editor at Knopf knew her identity and therefore accepted the book, but didn't tell anyone who she was. As a result, there were few reviews; the book sold only 1,500 copies in Britain and 3,000 in the

United States. Furthermore, professional evaluations before publication were both patronizing and nasty.

Because no one guessed that this novel was by Lessing, she brought out a sequel in 1984—and still no one guessed, not even the reviewers who have claimed to be Lessing experts. (She made sure that copies were sent to them.) If the books had carried her name, they would have had glowing reviews and high sales. Later in 1984 she revealed the hoax and reissued the books under her own name, having made her point—that the literary marketplace is usually not fair to people who are not already famous.

In the summer of 1991 a Florida journalist named David Wilkening bought a copy of the highly publicized novel *American Psycho* and was so disgusted by it that he tried his own experiment. He typed out an outline and the first three chapters of Marjorie Kinan Rawlings' wholesome novel *The Yearling* and submitted it to twenty-two publishers under his own name. When this beloved story of a Florida boy and his pet fawn was first published in 1938 by Scribner's, under the care of master-editor Maxwell Perkins, it promptly won a Pulitzer Prize. It was made into a 1946 movie starring Gregory Peck, and the book can still be found in libraries everywhere.

A Scribner's editor sent Wilkening's outline and sample chapters back to him with the message, "Unfortunately, I lack the necessary enthusiasm for the project to recommend its publication here at Scribner's." After Wilkening published an account of his hoax, the editor was called by Associated Press and explained, "We don't spend a lot of time on any one manuscript." When asked if she had ever read *The Yearling*, she hung up.

In spurning *The Yearling*, Scribner's was in good company; not one publisher was willing to look at the rest of the wonderful book. Twelve other publishers rejected it outright, and eight more didn't even bother to answer Wilkening's proposal. The only publisher to recognize the classic was the owner of tiny Pineapple Press, who said, "We caught it in the first few pages because it was so obvious."

### Bluffing

Perhaps most of today's American book editors have never found time to read the Pulitzer winners; if so, they could use a handy guide called *Bluff Your Way in American Novels*. Centennial Press offers twenty-five little paperback "Bluffer's Guides" to help uninformed people sound knowledgeable in football, psychology, computers, and various other specialties. For only $3.95 and the time it takes to read about eighty pages, one can acquire a useful overview of a given topic. More people are willing to buy a "useful overview" if it is called a "bluffer's guide," no doubt. (Similarly, most Americans will pay more for a ticket to a *theatre* than for a ticket to a *theater*.)

Bluffing is so common that Robert Mitchum once said, "Half the people in America are faking it." One night in 1928 at an Atlantic City party, a trio of song writers got an emergency call from Al Jolson. For his forthcoming film *The Singing Fool*, he needed a song about a little boy who died. The trio took the assignment as a joke and quickly wrote "Sonny Boy," laughing hysterically at its musical clichés. To them the song was a ridiculous satire on sentimentality; but when it came out the public took it seriously, and it became one of the first recordings to sell a million copies. The public never guessed that their tear-jerker was a leg-puller.

Law-enforcement officers often resort to bluffing. For six hours on July 23, 1992, drivers on Interstate 85 in North Carolina encountered flashing lights and the warning "Slow Down, Drug Checkpoint Ahead." About 200 drivers automatically took the next exit ramp, which led to almost nowhere except to the real checkpoint—where several were arrested for carrying cocaine, marijuana, and concealed weapons. There was no checkpoint on Interstate 85.

In an especially colorful sting operation in Corunna, Michigan, in 1990, a large-scale drug dealer named Danny Brown invited guests to his wedding to Debbie Leno, daughter of crime boss Fast Eddie Leno. At the door a sign asked guests to check their guns or leave them outside. Pretty blonde Debbie was there in her long white wedding gown, and the Reverend Billy Ray Hawk performed the service. Toasts were drunk, a band called SPOC began to play, and the wedding dance began. Matchbooks on the table said, "Debbie and Danny—Thank you for sharing our joy." But when the band played "I Fought the Law (and the Law Won)," a Port Huron police sergeant asked all police officers to stand. The bride and other police officers drew their revolvers, and almost everyone still seated was under arrest. All the members of the wedding party and many of the guests were armed law-enforcement officers with warrants for the arrest of the drug-dealer guests. And the band? Read SPOC backwards.

## Putting on Airs

Debbie Leno (officer Debra Williams) appeared in her bridal gown with gun in hand across the nation, courtesy of Associated Press. Almost every section of the newspaper is sprinkled weekly with hoaxes and frauds—not the least, the financial section. Editors have even had to screen letters by requiring addresses and telephone numbers that can be checked for verification because some letters to the editor are bogus. In the letters column of the book review section of the *Los Angeles Times* on July 22, 1991, Daniel A. Jenkins of Pacific Palisades stated his request: "I am writing my autobiography and would appreciate hearing from anyone who can remember anything interesting or exciting about me."

He got several amused answers. One began, "Jenkins? I remember the dear boy well. It was 1933; he was stalking lions in the African veldt with his Daisy air rifle . . ."

At about the same time, *Spy* magazine was spoofing people in the entertainment industry who bluff about who they remember. *Spy* tricked people by publishing a death notice in the *New York Times* for a nonexistent Jack Fine. Jack's obituary then ranked twelfth in importance out of forty-two in *Variety* on January 14, and columnist Liz Smith reported his passing. "A sad milestone in the world of show business: Jack Fine, personal manager of such golden greats of Hollywood as Betty Grable, Johnny Weissmuller and Jeff Chandler, passed away recently in Australia, far from his beloved New York. Jack founded Apex Management and ran it for 50 years before retiring. . . . He was known for his unflagging optimism, expressed in his signature line: 'Smile darling—somewhere it's opening night!'"

At a party that *New York Post* gossip columnist Cindy Adams gave for her comedian husband Joey Adams, a *Spy* journalist asked celebrity guests for their memories of the late Jack Fine and recorded the answers: "Oh, Jack! Are you kiddin' me? Yeah, what a nice man! I didn't know him very . . . y'know intimately, but I knew him—I knew of him. He was one of the finest men—" "Y'know, he passed on . . ." "I kno-o-ow, I know." "Well, he was a lovely man." "He was a lovely man. A good man. An honest man. A fair man . . ." "[I knew him] just in passing, but always kind and pleasant. And good." "I knew him very well. Well, in the business, y'know, same business."

The same issue of *Spy*, April 1991, reported on a 1988 hoax by someone who claimed to be Thekla von Stett-Vasary, an aged Hungarian princess. Thekla wrote to a variety of famous people, explaining that she was old and alone and sifting through her assets. In several cases she described meeting or dining with her correspondent many years ago. Now Thekla had an extra million dollars that she would like to give away; "As we say in Hungary: 'It is not worth being the wealthiest Lady at the cemetery!'" She received warm replies from Jerry Lewis, Michael Douglas, Ginger Rogers, Shirley Temple Black, Joan Baez, Tony Curtis, Pat Boone, Brigitte Bardot, Audrey Hepburn, Mamie Van Doren, Ed Koch, Erica Jong, and others. Some were eager for her gift for themselves, but several wanted it for a favorite charity. A few claimed to recall Thekla or agreed to travel in her jet. Along with friendly personal replies, some sent her their home addresses and telephone numbers, and even their bank-account numbers. The point in *Spy* was that celebrities are apt to drop their guard when approached by a stranger who wants to get rid of a million dollars. Jane Russell was the only one who felt sure from the start that Thekla was a hoax.

## Tricking Readers

There have also been hoaxes designed to show how careless people are about reading what they sign. A classic example was the bogus 1933 petition to nominate Giuseppe Zangara for the Omaha City Council. It was signed by over three hundred citizens, including some of Omaha's most prominent people. At that time Zangara had one of the most famous names in the United States because he had recently attempted to assassinate President-elect Franklin D. Roosevelt and had actually killed the mayor of Chicago. He was a homicidal madman.

Five years later some freshmen at the University of Michigan circulated a student petition requesting that a Saturday psychology lecture be changed to Wednesday so that it wouldn't conflict with the football game. It was signed, of course. The next day the wording of the successful petition appeared in the student paper: "We, the undersigned, hereby petition that the lecture in Psychology 2 be changed from Saturday to Wednesday afternoon. By signing this document without reading it we cheerfully disqualify ourselves as candidates for any degree conferred by this university . . ."

In 1983 the following summer workshops spoofing trendy self-help courses were listed in a newsletter for instructors at Santa Ana College: Creative Suffering, Overcoming Peace of Mind, The Primal Shrug, Dealing with Post Self-Realization Depression, How to Overcome Self-Doubt through Pretense and Ostentation, Ego Gratification through Violence, Money Can Make You Rich, I Made $100 in Real Estate, Filler Phrases for Thesis Writers, Tax Shelters for the Indigent, How to Convert Your Family Room into a Garage, Burglar-Proof Your Home with Concrete, Tap-Dance Your Way to Social Ridicule, and Self-Actualization through Macrame. No one was supposed to take the list seriously, but no doubt some did.

On May 7, 1991, an impassioned letter appeared in the *Dear Abby* column in newspapers across the country. Dr. Joe Weinstein of Somerville, New Jersey, reported that he had read in *Parade* magazine about six-year-old Brandy Oxenrider of Atlanta, Georgia, whose parents were allowing her to donate a kidney to an ailing chimpanzee in the Perkins Animal Clinic. Mr. Oxenrider, a forty-year-old health-food-store owner who took bananas to the chimpanzee, explained that he was one-hundred percent committed to animal welfare; he would like to donate his heart to a laboratory rat in California that needed a heart transplant, but his heart wouldn't fit into that tiny little chest cavity.

Dr. Weinstein considered Brandy's organ donation outrageous because a six-year-old could not possibly understand the risks of surgery and going through life with only one kidney. In a case where the donor child was dying anyway, the kidney should be donated to a needy human on a transplant waiting list. Besides everything else, the chimp would be better off if its new kidney came from another chimp, preferably a blood relative. Dr. Weinstein concluded by saying that he was at a loss to understand why human organs are being transplanted into animals.

Abigail Van Buren agreed with Dr. Weinstein and tried to call the Perkins Animal Clinic in Atlanta, but it does not exist. She then called *Parade* magazine and was told that the news item was only a joke. Her response was that organ transplants are not a joking matter. (The *Parade* writer was making fun of animal welfare fanatics, not organ transplants.)

Was Abby serious? Evidently so. Was Dr. Weinstein serious? I called cross-country to his office on the day of publication to find out. He is an idealistic young doctor in family practice. He explained that he had read the transplant item in a review of 1990 news in *Parade* at the end of December and had assumed that it was true. He said he was not without a sense of humor and had enjoyed occasional spoof editions of a student paper when he was at Rutgers University, but it never occurred to him that a writer at *Parade* might slip a single spoof into a page of historic facts. Dr. Weinstein learned the truth when he read his letter and Abby's reply in the paper that day.

# BLACK AND WHITE AND READ ALL OVER

*Has any reader ever found perfect accuracy in the newspaper
account of any event of which he himself had inside knowledge?*

—E. V. Lucas

Mark Twain advised journalists, "Get your facts first, and then you
can distort them as much as you please." Thomas Jefferson said that
newspapers should come in four sections: Truth, Probability, Possibility, and Lies. Journalists not only have to battle against errors and
inaccuracies, but they also have to contend with what *Newsweek*'s
Meg Greenfield calls "the eternal journalistic temptation to perpetrate
a hoax." Expert Curtis D. MacDougall claims that even with twisted
and inaccurate stories ruled out, a complete list of journalistic hoaxes
would be interminable. In addition to tricks played by journalists,
however, there are also tricks played upon journalists.

## Intentional Inventions

One of the earliest known newspaper hoaxes occurred in 1783,
when Paris was full of exciting scientific experiments. (Paris was also
full of malarkey at that time; according to author John Charles Cooper
in *The Black Mask*, "The so-called Age of Reason was a time of super-
stition and magnetic attraction to occultists, secret societies, and
frauds of every kind.") An anonymous watchmaker wrote to the *Journal de Paris* that he had developed shoes which enabled him to walk
on water with the speed of a galloping horse. For two hundred louis,
he offered to cross the Seine in public. The *Journal* willingly collected
for the project, and over a hundred aristocrats donated, including the
royal family. But when the great day came there were no special
shoes; there was not even any watchmaker. It was all a prank by a
well-known citizen, designed to mock the many charlatans who were
collecting donations for sham science projects. The embarrassed *Journal de Paris* apologized, "In a moment when the sciences offer us the
most imposing of phenomena, that of man boldly soaring in the

regions of the air [hot-air ballooning was the latest marvel], we did not think we could dismiss the idea of seeing him walk on the surface of the waters." In a display of good spirit, the gullible donors gave the money to charity.

In the 1930s, C. Louis Mortison, a Prospect, Connecticut, correspondent for the Waterbury *Republican* and *American,* invented a farmer named Lester Green whose preposterous experiences were often believed by educated readers. Green found that if he put two setting hens on his automobile on cold nights, the engine was warm enough to start without trouble in the morning; a hen's temperature is 102, and so the temperature of two hens is 204. Green devised a new way to hunt foxes: he taught his hound to run away from foxes and lure them to the farm, where Green would shoot them. He churned the juice of milkweed stems and produced butter.

Readers sometimes wrote to Farmer Green, and Mortison answered. Green discovered a fluid in pigs that makes their tails curl, and when his wife and daughter rubbed it into their hair it gave them permanent waves. (They were besieged with inquiries about the fluid.) He sprayed his apple trees with glue one fall and thus could pick fresh apples off the trees all winter. (American and Canadian glue companies wrote to Green to find out what kind of glue he used.) He flooded a field one fall, and in the ice months later he found a nest of frozen chicken eggs. He thawed them out, and a few days later they hatched eight chicks covered with fur instead of feathers. (A Canadian farmer tried to buy a pair of the furry chickens, but Morrison answered they had all died from overheating in warm weather.)

Newspapers have often printed fake news items to prove that other papers copy their articles without giving credit. In Pennsylvania in 1940 the *Kennet Advertiser* described the visit of a full-blooded Delaware Indian descended from the great chief Ffutsse Lpoepre Htognil Aets. After West Chester's *Daily Local News* published the same general story, the first paper's publisher told everyone to read the Indian chief's name backward: Stealing other people's stuff.

The most notorious modern newspaper fraud involved a young *Washington Post* reporter who first invented part of her resume in order to get her job, then invented an eight-year-old heroin addict named Jimmy and wrote a heart-wrenching article about him. The article was so dramatic that it won a Pulitzer Prize. When the news broke that the story was fiction, the proud *Washington Post* was humiliated and the ambitious reporter's career was in shambles.

One of the worst tales ever told about newspaper fraud is how publisher William Randolph Hearst intended to provoke a war with Spain over Cuba. He sent artist Frederick Remington to Cuba to draw pictures of Spanish atrocities for his papers. Remington wired Hearst from Cuba, "Everything is quiet. There is no trouble here. There will be no war. I wish to return."

Hearst wired back, "Please remain. You furnish pictures. I'll furnish the war." Remington did as he was told, and Hearst did as he promised. Readers failed to realize that Hearst repeatedly manipulated public opinion with intentionally false reports. (Ironically, this famous example of Hearst's fraudulence is said to be fraudulent.)

### No-news News

There is a serious book about the history of American journalism titled *If No News, Send Rumors.* That title speaks volumes.

"As the line between fact and fiction becomes increasingly blurred, the news business inevitably becomes more and more like show business," according to Paul Duke of television's *Washington Week in Review.* That is true in more ways than one. David Epstein, a Hollywood publicity man, invented an important Broadway producer named Ned Farrington, whose frequent imaginary dealings with Epstein's very real clients got their names into print over and over. Finally a columnist for the *Hollywood Reporter* caught on, and one morning he announced in his column "The many Hollywood friends of Ned Farrington, Broadway producer, were inexpressibly shocked to learn that he died in his sleep last night." Mr. Epstein was indeed shocked, and from then on he had to get along without his mythical Ned Farrington.

When journalist Jeremy Campbell began his career at London's *Evening Standard,* he had to contribute to the "London Last Night" page that reported on London high life, especially the doings of debutantes. Campbell was so bored that he invented a colorful debutante named Venetia Crust, whose high jinks enlivened his reports month after month. He eventually confided in someone who then reported the hoax to his editor, and he was fired. Later he was rehired at the *Evening Standard,* but not to write society news.

A student named Pearl Rubins once had the job of writing the gossip column for the University of Chicago daily paper, the *Maroon*. One dull day she and Robert Evans decided to liven up the column with activities of a coed they named Lillian Luther. Week after week they included tidbits like "Miss Lillian Luther, who had a date Friday night with Hart Perry, left with Bob Merriam and never showed up at her dormitory until 2:00 A.M. Saturday."

In the *Maroon*'s final story about Miss Luther, she slapped the face of her badly behaved escort Robert Evans in the middle of the dance floor at the prom. The campus reporter for Chicago's *Herald Examiner* knew it was all a hoax, but he saw the chance for a good story with a by-line and wrote it up. The senior Mr. Evans, a rather austere Chicago investment banker, saw the embarrassing news about his son in the *Herald Examiner* and was furious. No amount of explanation ever quite convinced Mr. Evans it was just a hoax.

In the 1970s, when Canadian Andreas Schroeder was assigned to write a column about local literary events for the *Vancouver Province*, there was little to write about. As a result, he invented a coffee house named L'Crash and reported colorful events that took place there. Schroeder located his coffee house in a strictly residential neighborhood, at the intersection of two streets that run parallel. Nevertheless, readers of his column often tried to find L'Crash and called the newspaper for directions. As this problem increased, Schroeder finally reported that the coffee house burned down.

At that time Toronto was boasting several new publishing houses, and Schroeder decided that Vancouver should have one also. So he invented a big one that had attracted investors like IBM. He named the new company Permanent Press (an idea he got from his shirt label) and announced forthcoming books. Hopeful writers who could not locate the address of Permanent Press started sending their manuscripts there in care of Schroeder. (Some of these were famous writers.) He had to close down Permanent Press.

Schroeder was also on the staff of the *Magazine of Contemporary Literature and Translation*, a journal supported by the Canada Council. A young Jewish writer in St. Louis, Missouri, submitted a fine manuscript of poetic Midrashim (words of wisdom); the trouble was that according to tradition Midrashim should be written by elderly men. In the spirit of satire, the editors created a ninety-year-old Jewish author and printed his photo and biography along with the new

Midrashim in a special section of their journal. They cited their author's fifteen previous books, literary criticism, and reviews. They also mentioned his nine-volume diary, yet unpublished.

Specialists were amazed that they had hitherto missed such a significant writer. At a convention of Jewish intellectuals in San Francisco shortly after the journal came out, interest was intense. Schroeder had to fly to St. Louis to help the frantic young author fend off a famous New York translator who was urgently demanding access to the nine diaries. In the end, the hoaxers had to confess, and the dignified Canada Council was not amused. That was the death of the *Magazine of Contemporary Literature and Translation*.

There have been many hoaxes in the sports world. *Chicago Tribune* sportswriter and humorist Ring Lardner tricked Chicago mightily once. The annual Chicago/Michigan Big Ten game on Thanksgiving Day used to be played alternately at Stagg Field and Ann Arbor, but the crowd (like today's soccer fans) got too unruly and the tradition was cancelled. When Thanksgiving week rolled around again Lardner wrote about the "approaching game" as if nothing had changed. As a result, it is said, on Thanksgiving afternoon, 10,000 fans showed up at Stagg Field to get tickets to the nonexistent game.

A New York stockbroker named Morris Newburger invented the Flying Figments football team of the imaginary Plainfield Teachers College in Plainfield, New Jersey. He provided them with coach Ralph Hoblitzel, a valuable tackle named Morris Newburger, and a star quarterback named Johnny Chung. Chung was a potential all-American who ate a bowl of rice between halves. All the news that Newburger called in anonymously about Plainfield Teachers games appeared on Sundays in the *New York Times* and *Herald Tribune* until reporters in search of Johnny Chung uncovered the hoax.

## Dipsy-doodle Reports

In retrospect, many articles in reputable newspapers seem fit only for tabloids like the *National Enquirer.* There have been newspaper articles about King Tut's solid gold typewriter; a red, white, and blue egg laid by a chicken on July 4; and a man who successfully chased away flies by painting a spider on his bald head. In 1962 a nonexistent set of octuplets in Chile was reported in serious newspapers around the world. A foreign correspondent once reported that a

British millionaire on the French Riviera supplied his guests with special bathing suits that dissolved in salt water. When his editor at home demanded some of the suits, the reporter sent finely pulverized cereal in a sturdy box, in order to give the impression that the bathing suits had dissolved in damp air on the way.

In about 1875 a Lacon, Illinois, editor named Willis B. Powell sent the Associated Press an announcement about a cat-and-rat ranch, and news of it was published across the United States. Here is the announcement:

> Glorious Opportunity to Get Rich—We are starting a cat ranch in Lacon with 100,000 cats. Each cat will average 12 kittens a year. The cat skins will sell for 30 cents each. One hundred men can skin 5,000 cats a day. We figure a daily net profit of over $10,000. Now what shall we feed the cats? We will start a rat ranch next door with 1,000,000 rats. The rats will breed 12 times faster than the cats. So we will have four rats to feed each day to each cat. Now what shall we feed the rats? We will feed the rats the carcasses of the cats after they have been skinned. Now Get This! We feed the rats to the cats and the cats to the rats and get the cat skins for nothing.

In October 1891 the *Great Yarmouth Mercury* reported an accident that had occurred near the Falkland Islands the previous February. Two sailors on Star of the East were knocked overboard while trying to harpoon a large sperm whale. The one named James Bartley disappeared; and when the crew killed the whale later and cut it open, there was Bartley, doubled up in its stomach. After several weeks he recovered from the ordeal of soaking in hot gastric juices, but his skin was permanently bleached deathly white. Investigators found that there was no shred of evidence that James Bartley existed, and the captain's widow denied the entire story, but it has been repeated over and over in books and magazines anyway.

In 1990 an English translation of a Norwegian newspaper article revealed an amazing event in the Soviet Union. Dr. Azzacov and other scientists on an oil drilling platform in the North Sea drilled a hole nine miles deep, then stopped when they smelled sulfur and heard millions of people screaming. The frightened scientists had discovered the location of hell. A translation of the Norwegian article was used by at least one American news announcer and appeared in a prophecy magazine called the *Midnight Cry*.

*Biblical Archaeology Review* published the news in a tongue-in-cheek report in its November-December 1990 issue, likening the discovery of hell under Siberia to purported discoveries of Noah's Ark and the Ark of the Covenant. Many readers took the spoof seriously and sent in comments, including the following: "To take at face value the report from the *Midnight Cry* as though it were reliable and free from prejudice and bias is naïve in the extreme. Then to report it without comment giving it an air of respectability is irresponsible" (Professor T. R. Hobbs, McMaster University Divinity College, Ontario, Canada). "I hope you will stop printing such nonsensical third- and fourth-hand information and stick to straightforward and helpful finds . . ." (Kerry Cort, Webster, New York). " . . . one would expect more from a scholarly journal" (Dr. Robert A. Box, Augusta, Kansas). "I would like to see *BAR* follow up and see if a Dr. Azzacov even exists" (Janis Hutchinson, Everett, Washington).

Editor Hershel Shanks answered that the article had been concocted by a hoaxer to test the American media and had never appeared in a Norwegian newspaper. "We thought . . . our readers would get a laugh over the story, just as we did. If hell is ever actually discovered, you may be sure that we will not confine our announcement to an item in [our miscellany page]. We'll give it a 72-point head across a spread—with the first color pictures of the place!"

## Two Top Newspaper Hoaxes

It is fair to assume that British author and scholar C. S. Lewis might have enjoyed the new Hell-under-Siberia hoax, since he greatly enjoyed reading about the old Lunar Hoax. In August 1835 the New York *Sun* ran a series of scientific articles purportedly reprinted from the *Edinburgh Journal of Science* (a journal that had ceased publication two years earlier). The articles were allegedly written by the distinguished British astronomer Sir John Herschel, who had gone to the Cape of Good Hope to try out a new telescope that could magnify things 42,000 times. Herschel's detailed descriptions of the moon were amazing. He saw lakes, immense fields of poppies, herds of buffalo with heavy eyelids, a temple made of sapphire, bears with horns, amethysts over sixty feet tall, thirty-eight species of forest trees, two-footed beavers, and tiny reindeer. Public excitement mounted with each new installment, and circulation soared.

The fourth installment from Herschel described furry, bat-winged, friendly people with intelligent faces. On the day that report was published, the *Sun* boasted the largest circulation of any paper in the world—19,360. Other papers were frantic and copied the articles from the *Sun*, claiming that they got the articles directly from the *Edinburgh Journal of Science*. A committee of suspicious scientists from Yale University hastened to New York to inspect the *Journal* but the *Sun* shunted them here and there in their search for the missing document, until they finally gave up and went home. At last, after three weeks, the *Sun* confessed its great hoax and scolded the papers that had copied its stories without giving credit. The moon story had been written by *Sun* journalist Richard Adams Locke.

Less than ten years after its spectacular Lunar Hoax, the *Sun* ran another hoax: the exciting story of a balloon that carried nine people across the Atlantic to South Carolina in only three days. This one was written by Edgar Allan Poe.

Hoax authority Curtis D. MacDougall considers the Wild Animal Hoax second to the great Lunar Hoax in the annals of American newspaper hoaxdom. On November 9, 1874, the *New York Herald* published a detailed eyewitness account of a catastrophe at the Central Park Zoo, where all the animals had escaped. Two hundred people were injured, sixty were in serious condition, and forty-nine were dead. (The names of twenty-seven of the dead were listed.) Twelve dangerous animals were still at large when the paper went to press, and the mayor warned citizens to stay at home while the beasts were hunted down by prominent New Yorkers in the area of Fifth and Broadway. Readers were frantic. The owner of the *Herald* collapsed in bed while reading the news and stayed there all day. The relatively few readers who finished the article learned in the last paragraph that the *Herald*'s managing editor had asked his staff to write this fictitious story to dramatize the need for improvements at the zoo.

That paper's founder, James Gordon Bennett, once advised a cub reporter not to let accuracy interfere too much with entertainment: "Remember, son, many a good story has been ruined by oververification."

## Traveling Stones

In 1865, readers of the *Virginia City Territorial Enterprise* read Dan De Quille's report on "traveling stones" found in the Pahranagat mountains of Nevada. These magnetic stones attracted each other and then huddled together in groups. Journalist De Quille, a friend of Mark Twain, eventually received inquiries from scientists across the United States and Europe. P. T. Barnum reportedly offered him $10,000 for some of the stones.

Thirteen years later, De Quille confessed in the paper, "It is becoming a little monotonous. We are growing old, and we want peace. . . . Therefore we solemnly affirm that we never saw or heard of any such diabolical cobbles as the traveling stones of Pahranagat— though we still think there ought to be something of the kind some- where in the world. If this candid confession shall carry a pang to the heart of any true believer we shall be glad of it, as the true believers have panged it to us, right and left, quite long enough."

But in 1892 De Quille brought up the stones again in his column in the Salt Lake City *Daily Tribune.*

> I once wrote an item about some stones supposed to have been found in Pahranagat that, when scattered about on a table, would run together and bunch up like a covey of quail. The stones were said to be rounded by the action of water, and largely composed of magnetic iron. The item was merely put forth as a "feeler." I thought there might be such rounded pebbles of magnetic iron, as I had seen a lump of such ore pick up several fragments of the same weighing as much as four or five ounces. My object was to set the many prospectors then ranging the country to looking for such things.
>
> My item was extensively copied, and finally it became the "Traveling Stones of Australia," some papers in our antipodes having localized it by using the name of some Australian mining region instead of Pahranagat. Meantime I was so bothered with letters from all kinds of people that I at last came out and said my item was a mere "fake," that I had seen no such stones. Hundreds wanted sample lots of the stones—small nests of them. One man desired to become my partner in the deposit. We were to run a train of

77

pack mules as freight trains to the nearest point on the railroad, and load several cars with the stones. . . . He would
first supply the demand in all the museums of this country,
and would then similarly favor the Old World. . . .

Shortly after I denied the existence of the traveling
stones, I began to receive assurances that such stones had
really been found in central Nevada. Among others who
had found and owned such stones were Joseph E. Eckley,
present State Printer of Nevada. Mr. Eckley has several
times told me of his having owned a lot of such stones while
he was a citizen of Austin, Lander county. He obtained them
in Nye county on a hill that was filled and covered with
geodes. Most of these geodes contained crystals of various
colors. These are not the traveling kind. Those that appear
to be endued with life are little nodules of iron. They are
found on the hill among the geodes, and it was only by
accident that Mr. Eckley discovered their traveling propen-
sities.

De Quille also reported on a letter he received from a J. M. Woodworth. Woodworth said that he had seen plenty of traveling stones in
Humboldt county about sixty miles from the Central Pacific Railroad.

If they are as rare as you and Professor Stewart seem to
think, Nevada should have some at the World's Fair. They
are from the size of No. 4 shot to quail eggs and generally
there will be one quite large and then several smaller ones
in a depression in the rock. It seems to be a volcanic rock,
with a large amount of iron in it. If they are taken away and
thrown around promiscuously they will loose [sic] their
magnetic quality in a few weeks, but if kept in a glass bottle
will retain it indefinitely. Take a handful of them, throw
them on the table or on a smooth floor and they will all run
together in less than thirty seconds, and the last one getting
there jumping a foot or more and sticking on the pile wher-
ever it strikes . . .

De Quille included an authoritative description of Nye county
geodes along with other factual detail and pseudo-facts.

78

Even when De Quille admitted that he had lied earlier about the traveling stones, readers believed in them all over again because he seemed so frank and candid.

## The Bathtub

American journalist H. L. Mencken's straight-faced hoax outdid De Quille's. On December 28, 1917, Mencken published in the *New York Evening Mail* some harmless levity titled "A Neglected Anniversary," to lighten the dark days of World War I. He pointed out that on December 10 the seventy-fifth anniversary of a great event in American history had passed unnoticed—the introduction of the bathtub. He explained that a wealthy American named Adam Thompson had met Lord John Russell in England in 1842 and decided to do for America what Russell had done a decade earlier for England.

Thompson had a splendid mahogany tub built, lined with lead to prevent rot, and introduced it in Cincinnati on December 10, 1842. At first his friends took turns trying it out. As this novelty spread, physicians protested. Boston banned the use of tubs except under medical supervision, and Philadelphia almost outlawed the use of bathtubs in winter. But the public learned to love baths anyway, and President Millard Fillmore had the first bathtub installed in the White House. There were many more details in Mencken's account.

Every bit of this history was entirely bogus.

Before long, Mencken saw his hoax appearing in news articles, scholarly works, and reference books. On May 23, 1926, he published his retraction of the bathtub malarkey, titled "Melancholy Reflections," in many major newspapers. But the hoax was over eight years old by that time and had a life of its own. Three weeks after publishing Mencken's retraction, the *Boston Herald* republished the bathtub fable all over again. Mencken wrote a second column refuting his hoax, and it also failed to turn the tide.

Year after year Mencken's hokum about the history of bathtubs appeared and reappeared in newspapers (including the *New York Times* and countless others), magazines (including *Scribner's, New Statesman* and *House Beautiful*), pamphlets (including one from the Domestic Engineering Company of Chicago), and books (including a best-seller by Dr. Hans Zinsser of the Medical School of Harvard University). It appeared in countless communications including a bulletin of the Department of Health of Kentucky and a radio address by New York City's commissioner of health.

On April 28, 1951, author John Hersey remarked in a profile on Harry Truman in the *New Yorker* that the President often included Mencken's bathtub history when he talked to visitors about White House renovations. But Hersey's revelation did no good. On September 16, 1952, President Truman repeated the story again in a Philadelphia speech praising our great progress in public health. That was thirty-five years after Mencken started the hoax and twenty-six years after his second retraction. H. L. Mencken died in 1956, but his bathtub blarney lives on.

# FORGING AHEAD WITH HISTORY

*History: an account mostly false, of events mostly unimportant, which are brought about by rulers mostly knaves, and soldiers mostly fools.*

—Ambrose Bierce

Newspapers sometimes print malarkey about history, and historians have been known to return the compliment, printing malarkey about newspapers.

For fifty years, copies of the world's first newspaper, the *English Mercury*, were prized possessions of the British Museum. It had been published under Queen Elizabeth to report accurately Britain's victory over the Spanish Armada in 1588, and it surfaced in the British Museum in 1782. It was soon a source of national pride because it proved that Britain had produced the earliest newspaper more than forty years before France, which had supposedly invented newspapers.

In 1839 the superintendent of the reading room of the British Museum announced sadly that the print type used in the *English Mercury* did not exist until the 1700s, and so the 1588 newspaper could not be genuine. There was no *English Mercury* or any other newspaper in Queen Elizabeth's day after all. (The honor of inventing newspapers bounced back to France.) Rummaging around in their files, the librarians found correspondence between a Dr. Thomas Birch and his friend Philip Yorke in the 1740s proving that Yorke had produced the 1588 edition of the *English Mercury* for Birch for fun. Birch's literary possessions, including that spoof, had ended up in the British Museum; but neither Birch nor Yorke had meant to hoax anyone.

## Inventing the Past

Eight hundred years ago, the great Jewish scholar Maimonides warned wisely, "Do not think a thing proved because it is in a book; the liar, who deceives men with his tongue, does not hesitate to

81

deceive them with his pen." But he warned in vain. People not only believe lies when they read them in a book; sometimes they even believe outright fiction when they read it in a book. No historical hoax was intended in 1980 when writer Harold Myra published his novel *The Choice*, which began with a preface that said:

> The news media accounts about the archaeologists' discovery near Beersheba of "Risha's story" have been largely accurate. The international interest, of course, has centered on the previously unknown substance of the 367 plates. . . . Some scholars were jolted to find the content an expansion of the early Genesis chapters. Did the plates come before the biblical account, or after? . . . *The Choice*—the publisher's title and not derived from the plates [*The drawings in this edition are a modern artist's conception and should in no way be construed as having been inspirited by marks in the plates*]—is being published simultaneously in fourteen languages, due to the intensity of world interest. Personally, we who have devoted our time to the translation work look forward to the initial furor over the plates finally giving way to interest in the remarkable tale itself.

In spite of the fact that the inside flap of the dust jacket calls the book a novel, some readers mistook it for the translation of an ancient historical document. I know, because a friend of mine with an M.A. in literature from a fine university read my copy all the way through and believed it was genuine. The playful preface had completely honey-fuggled her.

In 1926, *Diary of a Young Lady of Fashion, 1764–1765* was such a best-seller in the United States that it went through nine editions in two months. The girl who wrote the diary, Cleone Knox, gave an inside view of English and European society in her day; she told of meeting Voltaire in Switzerland and of being kissed on both cheeks by the King of France. The public loved the book, and prominent people praised it as a wonderful historical document. Then the truth came out; it had just been dashed off in a few weeks by nineteen-year-old Magdalen King-Hall, daughter of a British Navy admiral, who got her information about life in 1764 from library books. The author said she hadn't meant to deceive anyone; but it seems that her publisher did.

Unlike *The Choice* and *Diary of a Young Lady*, most historical hoaxes are intentional. The great violinist Fritz Kreisler confessed in February 1935 that for thirty years he had been playing his own compositions and attributing them to early masters like Vivaldi, claiming to have found them during his world tours. He explained that people wouldn't have listened if they had known that the music was contemporary. He created the music, then created the history that gave it prestige.

Fudging history is as old as history. In the British Museum there is a temple inscription from Babylon dated, in our terms, at 2000 B.C., telling how much the king had donated to the temple. Tests show that the inscription was really produced in 1000 B.C. The purpose of the priests in predating their temple was probably to increase prestige and donations. Their 3,000-year-old lie, which pretends to be a 4,000-year-old truth, ends with every liar's all-time favorite assurance: "This is not a lie, it is indeed the truth." Some things never change.

### Druidic Lore

At the very time when the British were enjoying the wonderful discovery of the long-lost *English Mercury*, they were also enjoying the wonderful discovery of the lost lore of the Druids. The true significance of the British Celts and their culture had finally surfaced in the 1700s, and things Celtic were fashionable after about a thousand years of neglect. Some people enamored with things Celtic yearned for a Celtic religion, but the unwritten wisdom of Druidic priests and teachers seemed to be irrevocably, tragically lost.

What if the ancient Bards had passed down Druidic lore in a tradition that had gone underground in 1282, when the Welsh lost their independence? What if Archdruids had been secretly appointed through the centuries? What if Druids were finally ready to reveal that they were not extinct after all?

Edward Williams was born in 1747 in the village of Pen Onn in South Wales. His family spoke English, but Welsh was the language of the region where they lived. Williams was an ugly little stonemason like his father, but he was also an eloquent and witty writer. He was so eccentric that he never rode horses, but took his own horse for walks like a pet dog. Politically, Williams was an ardent supporter of the French revolution, and theologically he was anti-Christian. He found his niche in Welsh literary circles, and his frequent discoveries of old Celtic manuscripts made him a leading authority on things Celtic. He dropped the English name Edward Williams and took the Celtic name Iolo Morganwg.

In 1792, forty-five-year-old Iolo Morganwg revealed that he was in fact the current Archdruid and custodian of the heritage of ancient wisdom. Followers flocked to him. He launched himself with a history-making bardic council in a stone circle on London's Primrose Hill. (No one thought of applying to Iolo the old Celtic proverb "Don't leave the fox in charge of the geese.") He was so successful that he eventually directed in detail the first annual National Eisteddfod, which is to this day the best-known cultural event in Wales.

Iolo was not only accepted by many as the best authority on the secret tradition of the Druids, but also the foremost expert on Celtic mythology. Until he died at the age of seventy-four in 1826, he worked tirelessly on his compilations and clarifications of ancient Celtic myth and poetry. Among other things, he revealed what came to be called the "Helio-Arkite" form of ancient Celtic religion, based on a sun-god providing an ark during a flood. Iolo also revealed a traditional Celtic egalitarianism and pacifism that other scholars had not yet discovered in their research. No one else found evidence of a Celtic sun-god, the high place of Celtic women, and a Celtic aversion to war and slavery.

During the nineteenth century, linguists learned much more about the Celtic language and gradually noticed so many mistakes in Iolo's literature that his scholarship became suspect. Finally in 1919 the Welsh periodical *Y Beirniad* announced that Iolo's work was a gigantic hoax, and the academic establishment had to agree. He had not been relaying history; he had been creating a great work of imagination, rather like that of J. R. R. Tolkien. Many of the Celtic manuscripts he had discovered were his own forgeries.

By the time that Iolo was proved a fraud, his material had thoroughly permeated the public perception of Celts. Lewis Spence spread Iolo's claims even farther in his popular 1928 nonfiction book *Mysteries of Britain*. Fifty years after he was debunked, Iolo's imagination was still enriching the work of writers who make creative use of Celtic mythology, such as Robert Graves in *The White Goddess*, Evangeline Walton in *The Island of the Mighty*, and Lloyd Alexander in his prizewinning *Chronicles of Prydain*.

A Celtic specialist named Alexi Kondratiev has analyzed Iolo and the possible motives behind "such painstaking and time-consuming deceit." In cases like this we are often dealing with a compulsive liar and his urge to manipulate other people's credulity. In other cases, Kondratiev believes, the main goal has been to gain respectability and power for some beloved cause that was perceived as weak and languishing. Deceit is especially apt to occur where long-standing institutions and traditions would strengthen a nationalistic, political, or ethnic movement. If there is no adequate written evidence of such history, one can seek it in oral folklore—or one can try to forge it.

## One Fairy Story Too Many

There were once two brothers who loved nothing as much as listening to stories which old women and young girls told them . . . and because friends encouraged them, they went deeper and deeper into the fairy-tale forest, and collected all the pretty leaves that they found, and took them home, and preserved them as a special treasure. [In plainer words, they] spent much of their time wandering about the country, gleaning from peasants and the simpler townspeople a rich harvest of legends, which they wrote down as nearly as possible in the words in which they were told.

This beguiling story about the Grimm brothers has been told and retold in almost ritual fashion for over 150 years, although it is all bosh and has been repeatedly and thoroughly disproved. It is one of the most successfully perpetuated literary frauds of all time.

Jacob Grimm (1785–1863) and his brother Wilhelm (1786–1859) were caught up in the spirit of German nationalism that ruled their day. They claimed to have written down faithfully the tales told to them by peasants and other simple folk, tapping into an authentic German oral tradition. In fact, however, their major sources were educated, middle-class, and French. The brothers gathered tales from well-to-do friends and relatives, radically rewrote them to their own taste, then passed them off as genuine German folktales. They lied blatantly about their sources, intentionally destroyed their basic material, and later lied about their own revisions to their own published texts.

Most scholars and children's literature specialists ignore the evidence and resort to highly implausible ideas to avoid admitting that the Grimm brothers consciously and deliberately deceived their public. (It is simply not true that standards for accuracy were lower in the 1800s.) John M. Ellis, professor of German literature at the University of California at Santa Cruz, gives a full account of the amazing hoax in his 1983 book *One Fairy Story Too Many*.

How did the Grimms succeed? Ellis says, "Experience shows that once misconceptions are really firmly entrenched in a body of scholarship, they develop a life of their own and are not easily eradicable; like a giant oil tanker, they have enormous directional momentum and take a very long time to turn around."

### Faraway Fakery

Bogus cultural traditions have often been foisted off on the public. For example, according to Thomas Sowell of the Hoover Institute, kindergarten children in Redwood City are taught about Kwanzaa, an "African-American celebration of the first fruits of harvest." Sowell explains, "Nobody in Africa ever heard about this holiday because it was invented in Los Angeles in the 1960s—long after most black people in the United States had ever seen a harvest. But this is one of the more harmless frauds of 'multicultural diversity.'" Sowell complains that many multicultural diversity programs are made up of cheap and superficial propaganda, "as phony as a three-dollar bill."

The man who invented Kwanzaa in 1966, a professor in Long Beach, California, claims that it is now celebrated by some 15 million people in the United States, Africa, Canada, the Caribbean, and parts of Europe. As an alternative to Christmas celebrations, it lasts from December 26 to January 1, and its decorative colors are red, black, and green. Whether Kwanzaa is an honest invention or a cultural fraud, history has always been contaminated with facts and artifacts as phony as a three-dollar bill.

Vancouver, British Columbia, has become the home of quite a few people from India. Some of them produce traditional kinds of Canadian souvenirs for tourists and market them as "made by authentic Indians."

In contrast to this new tribe of Vancouver Indians, Chief Seattle was a genuine American Indian leader from the Squamish tribe in

Puget Sound. In 1854, he gave a stirring speech that contrasted the Indian and "white" ways of life (as a Roman Catholic, he was not entirely opposed to the latter), and in 1855 he signed the treaty that ceded much of the land where the city of Seattle stands today. He died in 1866, one day after the city of Seattle passed a law making it illegal for Indians to live within the city limits. He remained just an admirable historical footnote until he was transformed into an environmental prophet.

In 1971, the Southern Baptist Radio and Television Commission produced a film on ecology by a screenwriter named Ted Perry. Perry, who now teaches at Middlebury College in Vermont, wrote a fictitious speech for Chief Seattle to deliver in the film. (A recollection of the chief's actual 1854 speech was published in 1887, and it was not about ecology.) In Perry's speech, Chief Seattle lamented the thousands of buffalo shot from passing trains and left to rot. In fact, however, there were no bison within 600 miles of Puget Sound, and no railroad crossed the plains until fifteen years after Chief Seattle's death.

After 1971, different versions of Perry's historically inaccurate speech circulated and appeared in print. In 1991, Dial Books for Young People published Susan Jeffers' version as a nonfiction book titled *Brother Eagle, Sister Sky: A Message from Chief Seattle*. In 1992, the Earth Day U.S.A. Committee sent out a similar version, identified as Chief Seattle's letter to President Franklin Pierce.

David Buerge, a historian of the Northwest who was writing a book about Chief Seattle at the time, said, "It's a classic case of a lie going twenty miles an hour when truth is just putting on its boots."

Another lie went twenty miles an hour early in 1985 when journalists rhapsodized about the discovery of the ruins of an ancient lost city in Peru. Readers were thrilled, until they learned later that the city had been known and visited for years. In fact, it had even been the subject of a television program, and all that was new in 1985 was one more archaeological dig.

For about five hundred years most people believed in a mythical island southwest of Ireland named Hi-Brazil, which used to appear on maps of the North Atlantic. When Columbus discovered the coast of South America, some people thought he had discovered the elusive Hi-Brazil. Various seafarers sought it in vain, but in 1674 Captain John Nisbet landed there and rescued some shipwrecked Scotsmen. He revealed that these men (who agreed with everything he said) had been held prisoner for years by an evil magician who lived in a castle on the island, which was populated mainly by large black rabbits. Nisbet and his men had overcome the magic by building a fire on the shore. When they got home they were treated like heroes.

Few people today have heard of John Nisbet and Hi-Brazil, but according to David Roberts, who wrote the Sierra Club's *Great Exploration Hoaxes*, some of our most famous explorers were frauds. He includes Sebastian Cabot, Father Hennepin, Donald Crowhurst, Frederick Cook, Samuel Adams, Cesare Maestre, Robert Drury, Robert Peary, and Richard E. Byrd. All of these men (few women are either explorers or hoaxers) wanted the genuine achievement very badly. Although admirable explorers like Eric Shipton on Mount Everest and Ernest Shackleton near the South Pole suffered defeat honestly, the hoaxers faked success in grim determination to fool the world. They could not bear to let other men get the glory.

### Early Americana

From exploration to explanation, the history of America has often been flavored with fakery. Christopher Columbus has inspired forgers to create many water-soaked parchments filling in his story with missing information. One of these was bought by a lawyer in Mexico City in about 1876. It had been soaked in salt water and was embedded with sand and shells, but the writing was clearly legible. Columbus explained that he was writing his log in German so that his crew members couldn't read it.

For centuries it has been popular to idealize Columbus. The 1955 children's book *Columbus* by Ingri and Edgar D'Aulaire gives him credit for discovering that the world is round, although every educated person in his day knew it is round. The book says Columbus and his men came to bring the Christian faith to the naked red-skinned savages, but it fails to mention they brought slavery and murder instead. Columbus's seizing six Indians for display in Spain is described happily: "He had even brought along some Indians to show."

In the 1991 controversy about whether Christopher Columbus was an Italian/Spanish Christian hero or a criminal, it became more obvious than ever that some people look at the past as raw material that they can transform for their own pleasure, profit, or political gain. Playwright Harold Pinter described that attitude clearly: "The past is what you remember, imagine you remember, convince yourself you remember, or pretend to remember." And according to George Orwell, since whoever controls the past controls the future, whoever is in power in the present tries to control the past.

Many people like to think of Puritans as far more strict and sour than they were. According to Richard Peters' 1829 book *The General History of Connecticut,* Puritan laws prohibited people from kissing their children on Sunday; from making mince pies; from playing any instrument except the drum, trumpet, or Jew's harp; and from many other innocent activities. The list of laws was so unreasonable that it was quoted far and wide. But those laws never existed.

North Carolina's 1775 Declaration of Independence from England is still on its statute books. The date of the Declaration, May 20, 1775, is emblazoned upon the state seal; and by legislative action May 20 is a state holiday. Never mind that Thomas Jefferson himself said that the Mecklenburg Declaration is a hoax. (If it is genuine, Jefferson plagiarized it.)

This declaration is named after Mecklenburg County, North Carolina. There John M. Alexander, allegedly the recording clerk at a convention of citizens in Charlotte in 1775, wrote out the five resolutions from memory in 1800. It was first published April 30, 1819, in the Raleigh *Register,* and in 1830 Thomas Jefferson declared it a fake.

The original document, if there was one, has never turned up. It was supposedly sent to England by Governor Josiah Martin. When James K. Polk was president, he ordered Ambassador George Bancroft to search for it in London, in vain. It has been said that on August 15, 1832, Ambassador Stevenson found the document in London; but there is no such report from Stevenson in the records.

On July 1, 1905, *Collier's* published an article by S. Millington Miller to prove the authenticity of the Mecklenburg Declaration. Miller provided a picture of the first page of the *Cape-Fear Mercury* newspaper for June 3, 1775, which presented the resolutions exactly two weeks after they were adopted. It seemed that Thomas Jefferson was wrong and the North Carolina legislature was right.

But nine months after Miller authenticated the Mecklenburg Declaration, the *American Historical Review* spoiled all the fun. An article by the secretary of the Historical Commission of South

Carolina and the chief of the Division of Manuscripts of the Library of Congress showed that the first page of the *Cape-Fear Mercury* was a hoax. There were several serious errors in it; and worst of all, that newspaper was no longer being published in June 1775.

## The Cherry Tree

There have been few American historical scenes so well known as George Washington and the cherry tree. Mason Locke Weems started his career as an ebullient itinerant Bible salesman, and he knew how to please simple, hardworking people. He was a preacher at heart, and more interested in patriotism, inspiration, and financial success than he was in accurate history—even his own. He claimed in print to have been the rector of George Washington's Mount Vernon Parish, but the closest he came to that was occasional preaching at a country church eighteen miles away.

In June 1799 Weems advised a publisher to issue a series of brief biographies of American heroes, beginning with one by Weems titled *The Beauties of Washington*. Washington had retired to his estate at Mount Vernon and was at the peak of his popularity. When he died that December, the nation was grief-stricken, and Weems wrote to his publisher again:

> Washington is gone! Millions are gasping to read something about him. I am nearly primed and cocked for 'em. Six months ago I set myself to collecting anecdotes of him. You know I live conveniently for that work. My plan! I give his history, sufficiently minute—I accompany him from the start, thro' the French & Indian & British or Revolutionary wars to the Presidents chair, to the throne in the hearts of 5,000,000 people. I then show that his unparrelled [sic] rise and elevation were owing to his Great Virtues. . . . We can sell it with great rapidity for 25 or 37 cents, and it would not cost 10. . . . it will be the first. I can send it on, half of it, immediately.

Actually, Weems' sketch of Washington was not the first, but it was the liveliest. He titled it *A History of the Life and Death, Virtues and Exploits of General George Washington,* and he dedicated it to Martha Washington on February 22, Washington's birthday. He pointed out in his dedication that Washington was the son of a second marriage, "which it is hoped will effectually stop the mouths of those enemies of American population who are eternally bawling against second marriages. And it is also hoped that it will comfort the nerves of those chicken-livered bachelors, who are afraid to wed . . . lest they should encounter a group of their own angel-faced children. Timid mortals! Depopulation of your own country! Take courage and be happy!" That set the tone.

The pamphlet sold wonderfully well and made Weems a minor celebrity. It said nothing about the hatchet and the cherry tree, about Washington's mother having a dream that foretold his success, or about his being discovered in prayer at Valley Forge. Those stories were added to the fifth edition, when Weems added his imaginary pastorate at Mount Vernon. In its ninth edition, published in 1809, it had grown from an 80-page pamphlet to a 228-page book titled *The Life of George Washington; with Curious Anecdotes Equally Honourable to Himself and Exemplary to His Young Countrymen.* He sold the copyright before he realized what a gold mine the book was, and he said more than once that he could have supported his family in high style on the royalties from that one book alone.

As Weems told the cherry tree story, George received a hatchet when he was about six years old and frequently chopped at things. One day he wounded a beautiful young English cherry tree which his elderly father valued highly.

"George," said his father, "do you know who killed that beautiful little cherry-tree yonder in the garden?" That was a tough question; and George staggered under it for a moment; but quickly recovered himself: and looking at his father, with the sweet face of youth brightened with the inexpressible charm of all-conquering truth, he bravely cried out, "I can't tell a lie, Pa; you know I can't tell a lie. I did it with my hatchet."—"Run to my arms, you dearest boy," cried his father in transports, "run to my arms; glad am I, George, that you killed my tree; for you have paid me for it a thousand fold. Such an act of heroism in my son, is more worth than a thousand trees, though blossomed with silver, and their fruits of purest gold."

The most charitable view of Weems is that in his enthusiasm he embroidered the truth. Researchers claim that he copied the cherry tree story from James Beattie's book *The Minstrel*, published in London in 1799. That book also contained a story about cabbage seeds forming someone's name, which Weems repeated also in his life of Washington. Although scholars have disbelieved the cherry tree story for generations, it is popular in Fredericksburg. On February 22, 1935, a white-haired descendant of George Washington's family joined a group of Virginians there and planted a cherry tree on "the exact spot" where the famous tree once stood.

P. T. Barnum added a new dimension to George Washington's life by exhibiting Joice Heth, Washington's 161-year-old nurse. People said that she recalled a great deal about George Washington, and she looked 161 years old; but a later autopsy set her age at about eighty.

Betsy Ross's famous little old house in Philadelphia is probably no more genuine than George Washington's little old nurse. The house existed in Betsy Ross's day, but there is no evidence that Betsy Ross ever lived there.

### Honest Abe

Abraham Lincoln's famous little old house didn't even exist in his day. The log cabin on display near Hodgenville, Kentucky, is preserved by the Interior Department as "Abraham Lincoln Birthplace Historical Site." But records show that the log cabin where Lincoln was born burned down before 1840, and the remaining logs were reportedly used for firewood. When Lincoln died, witnesses said that there was no sign of a log cabin on his family's old farm, and his son Robert agreed. But a man named John Davenport built a fake Lincoln cabin and sold it to a promoter who displayed it at an exposition in Tennessee. The promoter's partner, an evangelist named James Bigham, remarked to an inquisitive reporter, "Lincoln was born in a log cabin, wasn't he? Well, one cabin is as good as another." The cabin in question was taken apart, moved, stored, and reassembled about six times before it was finally rescued from storage in New York by some preservationists who donated it to the Interior Department. It has been a tax-supported historic shrine in Kentucky ever since.

One of the most touching memories of Abraham Lincoln is his beautiful letter to Mrs. Bixby, who lost five sons in the Union Army.

Lincoln's secretary John Hay claimed to have written that letter, but it is not clear whether he meant that he composed it or if Lincoln dictated it to him. The original is lost; but no matter who composed it, it was a response to a hoax. Only two of Mrs. Bixby's five sons were killed in the Union army. Of the others, one was honorably discharged, one deserted, and one was captured and became a Confederate. When Lincoln scholar William Barton tried to publish an article about this, editors said that the public wouldn't care to have its faith in the Bixby story disturbed.

Another touching story about Lincoln is his rushing to single-handedly stop the callous firing-squad execution of William Scott, a soldier who went to sleep on guard duty. William Barton discovered that seven captains of Scott's regiment and a Brigadier General had all petitioned for Scott's pardon, and it was General McClellan who signed the pardon, not Abraham Lincoln. Lincoln no doubt approved of the pardon.

At the end of 1928 the *Atlantic Monthly* published a collection of weather-beaten love letters written by Abraham Lincoln and his sweetheart Anne Rutledge. The suspicious executive secretary of the Abraham Lincoln Association tested the letters in five ways: where they came from, the ink and paper, the handwriting, general subject matter, and how the incidents in the letters tallied with historical facts. In all five areas he found the letters faulty, and the *Atlantic* admitted in April 1929 that they were probably forged. They were evidently forged by their original owner, a woman in San Diego named Cora de Boyer.

In 1936 the Republican National Committee quoted this statement from Lincoln: "If we buy a ton of steel rails in England for $90, America gets the steel rails but England gets the $90. If we buy the steel rails in the United States we have the steel rails and the $90 too." But Lincoln never said this. There were no steel rails in the United States until shortly after his death.

"You cannot help the poor by destroying the rich." In 1949 Lincoln's set of ten political maxims was read into the Congressional Record by a Republican Congresswoman. *Look* magazine published the list next to Lincoln's portrait, with a call to heed his advice. In 1954 the postmaster-general included the list in a speech. At that point the chairman of the Democratic National Committee announced that the list was a fake, and he was right; the list originated in a 1942 leaflet from an ultra-conservative lobby backed by publisher Frank Gannett, and it has been repeatedly denounced as a fake ever since 1949. Nevertheless, on August 17, 1992, retired President Ronald Reagan featured the entirely bogus Lincoln maxims in his speech at the Republican National Convention in Houston, Texas. He said that Democrats fail to understand "the principles so eloquently stated by Abraham Lincoln: 'You cannot strengthen the weak by weakening the strong. You cannot help the wage earner by pulling down the wage payer. . . .'" The audience cheered wildly, and the speech was considered a stunning success.

There were too few full-length photographs of Abraham Lincoln, and as a result much doctoring of Lincoln photos took place. Someone decapitated a formal photo of Lincoln's political enemy John Calhoun and placed the head of Lincoln on Calhoun's stylish body, producing a fake that was used in many schoolrooms. A paper on Calhoun's table that had said "The Sovereignty of the States," was changed to read "Proclamation of Freedom." It is said that Lincoln's head also appeared on the bodies of Henry Clay, Andrew Jackson, John C. Fremont, and Martin Van Buren.

### Legends, Lies, and Cherished Myths

Just as George Washington and Abraham Lincoln were exalted into demi-gods after their deaths, so Edgar Alan Poe has been portrayed as almost demonic. In the freewheeling first half of the 1800s, some New York literati were openly given to lies, rivalries, mudslinging, name calling, and insults. Poe and Rufus W. Griswold had an uneasy truce. Poe considered Griswold a literary charlatan, but neither was entirely dependable. (Poe first told Griswold he was born in 1811, then changed it to 1813. Poe was really born in 1809.)

In 1849 Poe died, and Griswold somehow got himself appointed executor. In 1850 Poe's missing trunk containing his manuscripts finally reappeared, and at about that time Griswold started a book about Poe. Griswold was editor of a sensationalistic newspaper then (belonging, appropriately enough, to famous huckster P. T. Barnum) and had hired some of his friends to work with him. One of them got into Griswold's desk for something and came across his book material about Poe; it was so hostile that the horrified man chose to burn it all up.

In his book *Poe Poe Poe Poe Poe Poe Poe*, Daniel Hoffman declares, "His literary executor . . . went to extraordinary pains, after Poe's death, to present the deceased writer in a manner designed to make his name a household word for the dissolute, immoral, recklessly debauched. Griswold falsified the facts of Poe's life, and he revised the texts of Poe's letters, always with his calumnious end in view." Pulitzer-prize winner Richard Wilbur, a Poe expert, has summed it all up, "Poor Poe: though himself given to hoaxing and misrepresentation, he has been much misrepresented, at first maliciously and then stupidly, ever since Griswold."

From Columbus to Poe to today, American history is full of fictions and false fronts. In architecture, the false front was an invention of the American West: a one-story building with the facade of a nonexistent second story. The "newly restored" Huntington Hotel in Pasadena has a different kind of false front. In spite of a long struggle by preservationists, the great hotel was demolished in March 1989; and in March 1991 a brand new hotel with a similar design opened in its place, with some of the old hotel's interior decoration saved and restored. This brand new building is promoted as a "vintage hotel" and "historic landmark."

The old and the new are often confused this way in the world of fakery, and Paul Bunyan is a perfect example. Paul Bunyan is the legendary lumberjack purportedly invented in folktales passed down through generations of humble working people. Curtis MacDougall evidently believed that, because in his book *Hoaxes* he referred four times to Paul Bunyan as the all-American symbol of enthusiastic exaggeration. But according to Richard Shenkman in *Legends, Lies, and Cherished Myths*, "Paul is about as authentic a folk hero as Mr. Clean or the Jolly Green Giant. . . ." An advertising man named W. B. Laughead has confessed that he wrote the basic Paul Bunyan stories in the early 1920s as part of an ad campaign for the Red River Lumber Company. Paul Bunyan is modern fakelore, not folklore.

Another interesting piece of American fakelore is the prose-poem known as the "Desiderata" (which is a Latin word for "things to be desired"). In recent years countless people have read and passed along to others this extremely popular and historic piece of inspirational advice, which contains the famous lines, "You are a child of the universe no less than the trees and the stars; you have a right to be here. . . ." This awesome message is supposedly 300 years old and

95

anonymous, almost always bearing the attribution "Found in Old Saint Paul's Church, Baltimore. Dated 1692." In the sixties and seventies it was popular among counterculture youth for its universalistic wisdom, and it was reprinted many times in books and periodicals, and on plaques, cards, and posters. It was even made into a popular spoken-word recording by radio and TV personality Les Crane.

The "Desiderata," however, was written and published in 1927 by an obscure Indiana poet named Max Ehrmann (1872–1945). It was eventually included in the posthumous *Poems of Max Ehrmann*, (1948), a volume that is still in print.

According to journalist Ralph Reppert in the *Baltimore Sunday Magazine* (November 10, 1968), the misattribution most likely occurred in 1956, when Rev. Frederick Ward Kates became rector of Old Saint Paul's. As a collector of inspirational literature, Reverend Kates had already published a booklet containing the Ehrmann piece, properly credited. Kates recalls that during Lent he also had the "Desiderata" printed on the cover of a mimeographed booklet of inspirational writings that he distributed to his parishioners, though no copy of it can now be traced. Also on the cover appeared the name of the parish and the date of its founding: "Old Saint Paul's Church, Baltimore, 1692."

Quite probably, someone innocently reprinted the poem from this source, mistaking the church's own founding date for the source and date of the poem. Once the wrong attribution was duplicated in dozens of other publications, it proved to be an almost impossible error to eradicate. Though the poem continues to be immensely popular, its author's name remains as obscure as ever, and it must possess one of the most widely violated copyrights in modern times.

*I do not mind lying, but I hate inaccuracy.*

—Samuel Butler

# CHAPTER 4
# WOWING AN AUDIENCE

*Most writers regard the truth as their most valuable
possession, and therefore are most economical in its use.*
—Mark Twain

Truth is stranger than fiction in the world's chronicle of canny confabulators,
imposing imposters and famous forgers. Intrepid inventors and beguiling
borrowers never let truth get in the way of a good story.

# TALE SPINNERS AS WINNERS

*To succeed in the world, we do everything we can to appear successful.*

—François, Duc de La Rochefoucauld

When deception is at its most innocent, some love to get fooled; but there are always others who fool to get loved. For example, the dashing Atherton Fleming, a retired major in the Royal Dragoons, successfully courted mystery writer Dorothy Sayers in 1926. In fact, his name was originally Oswold, not Atherton, and he had been a captain in the Army Service Corps, not a major in the Royal Dragoons. After they married, Dorothy Sayers ended up supporting him and his drinking habit for the rest of his life.

When Dorothy Sayers was adjusting to her unfortunate marriage and creating wildly popular detective fiction in the 1930s, she must have heard about the international celebrity named Grey Owl who was creating wildly popular books of another kind.

## Grey Owl

Grey Owl was born in Mexico in 1888, the son of a man from Scotland and his Apache wife. This couple had gone to England with Buffalo Bill Cody and his Wild West Show for Queen Victoria's Jubilee, then returned to North America for Grey Owl's birth. They eventually moved to Canada. At the age of fifteen Grey Owl traveled alone into Ontario and was adopted by the Ojibways, who taught him to be a trapper and river guide. They gave him the name Wa-Sha-Quon-Asin, which means He-Who-Flies-by-Night, or Grey Owl.

Grey Owl was a Canadian soldier in France in World War I, then returned to life as a trapper with his beloved young Iroquois wife. In spite of being uneducated and barely literate, he developed an uncanny skill as a freelance author and lecturer. After falling in love with some orphaned baby beavers, he began to devote his life to animals. The National Parks of Canada made a film about his work with beavers and gave him a job as a conservationist.

In 1931 Grey Owl published *Men of the Last Frontier.* He followed it with *Pilgrims of the Wild.* In 1935 his publisher had him tour England, where he was a sensation. He gave two-hundred lectures to more than a quarter of a million people in four months. *Pilgrims* was so popular that it was reprinted nine times in thirteen months, and Grey Owl went home rich.

In 1937 Grey Owl returned for a second tour of England, including a performance at Buckingham Palace—where he upstaged King George with his dramatic entrance and announced to him, "I come in peace, brother." Princesses Elizabeth and Margaret were thrilled, and when Elizabeth (the present Queen) cried, "Oh, do go on!" she was rewarded with an encore. Grey Owl's publisher described the scene: "He was more than ever the Indian, proud, fierce, inscrutable. Those fringed buckskins, the wampum belt, the knife in its sheath at his side, the moccasins on those polished floors, the long dark hair surmounted by a single feather . . ."

In April 1938 Grey Owl died at forty-nine, and his hoax exploded. One headline announced accurately, "Grey Owl had cockney accent and four wives." The man known as Grey Owl had been born Archibald Stansfeld Belamey in 1888 in Hastings, on the south coast of England—son of a notorious ne'er-do-well and the thirteen-year-old sister-in-law he married after one of his wives died under rather suspicious circumstances. Well-to-do relatives finally paid the rogue an allowance just to stay out of England, and Belamey never saw his father again.

Reared comfortably by his grandmother and maiden aunts, Belamey was a bright, impish boy with a flair for drama and a love of Indian lore. His school records state good-naturedly: "What with his camping out, his tracking of all and sundry, and wild hooting [like an owl], he was more like a Red Indian than a respectable Grammar School boy." He was already dying his skin dark. In 1906, when he was eighteen, his relatives agreed to pay his way to Canada.

Not everyone was fooled by Grey Owl; the Ojibway and other Canadian woodsmen knew that he was a fake. Furthermore, when he spoke in Hastings in 1935, there was a woman in the audience who recognized him. Mary McCormick had grown up in the house next door to his at 36 St. Mary's Terrace. She recalled his owl-hooting and the fact that he had once built a wigwam on her parents' lawn.

Although he was a charlatan and a bigamist several times over, with more than his share of brushes with the law, Grey Owl is still greatly admired for his work as a conservationist. In that area, he was genuine.

### Lone Cowboy

A wonderful cowboy named Will James burst upon the public at just about the same time as the wonderful Indian Grey Owl. He became an overnight success with his 1927 children's book *Smoky the Cowhorse*, which he wrote and illustrated. *Smoky* won the Newbery Award, has been filmed three times, and is a perennial favorite.

In 1930 Will James brought out his masterful *Lone Cowboy: The Autobiography of Will James*. (As R. Z. Sheppard has observed, "Autobiographies frequently contain more fancy than novels.") Will James' autobiography tells the fascinating story of how he became a cowboy. His parents died when he was a four-year-old in Montana in about 1896, and he was reared by a French-Canadian trapper called Bopy who drifted from Canada to Mexico with the seasons. The two trapped in winter and prospected in summer, lodging in cabins along the way. Bopy taught the little orphan to ride, track, shoot, trap, and skin. When Bopy disappeared, presumably drowned in a flooded creek, James was just old enough to join some cowboys and became a bronc buster.

In 1987, forty-seven years after *Lone Cowboy*, an author named Jim Bramlett dared to publish *Ride for the High Points: The Real Story of Will James*. It seems that Joseph Ernest Nephtali Default, son of a middle-class French-speaking family in the city of Quebec, fell in love with the American West by reading about it in pulp fiction. His most obvious talent was art. At the age of fifteen he left home and headed west to become a cowboy. He dropped the French language and used various aliases before he settled upon Will James.

Will James hoped to become a famous Western artist; but when his art did not sell, his wife Alice advised him to write down one of the tales he liked to tell and to send it off to *Scribner's* magazine. *Scribner's* snatched it up for $300, and the new author made a quick trip to Quebec to swear his relatives to secrecy about his true identity.

His life story could have been happy; Will James bought the Rocking R ranch in Montana and had friends and fame. But he went on benders, drifted downhill, and ended up destitute in Hollywood, where he worked on movie ideas and his final book *The American Cowboy*. He died of alcoholism at age fifty in Hollywood Presbyterian Hospital. His books are still praised and loved, however, and very few people realize that his autobiography was a fraud.

## Little Tree

In 1930, the very year Will James published his autobiography claiming that he had become an orphan in Montana at the age of four, a sweet Cherokee child named Little Tree became an orphan at the age of five in backwoods Tennessee. He was taken in by his grandparents: Granma Bonnie Bee was pure Cherokee, but Granpa Wales was part Scottish. This salty old couple taught Little Tree survival skills such as weaving baskets and brewing whiskey (the family recipe was several hundred years old), along with courage, self-reliance, and profound tolerance for other people. They lived largely on wild game and berries, made moccasins, read "Mr. Shakespeare" for pleasure, and endured racial hatred with unfailing good spirit.

Little Tree grew up without schooling, became a cowboy ranch hand, and then was appointed official Storyteller in Council to the Cherokee Nation. In 1976 Delacorte Press published *The Education of Little Tree* under his adult name, Forrest Carter; he was praised in the *New York Times*, and Barbara Walters interviewed him on the *Today Show*. Carter died prematurely in 1979; but thanks to his agent, Eleanor Friede, *Little Tree* ("A True Story") was reissued in 1986 by the University of New Mexico Press, with reports of a million copies in print. In 1991 the American Booksellers Association gave the book their ABBY Award because of its humanitarian values. It was at the very top of the *Times* paperback best-seller list for weeks, with royalties benefiting the Cherokees. Then a historian blew the whistle.

There is no record of any royalties going to the Cherokees. There is no such post as Storyteller in Council to the Cherokee Nation. There is not even any Forrest Carter. (Earl Asa Carter took on that name sometime after 1970, having already gone by Earl, Asa, Bud and Ace.) Asa Carter was from Alabama, not Tennessee, and was no more an orphan than Will James had been. (He very likely read Will James' books when he was a child.) He and his relatives were not Cherokee, but white; in fact, Carter was once head of a White Citizen's Council. The man who charmed readers as a politically correct Native American New Age guru really worked for the Ku Klux Klan.

The mainspring of Asa Carter's life was racism. After a stint as a nonconformist college student and radio announcer in Colorado, he threw himself into Alabama politics. In 1956 a group of his supporters assaulted Nat King Cole on stage at a Birmingham concert. (Carter commented, "I've swung on niggers myself.") He started a new branch of the Klan and was arrested for shooting a man, but the case was dropped because witnesses backed out. In 1957 six of his close associates abducted a black man and castrated him with a razor blade in a room decorated with Carter's political posters. In 1963 Carter wrote Governor George Wallace's famous inaugural address that proclaimed, "Segregation now! Segregation tomorrow! Segregation forever!" But Wallace softened; in 1970 Carter ran against him, stating for the record "I am a racist." It didn't work; Carter lost.

Indian chic was popular in 1973. When Marlon Brando won an Oscar that year for his role in *The Godfather,* he refused to attend the award ceremony and sent in his place an Apache princess named Sasheen Little Feather, in Indian dress, to protest the mistreatment of Indians. Brando didn't know it, but Sasheen Little Feather was really just an aspiring actress named Marie Cruz from Salinas, California.

In about 1973, Asa Carter selected the name Forrest (the name of a Klan founder he admired) and started filling *Little Tree* with fake Cherokee lore and tender sentiments like "Grandma said you couldn't love something you didn't understand; nor could you love people, nor God, if you didn't understand the people and God." In real life Asa was notoriously anti-Semitic, but one of the dearest people in *Little Tree* is a Jew. In real life Asa was a heavy drinker and a "gun-toting racist," according to the Emory University professor who exposed him; but *Little Tree* is all goodwill, humor, and courage. Carter's widow, who received twenty-seven different *Little Tree* film offers, denied vigorously that Carter was ever a white supremacist. But according to his brother Doug, Asa invented lovable Little Tree as the way to finance a political comeback. He was a skillful writer who knew how to tug at the public's heartstrings and purse strings.

Forrest Carter gives new depth of meaning to the most famous saying of La Rochefoucauld: "Hypocrisy is the homage that vice pays

102

to virtue." According to Charles Caleb Colton, it is easier to pretend to be what you are not than to hide what you are, but the person who can accomplish both is a master hypocrite.

## Crying Wind and Other Hot Air

Asa Carter was once a radio announcer in Colorado, and a Colorado girl named Linda Davison could have heard him. In 1976 he published *Little Tree,* and Linda Davison Stafford could have read it. Whether she did or not, in 1977 she brought out a similar book called *Crying Wind.*

This heartwarming autobiography was an immediate hit in conservative Protestant bookstores. *Crying Wind* described her poverty-stricken childhood on a Kickapoo Indian reservation where she was reared by her wise old grandmother. Like Little Tree, she was forced out of school after only a few weeks because of cruel prejudice against Indians. (Like Grey Owl, Will James, and Little Tree, she wrote very well for someone with no schooling at all.)

Unlike Little Tree, Crying Wind was converted to Christianity. When her first book came out, she was an ordinary church-going Colorado housewife with four children. The book enabled her to launch an evangelistic ministry, and she was soon appearing in Indian garb at churches and conferences around the nation. When there were 175,000 copies of *Crying Wind* in print, its publisher, Moody Press, issued a sequel in hardcover titled *My Searching Heart*; a third *Crying Wind* book was ready for publication, and a fourth was in progress.

There had been questions about Crying Wind's background all along, but she had assured Moody Press that any minor errors were due to her imperfect memory. As complaints mounted, Moody finally investigated and then suddenly canceled the series in August 1979, saying that the books "extend literary privilege beyond the editorial standards of Moody Press."

The truth was that Linda Davison grew up in Woodland Park, Colorado, not on a reservation. She was an honors student in high school, took part in the writing and drama clubs, and graduated in 1961. Linda's Uncle Paul Hamlet (whom she called "Uncle Cloud") reported that their family was not Indian and never used Indian dress or names. In spite of knowing all this, in 1989 Harvest House republished Linda Davison's two books, listing them as "biographical" novels under the catalog caption "Exciting True Stories."

*Little Tree* came out in 1976; *Crying Wind* came out in 1977, and *The Track to Bralgu* came out in 1978. This collection of twelve sensitive stories by B. Wongar has been praised in Australia, Britain, and the United States. Like Grey Owl and Will James, Wongar is the son of a European father and a native mother—in this case, an Australian aborigine mother. It seems that the only person who has ever met the dreamy aborigine poet is his editor and agent Streten Bozic, who is a Melbourne anthropologist and aspiring writer.

### Awful Disclosures

*Crying Wind*'s style of stretching the truth to teach religion seems to be a fairly common temptation. George Du Pre was a Canadian who started to give inspiring Christian talks to young people after World War II, and he gradually spiced them up with accounts of his daring exploits in France. At one point the Gestapo crushed his right hand in a vice and poured boiling water down his throat to try to force him to identify his friends. These stories thrilled audiences, and word spread. *Readers Digest* sent author Quentin Reynolds to spend a week with this war hero, and he got the details for a book: *The Man Who Wouldn't Talk.* The book immediately went into two printings as well as a *Readers Digest* condensed version. Then someone notified a newspaper that Du Pre had never even been in France. When a reporter challenged him, he promptly confessed; he wrote an abject apology to Reynolds, and reportedly retired from public view to lead a chastened and sincere Christian life. It seems that the Man Who Wouldn't Talk was simply the Man Who Shouldn't Talk.

Early in 1991 an Arizona newspaper revealed that Elder Paul H. Dunn of the Mormon church had been making Du Pre's kind of mistakes about World War II memories for thirty years or more. Dunn was the most prolific author in Mormon leadership; in his fifty-one royalty-producing books and cassette tapes, he reminisced in a folksy, grandfatherly, self-deprecating style. But Dunn's best friend did not really die in his arms in Okinawa (or anywhere else), and Dunn never played baseball for the St. Louis Cardinals. When confronted with the truth, Dunn explained that "simply putting history in little finer packages" served to better entertain his audience and convey his message.

He likened his method to the parables of Jesus. In October 1991 the embarrassed Mormon Church forced Dunn to state in print, "I confess that I have not always been accurate in my public talks and writings."

Du Pre and Dunn disappointed people, but their religious self-promotion was relatively innocent when contrasted to the tragic tale of Maria Monk—not the tale of a monk, but the tale of an extremely famous fake nun. Maria was a Canadian who burst upon the Protestant church scene in New York City in January 1836 at the age of nineteen, with a priest's baby in her arms. She had been rescued from a convent in Montreal and brought to New York by a man named Hoyt, who wrote a book for her titled *The Awful Disclosures of Maria Monk.* Hoyt told how the cellars of the Montreal convent were reached by tunnels from a neighboring monastery, and how some nuns who resisted the demands of lustful priests had been killed and buried there. Maria claimed, "Speedy death can be no great calamity for those who lead the lives of nuns."

The pastor of New York's Collegiate Dutch Reformed Church was much impressed and provided the money that was required before Harpers would publish the book; and he and his wife took Maria into their home to care for her. As soon as the titillating exposé became a best-seller, Maria met another enterprising clergyman, named Slocum, and went away with him. He realized that all the royalties from her book were going to the Dutch Reformed pastor's ministry, and he sued Harpers for part of those royalties. Harpers' lawyer in this case was William Emerson, Ralph Waldo Emerson's brother.

The trial brought out the truth. Maria Monk's mother testified in an affidavit that Maria had been a pathological liar ever since a head injury when she was seven. She had lost all her jobs because of lying, had served several terms in reformatories, and was a prostitute. Her baby was most likely the offspring of a certain Montreal policeman. The court found that Hoyt and an editor had expanded Maria's own story with lore from European rumors about convents and torture. Newspapers announced the hoax, Slocum lost his case, and the Dutch Reformed pastor washed his hands of Maria.

After her next enslavement, which was in a Philadelphia convent, Maria brought out a sequel: *Further Disclosures of Maria Monk.* Slocum tricked her, hurried over to London, and became rich by selling the foreign rights to both her books. She got nothing for them and was soon living as a drunken prostitute on the Bowery, telling her tales to anyone who would listen. In 1849 she went to jail for pickpocketing and died there at the age of thirty-two. But her first book lives on. It has sold 300,000 copies and is still believed by many Protestants; it confirms their worst fears about the Catholic Church, and they are inspired by Maria Monk's valiant escape.

Back in the 1800s another female fraud became a celebrity with her autobiography; she told about her life as Sacajawea, Indian guide for Lewis and Clark. Although historians believe that the real Sacajawea was long dead, the imposter was probably the most famous woman in America in her day. No one seems to know who she really was. Like her followers Grey Owl, Sasheen Little Feather, Little Tree, and Crying Wind, Sacajawea gave people the Indians they wanted.

## International Successes

A book called *Anna and the King of Siam* gave people the proper Victorian governesses and cruel Oriental potentates they wanted. This 1944 novel by Margaret Landon was promptly made into a film starring Rex Harrison and Irene Dunne. In 1951 the story opened on Broadway as the successful Rogers and Hammerstein musical comedy *The King and I*, which then became a popular film starring Yul Brynner and Deborah Kerr.

The story is based on the experiences of Anna Leonowen, who went to work for Mongkut, King of Siam, in 1862. Anna told her own story in *The English Governess at the Siamese Court* (1870) and *The Romance of the Harem* (1872), and that is where Margaret Langdon got the ideas for her novel. But Anna had already fictionalized the story herself. It seems that she vilified the late Mongkut (1804–68) for dramatic purposes; he was a moderate reformer who was apparently innocent of the grisly deeds that Anna attributes to him. In fact, Anna plagiarized several of his atrocities from stories and legends about earlier Siamese rulers. Anna was not from Wales as she claimed, but from India. Her father was not the fine Captain Crawford she claimed, but a poor army sergeant named Edwards. Her deceased husband was not Major Thomas Leonowens of the Indian Army, but a hotel manager in Penang named Thomas Leon Owens. (She never mentioned him in her books; so much for the widow's tender song "Hello, Young Lovers.") Furthermore, the Mrs. Badger who once accompanied her husband and the teenage Anna on a trip through the Middle East did not exist. Mr. Badger was single, and he and Anna traveled alone. Evidently, Anna was a rather racy character for a Victorian governess.

How much of Anna's beloved story as told in *The King and I* is true? Believing a musical comedy based on a novel based on a dishonest autobiography is probably an exercise in sentimentality.

Hoax expert Norman Moss has remarked, "Every age has its own sentimentality. Jack Bilbo evidently gave the 1930s the gangsters it wanted, and he was rewarded for it." Bilbo was really twenty-four-year-old Hugo Baruch, son of a wealthy German father and English mother, a kind of playboy-adventurer. He wanted to be a writer, but didn't sell anything until he pretended to be a Chicago gangster. (Bilbo had never even been to Chicago.) *Carrying a Gun for Al Capone* (1930) came out first in Germany, then in many other countries including the United States. Burly and bull-necked, Bilbo posed for his publicity photo in a raincoat and a hat with the brim turned down, holding a pistol.

Four years after his book came out, Bilbo admitted in a newspaper interview that he had never carried a gun in his life, but the public overlooked that. In 1939, when he exhibited paintings in London, *Time* identified him as a Chicago mobster, and a London paper mentioned that he had killed at least a dozen people. His book had such huge sales that it was still being republished in the 1940s. His sentimental balderdash about Al Capone and the life of mobsters fooled reviewers because it appealed to their emotions: "I thought afterwards of our gang, men who when they say 'yes' mean 'yes.' No shifty-eyed standards, no hypocrisy. They are not interested only in prying you loose from your money. They are natural, not hypocrites. I am a gangster, and damned proud of it."

Another remarkable book that was successfully published in several countries and honored by reviewers who should have known better was *My Uncle Joe* (1952) by Budu Svanidze. It was purportedly written about Josef Stalin by a loving nephew who defected from the Soviet Union only because he fell in love with a German girl. He presents a benign portrait of Stalin as a warm, dedicated, patriotic man of simple tastes and unassuming manner. At the height of the Cold War, this warmhearted fantasy must have been comforting.

Yet another international literary success was *The Third Eye* (1956) by Lobsang Rampa, a Tibetan lama; it promptly sold 40,000 copies in Britain and was translated into ten languages. Rampa was a mystic brought up in Lhasa, capital of Tibet. He had undergone brain surgery that opened his "third eye," an organ which gave him spectacular psychic powers. He had also traveled abroad, had been tortured by the Japanese in World War II, and had seen the Communists take over China. His book was reviewed seriously in many places, and *Readers Digest* considered publishing excerpts.

Some Oriental scholars were so annoyed by the book that they hired a detective to track down Lobsang Rampa. They found him in Plymouth: a tall man named Cyril Hoskins who had never been out of England. This was announced in the newspapers, but it made no difference to book purchasers. Then Hoskins published a second book claiming that the first one was genuine in spite of the fact that he was not a Tibetan lama, because it was written through him by a genuine Tibetan lama. Hoskins published fourteen books altogether, about the occult, life after death, flying saucers, and a secret world inside the earth reached through tunnels at the North and South Poles. According to hoax authority Norman Moss, "It seems that for many people in need of some dimension of life beyond that of the material world about us, a fake lama is better than no lama at all."

## The Fake Formosan

Like Cyril Hoskins, George Psalmanazar had never been to the Orient. He is one of history's most intelligent, colorful, and amazing frauds. By the time he was twenty-two, Psalmanazar had specialized in posing as a "Japanese-Formosan," although he was a blond and blue-eyed European. (He explained that Formosans don't look very Oriental.) He went nearly naked under his cloak, ate his meat and vegetables raw, and muttered "Formosan prayers" in gibberish.

Alexander Innes, a cynical Scottish army chaplain, met Psalmanazar in the Netherlands and saw through his act. Here was a good chance for Innes to profit. He got Psalmanazar to fake a conversion to Christianity and took him to London to show him off. Sure enough, the delighted Bishop of London promoted Innes for his evangelistic work. According to an article by Christopher Howse in the *Spectator* (August 10, 1991), Innes later stole a manuscript about ethics from a

Scottish clergyman and published it as his own under the title *An Inquiry into the Original of Moral Virtue.*

The Bishop sent Psalmanazar to Oxford to teach the Formosan language to missionaries (he taught them nonsense). Basking in popular success, Psalmanazar published his best-selling *Description of Formosa* in 1704. He said that people on Formosa live to be a hundred, that they have much gold and silver, and that the island is inhabited by giraffes and elephants. He described what must have been the world's cruelest religion, which required cannibalism and the sacrifice of 18,000 young boys every year. For a decade Psalmanazar was a celebrity in church circles and society, and he contributed about fifteen sections on ancient history to *Bower's Universal History.*

Not everyone was fooled by the fake Formosan. A Dutch Jesuit who had been to Formosa challenged him, but Psalmanazar convinced people that the poor man was a fraud. London's Royal Society realized that Psalmanazar was the fraud, but for some reason chose not to expose him. Edmund Halley (of comet fame) questioned him about the direction of sunlight and length of twilight in Formosa and realized that he had never been there, but kept quiet.

In 1728 Psalmanazar read William Law's classic *Serious Call to a Devout and Holy Life* and was really converted. He went on to write articles about thirty countries for *Bowen's Complete History of Geography* and used his accurate new essay on Formosa to apologize for "the falsehood and imposture of my former account of that island." He lived to old age, but he never revealed his exact origin or his real name.

Was Psalmanazar's second conversion to Christianity genuine? Samuel Johnson once said, "Seldom any splendid story is wholly true," but he had no doubt about it; he counted Psalmanazar as the friend he treasured most. He was once heard to say that Psalmanazar's piety, penitence, and virtue almost exceeded those of the saints.

It's a long way from *Description of Formosa* to *The Amityville Horror,* but both were phony thrillers that titillated the public and made lots of money. The latter is a simple story.

### Haunted House Humbug

In 1974 a domestic crime that echoed ancient Greek tragedies occurred in Amityville, New York. A man named Ronald DeFeo murdered both parents and his brothers and sisters in cold blood.

A year later a family of four moved into the house and was driven out in four weeks. George and Kathy Lutz and their two boys were harassed by strange music, green slime, damage to doors and windows, and odd hoof tracks in the snow around the house. Kathy was lifted into the air above her bed. A priest who blessed the rooms with Holy Water heard a voice say "Get out!" The Lutzes repeatedly called the police for help. After they moved, Jay Anson, a scriptwriter who had worked on *The Exorcist*, wrote *The Amityville Horror* for them. The film that followed added new events, including an ax attack upon Kathy Lutz.

Investigators of the paranormal went to Amityville to check out details. They found that the priest denied ever going into the house. The police denied that they had ever been called to investigate there. The doors and windows were in good condition and had not been replaced or repaired. Weather records showed that there had been no snow on the ground when the hoofprints allegedly appeared in the snow.

The lawyer for Ronald DeFeo eventually admitted that he had first intended to make money by producing a factual book about the DeFeo murders. Then he and George Lutz, a confidence artist, concocted the idea of the haunted house and got Jay Anson to write the story for them. They did it for the money.

People lie in their books for two main reasons: for love or for money. When they do it for money, everyone understands. But when they do it for love, there is psychological mystery involved; perhaps they write for the love of attention, the love of excitement, the love of a social cause, or the love of the lie itself.

# BEGUILED AND BEGUILERS

*No man, for any considerable period, can wear one face to himself and another to the multitude, without finally getting bewildered as to which may be the true.*

—Nathaniel Hawthorne

All around us there are lies that are lived instead of written. Some of these lies are fleeting, and others are lifelong pretenses. Some are funny, others are tragic, and quite a few are both.

History's briefest and funniest criminal imposture was launched in 1906 when a scrawny shoemaker named Wilhelm Voigt bought the flashy second-hand uniform of a captain in the Prussian Guard. He wore it to a section of Berlin where he would find plenty of soldiers wandering about, and rounded up about ten of them for special duties. Then he marched them to the little town of Kopenick and arrested the mayor, announcing, "At the command of His Majesty the Kaiser, you will be taken to Berlin as my prisoner." He ordered the police inspector to control the gathering crowd and ordered the town treasurer to turn over all the cash at hand; then he sent the mayor and treasurer off in carriages to Berlin, changed his clothes in the train depot, and went home with the money. He was caught, but the trial was so comical that he was sentenced to only four years and released in less than half the time. In the meantime he received offers of marriage from Britain and America, and a Jewish woman in Berlin gave him a pension of 100 marks a month for life. He entertained briefly in a colorful uniform in New York and London music halls, and then retired happily to Luxemburg for the rest of his days.

Golden-tongued Ignacz Trebitsch was born in Hungary in 1879 and tricked people until his death in 1943. He moved to England, took the name Lincoln, and "converted" from Judaism to Christianity. He worked in missions to Jews in Montreal and elsewhere. He manipulated a wealthy British patron and was elected to Parliament. During World War I he worked as a spy for both England and Germany and

111

wrote some sensational false memoirs. He bilked both English and Americans, spent three years in a British prison, then dabbled in extreme right-wing politics in Central Europe. He finally ended up in China as an abbot for a tiny sect of European converts to Buddhism. Buddhism's loss was Christianity's gain.

Female imposters are less common than males. In the 1980 Boston Marathon Rosie Ruiz dashed across the finish line with the third fastest time ever run by a woman, winning the cheers of the crowd, a laurel wreath, and instant fame. In fact, however, she had sneaked into the race at the end and was soon exposed as a fraud.

In 1989 a twenty-year-old prodigy named Lorenzo Jackson joined the Angels baseball team. Although he was the half-brother of two collegiate basketball stars, Lorenzo suffered from epilepsy and was a ninth-grade dropout with no previous background in any team sports. He looked so promising that he was featured in *USA Today* and was lined up for *Good Morning America* and the *Today* show. Then the truth came out. He was twenty-nine-year-old Andre Lorenzo Jackson, who had years of college baseball experience and had played bit parts in two baseball movies. He was not a ninth-grade dropout, had no famous half-brothers, and had no epilepsy. He struck out.

In 1990 Gunther Russbacher's luck ran out. Although he was born in Salzburg, Austria, he had moved to the United States at the age of twelve and eventually developed a flair for posing as officials. He allegedly convinced people that he was an Assistant U.S. Attorney, an employee of the CIA, a U.S. marshal, and an Army major. He allegedly leased a jet for his honeymoon at government expense and used up over $8,000 worth of jet fuel. In 1990 he was allegedly passing for a Navy captain awaiting promotion to admiral. He had entered Castle Air Force Base in central California in white dress military uniform, en route to Oak Harbor Naval Base in Seattle, where he said he was going to assume command. He and his wife were enjoying VIP guest housing at Castle when they were arrested by the FBI. Russbacher happened to be wearing his captain's bars upside down at the time. After indictment by a federal grand jury, he claimed that he had sold rights to his life story to a movie production company.

Early in 1991, a less ambitious imposter was caught and arrested on retreat at a monastery. He had worked in many places as an Episcopal priest, education director, and high school teacher. Colleagues had considered him a caring priest and a great teacher, but in fact he was neither ordained nor credentialed. After his arrest he explained: "The kaleidoscope concept has always cut across my life, deliberately smashing the neat pattern society dictates."

Later in 1991 a nun managed to get into the receiving line in Brasilia when the Pope met the president of Brazil. She embraced the Pope in a religious rapture, and then had her picture taken embracing the president and his wife. She told reporters that her name was Sister Salete, and she had emerged from twenty-four years in a cloister for this occasion. When her picture appeared in the papers the next day, however, she was identified as the same fake nun who had negotiated release of hostages and an escape for a team of trapped bank robbers in 1988; she had then disappeared with the $9,000 reward they gave her from their loot.

## Chosen Poses

U.S. Navy veteran Robert Fife of Salt Lake City, Utah, committed suicide in the summer of 1989 and left a 449-page manuscript describing his Vietnam experiences. His wife, Nancy, never doubted that he had been scarred physically and mentally by his Viet Cong captors back in 1966, shortly before she met and married him. She considered him a casualty of the war and arranged to have his name inscribed on the Utah Vietnam War memorial.

Fife had a certificate from the USS Ranger Committee stating that after 130 missions over enemy territory, he was "one of only four naval aviators to escape from enemy prison camps." The certificate listed Fife's medals, including the service's highest award for valor, the Navy Cross; but he had burned his medals in protest against the neglect of Vietnam veterans. Suffering from post-traumatic stress syndrome, he had drifted from one failure to another in civilian life.

Wanting to honor Fife, a reporter asked the Navy to track down his records. The records showed that Fife was in the Navy only eight months, won no awards, was never captured, and hadn't even been near Vietnam. When the reporter broke the news to Mrs. Fife, she said, "I feel like I've been raped." She had believed her husband's victimization story and his fake certificate for twenty-three years.

Many people enjoy playing hero or victim or both. Robert Fife actually went to a psychologist for counseling about his ongoing Vietnam trauma. (The psychologist believed all that Fife told him and tried in vain to help.) The most bizarre victim impersonators are those who make a specialty of lying about physical ailments to obtain useless treatments and surgeries. They have what is called the Munchausen Syndrome. These people are not hypochondriacs who think they are ill; they know they are lying about their symptoms.

In contrast to people who fake illness, those who fake desirable social status are fairly easy to understand. *Newsweek* observed in its August 31 issue in 1987, "There is a kind of American frog that dreams of becoming a European prince." Sherman Suchow put behind him his origin in Brooklyn, changed his name to Charles Merrill Mount, and spoke with an English accent. He considered himself a "perfectly normal Edwardian gentleman," dressed elegantly, and carried a walking stick when no one else did so. During one happy period he functioned in Europe as an art dealer.

In the 1960s Mount was accused of authenticating forged watercolors by his favorite artist, John Singer Sargent; and because the suspicious watercolors resembled Mount's own paintings, some people thought he forged them. No action was taken.

Twenty years later Mount was living in a seedy rooming house on Capitol Hill, spending his days as a dignified European-style browser in the Library of Congress and the National Archives. He appeared to be nothing but a charming gentleman-scholar. Then one day in 1987 the FBI arrested him—not for forging Sargent paintings, but for gradually stealing hundreds of national historical treasures worth about a million dollars. He had been selling them bit by bit to document dealers.

*Newsweek* concluded that Mount was a curiously sympathetic character. "Americans like a man who invents himself—it's an old American custom—and if there's some humbug that just adds to the spice."

When some people invent themselves, they use another person's blueprints. One of the most dramatic impostures in history took place in 1556 in the small French village of Artigat. Martin Guerre, who was fairly well-to-do, had gone to Spain eight years earlier and never returned to his wife Bertrande and their son. Thus Bertrande was neither wife nor widow and lacked property rights. A handsome and charming peasant named Arnaud du Tilh heard that he resembled the missing Martin Guerre and set out to learn all about him. Then he sent word to Bertrande that he was coming home to her. When he arrived,

Martin's uncle insisted that this was an interloper; but Bertrande claimed him as her long-lost husband. They lived together as man and wife for three years, until Martin's uncle uncovered Arnaud's original identity and forced the matter into court.

The trial went surprisingly well for Arnaud because he knew every detail of Martin's life and was extremely convincing. But at the last minute a one-legged man entered the courtroom: Martin Guerre, home from Spain, minus a leg. Now there was a contest between the two men who both claimed to be Martin Guerre, and the two-legged Martin knew even more correct details about Martin's life than the one-legged Martin. But when Bertrande was brought into the court-room, she burst into tears and embraced the one-legged man. Arnaud was hanged on September 16, 1560, and he went to his death convincing the village that Bertrande had not realized that he was an imposter. That in itself was probably his best deception. (Their story is movingly told in the French film *The Return of Martin Guerre*.)

## The Claimant

Three-hundred years later an even stranger case occurred, that of "the Tichborne Claimant." No soap opera could match it. The young Sir Roger Charles Doughty Tichborne had been declared dead in 1856, three years after his ship sank in the Atlantic; the English title and estate that would have come to him went to his infant nephew. Although there were no known survivors from the sunken ship, Roger's widowed mother eventually advertised in distant newspapers for information about her missing son. Twelve years after Roger's ship sank, she received a letter from him that began, "My Dear Mother." It was from a butcher who called himself Thomas Castro, in Wagga Wagga, Australia. He asked for money.

Lady Tichborne was a beautiful and wealthy French aristocrat who was used to getting whatever she wanted. Her husband had been James Tichborne, an English aristocrat. Roger had grown up in Paris, but he moved to England when he was sixteen to attend Stony-hurst, an elite Catholic boarding school. At the age of twenty-three, Roger had fallen madly in love with his English cousin Katherine; but his father made him promise to stay away from her for three years before seeking a Catholic dispensation that would allow cousins to marry. Roger went traveling to pass the time, and when he was on a trip to South America his ship sank. Eventually Lady Tichborne lost all four children as well as her husband. Roger was the only one who could still be alive, and so she clung to that possibility.

The Tichbornes' old Negro servant named Bogle was living in Sydney, and she asked him to decide for her if the Wagga Wagga butcher was really Roger. Castro gathered information about the Tichbornes and then went to Sydney to greet dear old Bogle, who was duly impressed by the friendly attention. Next, Lady Tichborne sent money so that Roger could return to her, with his illiterate wife, two children, and Bogle in tow.

During his absence, Roger had changed from a slender young aristocrat to a fat middle-aged butcher who weighed 289 pounds. He regretted neglecting to contact his family during his eleven years in Australia; he had been busy, and the time had slipped by. His English grammar and spelling had gone downhill, and he could no longer understand a word of his native French. Neither his old tutor nor his closest friend could believe that this was really Roger; but Lady Tichborne, her attorney, and some neighbors were convinced. She gave her long-lost boy a huge allowance.

After reacquainting himself with his earlier life, Roger filed a claim for the magnificent family estate that had gone to his nephew. In court hearings, Roger recalled the name of his old servant Bogle, but not the names of any of his boyhood friends, his Stonyhurst teachers, or the title of even one book he had read there. But he was self-assured; he never faltered, wavered, or blinked. When quizzed about his sweetheart Katherine, who was now Mrs. Radcliffe and very much alive, he revealed that she had tried to trick him into an early marriage by pretending that she was pregnant.

Roger was openly accusing his cousin Katherine of sexual immorality as well as dishonesty. As in the well-publicized 1991 conflict between Anita Hill and Clarence Thomas, the amazed public split into those who believed Katherine and those who believed Roger. In the midst of this brouhaha, Lady Tichborne died; Roger managed to position himself at the funeral as principal mourner.

Roger's supporters were so ardent by now that they raised money to pay for his legal expenses. He took a lawyer and an assistant all the way to Chile to search for proof that he had visited there before his ship sank. Unfortunately for him, this led to discovery of the fact that in about 1850 a London butcher's son named Arthur Orton, from

**116**

Wapping, had visited Chile. There was evidence that Arthur Orton went on to Australia, stole a horse, and changed his name to Thomas Castro. Roger's opponents proved that Roger was chummy with the Orton family in London and suggested that he was really the missing Arthur Orton. But there was such an overabundance of witnesses and claims in the case that few people could analyze it all rationally.

The main trial went on for 102 days. Roger was so convincing that ninety earnest witnesses testified in court that they recognized him from the old days. Others, including two of his aunts, testified against him. When witnesses finally revealed that the genuine Roger Tichborne had had his initials tattooed upon his arm, the jury had heard enough, and he lost his case. But when he was arrested for perjury, a crowd gathered to cheer for him. He was their victim-hero.

The perjury trial had to be delayed for a year while witnesses were sought in Australia. During that time, Roger spoke to large crowds and was cheered at music halls and fairs. A defense fund was created for him. There were countless Roger Tichborne buffs, and Roger's fans bought thousands of stout pottery "Claimant" figurines.

The trial for perjury lasted 188 days, at that time the longest criminal trial in British history. The defense attorney's summing-up alone took twenty-three days. One of the surprises in the new trial was false testimony from a sailor who claimed to have been rescued from the sinking ship in 1853 along with Roger; it turned out that he had been in jail at that time. The most amazing single piece of evidence was a notebook from Australia that had once belonged to Thomas Castro. In what looked like Roger's handwriting, it said "Rodger Charles Tichborne, Bart, some day, I hope." It also contained what could be called the swindlers' creed: "Some men has plenty money and no brains, and some men has plenty brains and no money. Surely men with plenty money and no brains were made for men with plenty brains and no money." The jury decided that Roger was really Charles Arthur Orton and that, in addition to other lies, he had lied about Katherine. He went to prison for about ten years.

Roger's supporters formed a society that for some time held meetings attended by thousands. His defense attorney started a weekly paper about him called *The Englishman* and won a seat in Parliament for his efforts. But he died before Roger got out of prison, and so did public enthusiasm for the cause. Roger spent his last years drifting from job to job, calling himself "Sir Roger Tichborne" until the day he died in 1898.

### The Son of Lord Byron

Major George Gordon Byron lived at the same time as Sir Roger Tichborne. He was the illegitimate son of Lord Byron, the poet, born to a Spanish noblewoman in 1810. In 1843 he surfaced in Pennsylvania and wrote to the son of Byron's publisher requesting a set of Byron's works and a Byron autograph. Then he contacted others who had materials that would help him to write a biography of his illustrious father. He solicited financial backing, and he moved to England.

In 1845 Byron contacted Mary Wollstonecraft Shelley, the widow of poet Percy Bysshe Shelley, and offered to sell her some of her late husband's letters that he had acquired. She saw him as a rogue and a swindler; but she believed that he owned important letters that she had lost, and so she paid him for quite a few. In 1847 Byron advertised his forthcoming book about his father, which would include over six-hundred previously unpublished letters. Lord Byron's half-sister Augusta Leigh, who controlled his literary estate, was furious and blocked that plan.

Soon a young woman who identified herself as the daughter of Lord Byron's doctor entered William White's Pall Mall bookshop with letters for sale. Week after week, White bought dozens of Lord Byron letters and Shelley letters from her. Eventually she had to admit that she was in fact Mrs. Byron, and that Byron had collected the letters on his travels. At this point Byron and his family returned to America by falsely persuading a ship captain that their fare would be paid in New York by a major publisher. When Byron launched a libel suit against the editor of the *Evening Mirror*, he was publicly portrayed as a fraud and swindler and lost his case; so the Byrons returned to England.

In 1852 Edward Moxon published twenty-five of the Shelley letters in a slender volume with a long introduction by Robert Browning. He sent a gift copy to the new Poet Laureate, Lord Tennyson. A friend of Tennyson's happened to glance at the Shelley letters and saw a passage that his own father had written and published in 1840. When Moxon realized that the letters were forged, he withdrew his book from the market within a week. White eventually bought back the forged letters that he had sold and donated them to the British Museum. The Byrons returned to America.

In 1869 Major Byron entered the literary world again, publishing questionable Lord Byron materials and trying to gain recognition as Lord Byron's son. There was some physical resemblance; he was a short, dark man with a waxed moustache and a superior attitude. He was a skilled raconteur with an inexhaustible fund of details about Lord Byron and his friends, and he was at home in several languages. He used the Byron crest on his stationery and dinnerware and on his silver cigarette holder. But his aliases, bogus military titles, and forgeries discredited him, and he ended in poverty, insisting to his dying day that he was Lord Byron's son.

Like many other forgers, Byron sold authentic documents along with those he forged, and it seems that he sold both kinds to Mary Shelley. The key letter was written on December 16, 1816, six days after Harriet Shelley's pregnant body was found in London's Serpentine. (Shelley had abandoned Harriet to alleged prostitution and despair when he left her for Mary.) There are four almost identical copies of the letter: at least two sold to the Shelleys by Byron. If he accomplished nothing else, Byron left Shelley scholars a maddening controversy that can never be settled; and he probably left Lord Byron scholars with a heritage of forged letters also—some that are copies of real letters, and others that are completely fictitious.

## The Great Imposter

The most outstanding imposter of twentieth century America was Ferdinand Waldo Demara, Jr. (1921–82). A high-school dropout, he forged documents, degrees, certifications, and letters of recommendation for himself. He figured out from his reading how to function successfully as a biologist who did cancer research, a zoologist, a deputy sheriff, a prison counselor, a soldier, a sailor, a Trappist monk in Kentucky, a doctor of philosophy who taught college psychology courses, a hospital orderly, and a military surgeon.

The latter was his most dramatic feat. He masqueraded as a lieutenant surgeon in the Canadian Navy in the Korean War and performed major operations under battle conditions. He never lost a patient. His surgical exploits were so outstanding that tributes in Canada led to the revelation that he was not what he claimed to be.

Demara was so charming, multitalented, and successful in most of his brief careers that in 1959 he became the subject of a book: *The Great Imposter* by Robert Crichton. In the Hollywood film adaptation he was played by Tony Curtis. Then he became an actor and played the part of a doctor in another film, *The Hypnotic Eye.* No one knows what he was up to after that, during the last twenty years of his life.

When he was asked about the motivation behind his compulsion to hoax people, Demara answered, "Rascality, pure rascality."

Mark Twain had a little streak of rascality too. By 1900 he had been a celebrity author for a long time, and his distinctive looks were well known. One day a stranger looked him over carefully in a train compartment. When he had almost reached the station where he was going to get off, the man finally said, "Now I am going to say something to you which I hope you will regard as a compliment. . . . I have never seen Mark Twain, but I have seen a portrait of him, and any friend of mine will tell you that when I have once seen a portrait of a man I place it in my eye and store it away in my memory. And I can tell you that you look enough like Mark Twain to be his brother. Now, I hope you take this as a compliment. Yes, you are a very good imitation. But when I come to look closer, you are probably not that man."

Mark Twain answered humbly, "I will be frank with you. In my desire to look like that excellent character I have dressed for the character. I have been playing a part."

The stranger smugly assured him that he had done a good job on the externals, but he had not caught the inner essence of Mark Twain.

# CROOKED BYLINES

*Forgery must be almost as old as writing, and plagiarism as old as literature.*

—Norman Moss

Mark Twain liked to pull people's legs. Once after a sermon he told the minister that he had a book at home with every word in it that the man had just preached. The minister was horrified, wondering if he could have plagiarized his entire sermon without knowing it. A few days later he received the book in the mail from Twain. It was a dictionary.

Taking credit for other people's work is so common among some preachers that they have a professional wisecrack about it: "When better sermons are written, I'll preach them." Florida author Jamie Buckingham admitted that when he was a young Baptist preacher he read all of Charles Allen's books of sermons; and because he had to preach three times a week, he preached most of them. One week Allen came to town to speak several times at the Methodist church, and some of the Baptists went to hear him. One of them came back and told Buckingham, "You'll never believe it, but that fake is preaching your sermons and didn't have the decency to give you credit. He even told some of your stories as if they happened to him."

Jamie Buckingham died in 1992, shortly before Jesse Jackson got caught telling another preacher's personal anecdote in his speech at the Democratic National Convention. That is also the year that best-selling apocalypse author Hal Lindsey got caught plagiarizing an Ohio history professor named Edwin Yamauchi in a new Lindsey manuscript titled *The Magog Factor*. What did Lindsey lift from Yamauchi? Part of a little-known 1982 book called *Foes from the Northern Frontier,* in which Yamauchi sought to show that Lindsey had mistakenly identified Russia in biblical prophecies in Lindsey's previous books. Without a nod to Yamauchi, Lindsey and his co-author Chuck

Missler copied sections of Yamauchi's scholarship, footnotes and all, as if they were their own.

## Stolen Property

Journalists sometimes plagiarize to fill space, just as preachers plagiarize to fill time or to puff up their prophecies. One day in the mid-1700s, Arthur Murphy didn't want to write his daily page for *Gray's Inn Journal*, and so he picked up a French journal and flipped through it for an idea. He spotted a story he liked, translated it quickly into English, signed it, and turned it in to his London editor as if it were his original work. After it was published, he learned to his horror that he had stumbled upon the French translation of an article by Samuel Johnson from *The Rambler*. He had turned Johnson's well-known essay straight back into English and published it under his own name. He immediately rushed to Johnson's house, introduced himself, and confessed the truth. That was the beginning of a twenty-year friendship.

English poet Samuel Taylor Coleridge was brilliant but eccentric, and he eventually slipped into a mental disorder that one perceptive scholar has called "literary kleptomania." He plagiarized German literature by translating it into English and pretending that he had orginated the ideas. That happened to give the ideas acceptability they wouldn't have had if they had been labeled German. Coleridge expert Richard Holmes observed, "If psychologically it was a form of kleptomania, then intellectually it was a form of smuggling valuables across a closed border." One of the odd things about Coleridge's plagiarism is the fact that he said, "Plagiarists are always suspicious of being stolen from."

Plagiarism is the use of someone else's words or ideas without giving credit, robbing the author and deceiving the reader. It begins in elementary school and can run on through adulthood. Although adult plagiarizers are often embarrassed enough to lie about what they did, they also insist sometimes that literary larceny is both unavoidable and desirable. "I didn't do it, I couldn't avoid it, and there is nothing wrong with it anyway." People sometimes excuse a plagiarizer by pointing out that not everything he published was written by someone else. As Thomas Mallon remarks in *Stolen Words*, that is like excusing a burglar by pointing out that only part of his possessions were taken from other people's houses.

According to Lance Morrow, the word *plagiarius* is kidnapper in Latin. "The plagiarist snatches the writer's brainchildren, pieces of his soul." Morrow claims that plagiarism is a squalid, grubby act that makes us turn aside in embarrassment, and he puts it into the same category as obscene phone calls or shoplifting. It is probably at least that common. Many writers are as shocked as Lance Morrow was when they stumble across their ideas, phrases, assembled materials, original insights, or entire essays published under other authors' names. They usually do nothing about it because there is not enough money involved for hiring a lawyer. Furthermore, anyone who dares to publicly cry "plagiarism!" is apt to be branded petty and mean-spirited. When we complain about being plagiarized, we are often told that we should feel flattered that someone thought our property was worth taking. (No one tells people that after they have had their cars stolen.)

On December 3, 1989, California's *Orange County Register* published an interesting freelance article about a Mexican train trip by Luther Enitsmus. An alert reader notified the *Register* that the article had been published earlier as a short story in the *New Yorker*; but then the train was in Spain and the author was Truman Capote. The *Register* contacted the apartment house in Phoenix where Mr. Enitsmus supposedly lived; a man named Wayne Sumstine (spelled backward, Enitsmus) had lived there and moved to Sao Paulo, Brazil. When the *Register* called Sumstine in Brazil, he said quietly that he had copied the story and didn't know why. Then he evidently reinvented himself as a social critic and wrote in for a free copy of the paper, explaining that he had played this trick on Orange County because of its boorish self-centeredness. As Carolyn Wells has put it, "A guilty conscience is the mother of invention."

Such plagiarism is common, but it would rarely pay to sue. Gail Sheehy, author of *Passages*, was forced to pay a large sum to the California psychiatrist whose research she had popularized without giving him credit. According to the *New York Times*, Alex Haley, author of *Roots*, had to pay a large sum to author Harold Courlander. In 1988 the Canadian estate of Lucy Maud Montgomery, author of *Anne of Green Gables*, complained about best-selling Australian author Colleen McCullough because her 1987 novel *The Ladies of Missalonghi* was

**123**

much like Montgomery's 1926 novel *The Blue Castle*. McCullough explained that her novel had "merely pleasant echoes" of Montgomery's novel, which she had read when she was young.

In 1979 Jacob Epstein, the Yale-educated son of two of New York's most powerful editors, received rave reviews for his first novel, *Wild Oats*. British author Martin Amis had met Epstein a couple of times, and when he saw him again he apologized for not yet reading *Wild Oats*. Epstein answered nervously, "Oh, that's okay. I'm a great admirer of your work, by the way." In 1980 *Wild Oats* started selling in England, and the friend who gave a copy to Amis said, "You'll like it." Indeed, Amis liked some of the passages as if they were his own, because they were. Epstein had copied them word-for-word out of Amis's 1974 novel *The Rachel Papers*.

Jacob Epstein's father, Jason, an editor at Random House, claimed hotly that what his son had done was not "plagiarism"—just a common literary "accident." Four years later, Jason Epstein was planning to publish a book that had been highly recommended to Random House in a letter from the chairman of the Department of Philosophy at Harvard. The book was by an author named Timothy J. Cooney, and the Harvard philosopher's letter was by Cooney also. It was a forgery. Epstein considered the matter for several weeks and regretfully decided not to publish Cooney's book after all. It was a book on moral philosophy titled *Telling Right from Wrong*.

In 1988 psychiatrist Shervert Frazier was caught republishing other people's psychiatric articles under his own name; one of the articles came right out of a recent issue of *Scientific American*. Frazier's plagiarism attracted attention because he was former Director of the National Institute of Mental Health, former president of the American College of Psychiatrists, psychiatrist in chief at Boston's McLean Hospital, and professor of psychiatry at Harvard Medical School. He had to resign from his post at Harvard. As a psychiatrist, he may have been aware that psychiatrists like Dr. Arnold Cooper, head of the American Psychoanalytic Association, attribute plagiarism to an unconscious desire to be publicly shamed.

In 1991, H. Joachim Maitre, a Boston University dean, was demoted after he delivered a commencement address that was copied from a *Reader's Digest* article by the popular film critic Michael Medved. After journalist Fox Butterfield published an article about

Maitre's plagiarism in the *New York Times,* he was suspended for copying part of his article from an article in the *Boston Globe.*

In 1991 literary wit Art Buchwald was disgusted at a Hollywood studio for rejecting a plot he had submitted and then secretly using it for Eddie Murphy's smash hit *Coming to America.* Buchwald sued and won, but it was a bitter victory because of what it cost him. Hollywood studios have never been noted for idealism. As literary wit Dorothy Parker observed long ago, "The only 'ism' Hollywood believes in is plagiarism."

Literary wits have given us a large assortment of barbed comments about plagiarism. William Mizner said, "When you take stuff from one writer, it's plagiarism; but when you take it from many writers, it's research." George Moore said, "Taking something from one man and making it worse is plagiarism." Jules Feifer said, "Good swiping is an art in itself." William Ralph Inge said, "Originality is undetected plagiarism." Austin O'Malley said, "It is a mean thief, or a successful author, who plunders the dead." George Gregory said, "All his best passages are plagiarisms." Jonathan Swift said, "Fine words! I wonder where you stole 'em." And Samuel Johnson told one aspiring writer, "Your manuscript is both good and original; but the part that is good is not original, and the part that is original is not good."

In 1989 Dallas's seventy-nine-year-old Baptist pastor W. A. Criswell was accused of committing plagiarism thirty years earlier. His book *Why I Preach that the Bible Is Literally True,* which is still selling, reportedly included fifteen sections where material had been copied directly out of R. A. Torrey's 1907 book *Difficulties and Alleged Errors and Contradictions in the Bible.* Criswell answered that he could not recall ever reading Torrey's book. Perhaps someone who helped him compile his research had read Torrey.

The overabundance of contemporary plagiarism is partly due to the fact that today almost everyone who is anyone hires a ghostwriter. Most of these ghostwriters feel like underpaid hacks, and some of them plagiarize to get their work done. If the plagiarism is eventually made public, the supposed author is in a pickle because although he didn't commit the plagiarism, he won't admit it. Some people would rather be blamed for plagiarism than to admit that they hired a ghostwriter. The plot thickens when someone notices that a ghostwritten book has been plagiarized; that situation accounts for the fact that some people who have been plagiarized brush it off nervously and say it doesn't matter. If they didn't write their own books in the first place, they don't welcome investigations that aim at giving credit where credit is due.

Plagiarism is both a lie to the public and theft from an author. In contrast, unacknowledged ghostwriting is only a lie to the public. Whether the ghostwriter is fairly paid or not, he knows all along that the work will be published under someone else's name, not his own; thus ghostwriting is far more ethical than plagiarism, although both intentionally hoax the reader. Readers of Christian literature might be surprised to learn that some of their favorite contemporary authors don't do their own writing, and some haven't even met their own ghostwriters.

No one has publicly analyzed the mindset of ersatz authors who deny that they use ghostwriters, although their numbers are legion. Adolf Hitler used ideas and actual wording from friends who helped him write his autobiography, *Mein Kampf*. Quite a few men have wives who do their writing. When Dr. Benjamin Spock and Michael Esses left their wives, Mrs. Spock and Mrs. Esses revealed that they had secretly borne the men's books as well as their children. In most cases of spousal ghosting, however, the news never gets out.

Many celebrity authors are secure enough to have the name of the real writer on the front of the book in small print, after the words *with* or *as told to*. Unfortunately, this sometimes leads to an extra layer of deception. Sometimes neither name on the cover is the name of the author; someone anonymous did the writing for both of them. I know personally a couple of those ghostwriters' ghostwriters and their famous books.

### Forgery: Reverse Plagiarism

As bad as plagiarism is, forgery is worse. As Samuel Butler put it, "It is bad enough to see one's own good things fathered on other people, but it is worse to have other people's rubbish fathered upon oneself." Creating rubbish and foisting it off on other people is an almost addictive pleasure for some forgers.

In ordinary cases of forgery, relics and documents with no particular literary interest are created for fun or for their financial value or their message. The earliest case I know of is recorded in the Bible, in

1 Kings 21:8, when Queen Jezebel forged letters from King Ahab to instigate a murder in about 850 B.C. The most recent case I know of is a page purportedly by C. S. Lewis that surfaced in 1991, offered by a dealer at almost $3,000. The broken scribbles say nothing, but the edge of the page is burned away, which enhances the value of the relic.

In 1991 the widow of a Dallas policeman named Roscoe White made public her husband's diary that he wrote from 1956 to his death in 1971. In it he told about shooting John F. Kennedy for the CIA. "They want me to kill the president. God help me. They say he's a threat to the United States." This particular hoax did not get much attention because of obvious anachronisms: whoever the author was, he referred to the Watergate break-in long before it occurred, and he wrote in the 1950s with a type of pen that did not exist then.

In literary forgery, there are two common patterns: an ordinary writer tries to mimic a famous writer, or a real author creates the writings of an author who never existed. But the cases of literary forgery by Jonathan Swift, Vrain Lucas, and William Lauder were different.

Jonathan Swift once served as private chaplain to a lady who always had him read to her from a book of pious meditations that he disliked. He finally sneaked the book away and fastened into it a page of his own, then returned it. The next time she asked him to read, he opened her book and solemnly read his own silly essay "Meditation on a Broomstick." When she described this odd meditation to some visitors who had read the book, they opened her copy and found the essay there in Swift's handwriting. His joke was enjoyed by everyone, and she never asked him to read from those meditations again.

Vrain Lucas must have been the most audacious forger of all time. In the mid-1800s this Frenchman forged and sold more than 27,000 pieces of manuscripts. They included letters from Pontius Pilate, Cleopatra, Alexander the Great, Cervantes, Pascal, Newton, Shakespeare, Boccaccio, Mary Magdalene, Luther, Ovid, Aeschylus, Judas, and Dante. He wrote them for an eccentric Francophile (that is, a person who loves all things French) "whose gullibility remains one of the wonders of history." The forgeries tended to rewrite history to praise France, and they were all written in beautiful French.

William Lauder used real forgery to create fake plagiarism. Right after William Lauder earned an M.A. from Edinburgh University in 1695, his knee was hit by someone's golf ball; and due to infection he finally had to have his leg amputated. His life was full of career disappointments, and to add to his pain he took Alexander Pope's lines about Milton and crutches in *The Dunciad* as mockery. Perhaps he wanted revenge. After ingenious preparation, in 1749 he brought out a scholarly book, with a preface by Samuel Johnson, setting forth eighteen obscure writers whose Latin had been plagiarized by Milton when he wrote *Paradise Lost*. (In reality, Lauder had translated bits of Milton into Latin and inserted them into Latin passages by these writers, then quoted the passages to show that Milton stole from them.) The hoax lasted three years before Johnson and other scholars caught on. Lauder's publisher cut off his royalties but went on selling his book anyway—as "a Masterpiece of Fraud."

The forgeries of Swift, Lucas, and Lauder were interesting flukes. In the annals of fakery, the three most famous literary forgers are probably James MacPherson, Thomas Chatterton, and William Ireland. The three most famous document forgers are probably Antique Smith, Thomas J. Wise, and Mark Hofmann. And the two most famous "forgees" in our day are Howard Hughes and Adolf Hitler.

## Manufacturing Antiques

Ten years after William Lauder's hoax was published, James MacPherson said he discovered some fragments of ancient Gaelic poetry by a long-forgotten epic poet named Ossian, and he translated them into English. He kept publishing more, and excitement spread abroad. On the continent both Goethe and Napoleon became great admirers of Ossian. MacPherson had found a way to fame and fortune.

Samuel Johnson was convinced that Ossian was a hoax and said so. (Johnson used to carry an oak cudgel for fear of being attacked by MacPherson.) No one ever saw MacPherson's ancient documents until 1775, when pressure from Johnson forced him to produce a few for examination. They looked phony, but by then MacPherson was a popular institution with powerful defenders who believed in him.

MacPherson never confessed and was never punished. He eventually became a Member of Parliament, and when he died he left money for a monument to himself in Scotland and was buried in Westminster Abbey. Joseph Ritson, an authority on Scottish literature, observes an odd fact: "The history of Scottish poetry exhibits a series of fraud, forgery and imposture, practiced with impunity and success."

Thomas Chatterton (1752–70) was born just sixteen years after the birth of James MacPherson, and he died sixteen years before the death of MacPherson—at the age of seventeen. His mother was the widow of a teacher. He was a prodigy, and he became England's favorite forger.

Antique literature was popular in those days. Before Chatterton was twelve, he was already forging historical documents. One of his early projects was "proof" that a local family could be traced back to the Norman conquest. At the age of fourteen he produced a convincing historical manuscript which he claimed to have found in a chest in an old church. He produced deeds, letters, and seven writings by the fictitious Ossian, as well as contemporary political verse and obscenities. His most striking production was 300-year-old poetry he attributed to a monk named Thomas Rowley.

In April of 1770 Chatterton went to London with high hopes for document sales and a brilliant career in journalism, but success didn't come fast enough. Afflicted with poverty and very likely ill with syphilis, he either intentionally or accidentally poisoned himself and died in August. His Rowley poems were first published in 1777, and their authenticity was first questioned in 1778. They were ardently defended by some experts and attacked by others, and the controversy raged for decades.

Once everyone agreed that Chatterton was a forger, he became a hero to the Romantics. Wordsworth referred to him as "the marvelous Boy," and Keats dedicated the poem *Endymion* to Chatterton's memory. A famous 1856 painting of his death hangs in the Tate Gallery in London. Appropriately enough, the painting is completely imaginary, because Chatterton left no portrait or description of himself.

Writer and publisher Horace Walpole, the first person to declare Chatterton's poetry a hoax, was himself a literary imposter. In 1765, he published his most famous novel, *The Castle of Otranto*, with the claim that it was translated by Williams Marshall from the original Italian of Onuphrio Muralto, who first published it in Naples in 1529. Walpole said the book had been found in the library of an ancient Catholic family in the north of England. But Williams Marshall, Onuphrio Muralto, and the ancient Catholic family were all fictitious. Walpole wrote the book in English, and it never existed in Italian.

129

In Murray Warren's 1977 book *A Descriptive and Annotated Bibliography of Thomas Chatterton*, he lists some other British literary imposters, including Charles Betram (1723–65), who made an "ancient" manuscript by Richard of Cirencester; John Pinkerton (1758–1826), who wrote fraudulent Scottish ballads; Allan Cunningham (1748–1842), who wrote fraudulent Irish songs; and John Jordan (1746–1809), who wrote false stories about Shakespeare.

### Improving on Shakespeare

William Henry Ireland was born seven years after Chatterton's death, one year after the end of the American Revolution. He grew up the motherless son of an antiquarian bookseller named Samuel Ireland, who reportedly considered him stupid. In 1793 the two of them visited Stratford, which was a literary shrine, and young Ireland bought a few Shakespeare relics that were almost surely bogus.

Knowing how much his father wanted a Shakespeare document, seventeen-year-old William made a Shakespeare property deed on some old parchment. He said that a gentleman who demanded anonymity had invited him to his country home and had allowed him to take any papers he found there.

After an expert declared the deed genuine, Ireland produced a Shakespeare business letter, a receipt, and a thank-you letter. In one busy month Ireland produced more Shakespeare letters, a love poem to Anne Hathaway, and letters of appreciation to Shakespeare from Queen Elizabeth. Shakespeare's letter to Anne Hathaway contained a lock of his hair. Next, Ireland produced handwritten copies of Shakespeare's plays *King Lear* and *Hamlet*, with some improvements added. He even came up with Shakespeare's statement of his Christian faith, which made Anglican clerics happy.

All these relics were displayed in Ireland's shop, and Samuel Johnson's friend James Boswell knelt and kissed them there. The shop became a shrine, and all the luminaries who visited there acclaimed the relics genuine. Along the way, Ireland forged some letters from the fictitious gentleman who purportedly gave him all these treasures, praising himself to his critical father. The two were celebrities. Edmund Malone, a leading Shakespeare scholar, was attacked and scorned for claiming that the Ireland materials were forged. In time, however, a few people agreed with him.

By now eighteen-year-old Ireland was busy producing a long-lost Shakespeare play never heard of before—*Vortigern and Rowena*. He got the idea from a drawing of Vortigern and Rowena that hung in his father's living-room, but no one found the coincidence at all suspicious. Writing the play was hard enough, but forging such a long document on old paper with old ink, in Elizabethan spelling, turned out to be too much work. So Ireland explained that he was only allowed to copy the play at his benefactor's country house rather than bring it home.

When playwright Richard Sheridan read the play, he remarked that Shakespeare must have been extremely young when he wrote it; but he agreed to produce it at his Drury Lane theater and to pay Ireland £300 plus half the takings.

Unfortunately for Ireland, Sheridan's producer and lead actor John Kemble was sure the play was a fraud. Bound by his contract, he tried to open the play as a joke on April 1; but Sheridan would not permit that and opened it on April 2. Kemble retaliated by planting scoffers in the audience and turning the tragedy into a farce. He stressed his line "And when this solemn mockery is ended," and the audience howled with glee. (A century and a half later, *This Solemn Mockery* became the title of a book about forgeries.) At the end of the play the scoffers and the true believers got into a fight, and the play was never performed again. Public laughter did what serious scholars could not do, and turned the tide against Ireland's Shakespeariana.

Ireland confessed, lost his father's favor, and married. Collectors were attracted to his forgeries, and he obliged by flooding the market with copies. He sold mock Elizabethan manuscripts as curios, started a rental library, became a translator, was an educator in France, and wrote more than a dozen novels and plays. His father, however, went to his grave in 1799 insisting that his Shakespeare material was genuine and that his son's confession was a bizarre hoax.

**Antique Smith**

A little over a century ago, a brisk and friendly shopper bought up dozens and dozens of old books of any kind in Edinburgh used book shops. But he chose only the books that had blank pages in them. Before long, some hawk-eyed skeptics started questioning the great abundance of rare manuscripts in Edinburgh. There were hundreds of old letters, poems, and historical documents. For a few shillings one could pick up handwritten manuscripts by such famous people as Burns, Scott, Thackeray, Cromwell, Lord Nelson, or Mary Queen of Scots. It was too good to be true.

In August 1891 the *Cumnock Express* printed a newly surfaced letter from Robert Burns to his old friend John Hill in Cumnock. An enthusiastic reader tried to trace the history of John Hill and found that no such person had ever lived in Cumnock. The researcher challenged the letter's owner, a manuscript dealer named James Mackenzie. Mackenzie's cocky answer was to print two previously unpublished poems by Burns that he had in Burns' own handwriting.

Unfortunately for Mackenzie, a reader identified the two newly published Burns poems. They were really by a minor writer who lived a generation before Burns. At that point the embarrassed Mackenzie claimed that he had found his manuscripts in a secret drawer in an old cabinet, and he and his document business became a laughing stock.

Eighty-eight-year-old James Stillie was also selling forged documents at that time. Stillie claimed that he had been a friend of Sir Walter Scott for fifty years (which would have made him 107 years old). A worried American who had paid Stillie £750 for 202 Burns manuscripts sent them to the British Museum for authentication and learned that 201 of them were fakes. He started to sue for a refund, but Stillie begged mercy because of his old age and was spared.

In November 1892 the *Edinburgh Evening Dispatch* printed a series of articles about these mysterious forgeries, with illustrations. A keen-eyed reader responded; some of the handwriting in the case was that of a law office clerk named Alexander Howland Smith, known as "Antique" Smith because of his interest in old documents. When questioned, Smith claimed that he had once been given all the old documents in the cellar of a law office, which he sorted and sold. Then, he admitted, he had started creating and selling old documents. He aged them by dipping them in weak tea.

In June 1893 Smith was charged with "selling and pawning spurious MSS as genuine, obtaining money by pretending that certain documents were genuine and what they purported to be." The judge explained that it is not a crime to forge a document and it is not a crime to lie, but using forgeries to steal money from people is a crime.

The jury found Smith guilty but sentenced him to only one year in jail. Forgery on such a massive scale had never occurred in Scotland before, and it caused a sensation.

## Prince of Collectors

At the very time of Antique Smith's trial, the collector's market in England was being infiltrated with dozens of like-new copies of over fifty pamphlets from famous Victorian authors, such as Ruskin, Browning, Swinburne, Kipling, and Tennyson. The oldest of the pamphlets were dated in the 1840s, but for some reason no copies had appeared on the market before 1890. None were autographed, none were mentioned anywhere by their authors, and none were listed in bibliographies before the 1890s. Yet they fetched high prices and took their place in the reference books about their authors. This was the beginning of a forgery scandal that dwarfed that of Antique Smith. This was the scandal of Thomas J. Wise, a wealthy scholar, England's highly venerated prince of book collectors, and the ruling authority on rare books.

From the heights of success, Wise piously deplored Major Byron's forgeries and fraudulence; but in fact his own spectacular career as a forger and cheat was just starting when Major Byron died in 1882. Perhaps Wise was inspired to succeed where Byron failed.

In 1932 John Carter and Graham Pollard of the London rare-book trade got together. Pollard believed that some valuable first-edition pamphlets by Ruskin were forgeries, and Carter was concerned about the earliest edition of Elizabeth Barrett Browning's *Sonnets from the Portuguese.* Elizabeth had brought the poems to her husband as a surprise gift at the breakfast table one morning. He declared them the best sonnets since Shakespeare and then allegedly insisted upon a small private printing for close friends. According to the title page, they were printed in Reading, England, in 1847. Carter didn't doubt the breakfast-table story; but according to Robert Browning it had taken place in 1849. That meant that the sonnets were published in Reading two years before the poet wrote them.

Wise had supposedly proved the pamphlets genuine, and in the 1920s about thirty of them had brought up to $1,250 apiece. Carter and Pollard had the "1847" paper tested and found that it was made of chemical wood pulp that could not have been produced before the

1880s. Next, they discovered that the type font used in the booklet did not exist before 1880. They also discovered that Wise had donated some of the forged pamphlets to the British Museum and Cambridge University to "authenticate" those that he was selling.

In 1934 Carter and Pollard shocked the document world by publishing the tale of their exciting detective work and Wise's fraud. Wise's response was to call the two authors "sewer rats." At that point an American bookseller recalled opening the wrong drawer in Wise's library once and seeing a whole pile of pages from the "1847 edition" of Browning's sonnets. Wise's defenders launched a bitter counterattack, but a confession by Wise turned up in an old letter in his own handwriting and cinched the case. It seems clear that Wise began forging and faking before 1900 to make money, but once he was rich he continued for the sardonic pleasure of outsmarting and cheating other collectors.

In the end, it has been said, Wise was more forged against than forging: Long before he was exposed, copies of his forged pamphlets were being forged by others. Thus it is that in 1992 a genuine Thomas Wise forgery—a bogus 1869 pamphlet of George Eliot sonnets, probably printed by Wise around 1888—was offered for $400. In the bookdealer's catalog, an American counterfeit of that pamphlet produced in about 1920 was offered for $200. One could order either the genuine Wise forgery or the forged Wise forgery.

Thomas Wise was a crook, but he was sincere in his passion for rare books. When his own rare books had pages missing, he inserted pages that he stole from copies in the British Museum.

## The Utah Forger

Both Antique Smith and Thomas Wise have been eclipsed now by the lurid career of a quiet Mormon murderer. From 1980 to 1985 Mark Hofmann was known as a phenomenally successful young dealer in rare documents, but he was really a phenomenally successful forger. The only reason his secret career was ever uncovered was that he was being investigated for murder. All the elements of a spellbinder are present in his story—rigid religion, secret atheism, the passion for risk, a double life, immense amounts of money, fraud, betrayal, blackmail, murder, horrible accidents, bankruptcy, mental breakdown, heroic detective work, a desperate legal battle, and—

134

evidently—an attempt to commit more murder from a prison cell. It is the story of a fiendishly clever and morally idiotic man; but it is also a story of the world of document collectors in which he operated.

As a teenager Hofmann allegedly added a D to an ordinary dime and fooled the experts at the U.S. Mint in Washington into thinking that it was one of a few from Denver worth thousands of dollars. Years later he convinced the American Antiquarian Society that he had found the long-lost "Oath of a Freeman" worth hundreds of thousands of dollars (he asked over a million for it). After his imprisonment, he claimed that aside from a few exceptions all the hundreds of documents he had sold were his own forgeries. He had forged the handwriting of at least eighty-three historical figures including John Milton, Paul Revere, George Washington, Daniel Boone, Mark Twain, Francis Scott Key, Abraham Lincoln, Joseph Smith, and poet Emily Dickinson.

"I just made up a poem and signed it—and I'll be darned if a year later I saw the poem published in a magazine as a 'newly discovered poem' by Emily Dickinson."

Who knows if that claim is true? It certainly could be.

The crux of Hofmann's career was his famous "salamander letter," which was part of his game of producing historical documents that could undermine the Mormon Church and then selling them to Mormons who wanted to hide them from researchers. Posing as a friend to the Church, he especially enjoyed cheating the Church. He could have succeeded if he had been prudent; but when his grandiose business maneuvers ran into trouble, he bombed two innocent bystanders in order to delay a financial accounting. The entire story is told by William Lindsey in his book *A Gathering of Saints*.

Charles Hamilton of New York is the dean of autograph collectors in the United States. His book *Great Forgers and Famous Fakes* has often been used by detectives and prosecutors who want to understand how forgers operate. Yet he was completely fooled by Hofmann's forged documents. He has reflected ruefully, "Hofmann is unquestionably the most skilled forger this country has ever seen, not just because he was a good technician. He got away with it because he had a knack for making people like and trust him. He fooled me, he fooled Ken Rendell, he fooled the whole world. He packaged himself as a bespectacled, sweet, unobtrusive, hard-working, intelligent

**135**

scholar dedicated to the uncovering of history. We now know he was something more than that."

Rare documents may be false, but false documents are not rare. They are everywhere; as dealer Anthony Roca remarked, "Forgery is the symptom, and greed is the disease." Whistle-blower Thomas Taylor warned, "The curators have not looked closely because . . . you don't look a gift horse in the mouth. So who can you trust? Not the greedy bookseller, not the shady bibliographer, not the timorous librarian." Many Hofmann forgeries are scattered across the land, inflating the value of public and private collections. Every time a forgery is sold as genuine, the buyer is stung; but every time a forgery is donated to a library as a tax write-off, the public is stung.

## Howard Hughes

Document forgers are artisans, and literary forgers are authors. Clifford Irving combined both kinds of forgery and topped them off with plagiarism when he sold his bogus authorized biography of billionaire Howard Hughes to McGraw-Hill for $750,000. The most amazing part of his scam is that he did it while Howard Hughes was still alive.

Irving was born in New York in 1930 and published his first novel in 1956. (In 1957 billionaire Howard Hughes disappeared from public sight.) Novel followed novel and marriage followed marriage, and Irving did not get rich as he had planned. In the 1960s McGraw-Hill published his book *Fake!*, which was the true story of a master hoaxer, art forger, and imposter named Elmyr de Hory.

In 1968 Irving told McGraw-Hill that he had sent Howard Hughes a copy of *Fake!* and that Hughes liked it so much he was granting permission for Irving to write a Hughes biography. Irving copied the style of Hughes' handwriting that he saw in *Newsweek* to forge twenty pages of letters from Hughes. They were authenticated by five of America's top handwriting experts, and Irving's editors paid him a gigantic advance. He insisted upon being the only person in contact with Hughes and upon receiving all his money before news of the book could be made public. Then he got hold of a manuscript by a longtime Hughes associate and copied much of it into his own book.

On December 7, 1971, McGraw-Hill announced its coming blockbuster. The book was first-page news. *Life* magazine planned to buy rights to the story until one of its journalists got a call from Hughes himself, announcing that the book was a hoax. *Life* confronted Irving, who seemed self-assured and convincing when he explained that the caller had been an imposter.

On January 7, 1972, Howard Hughes announced to the whole world that Irving's book was a fraud. Irving returned what was left of the money, and after a trial in New York he went to prison for two years. Later he brought out a book explaining his adventure, titled *What Really Happened*, but some readers didn't believe him.

### Adolf Hitler

In April 1983 the world was told of a forthcoming book more exciting than any Howard Hughes biography: the diary of Adolf Hitler. It seems that on April 21, 1945, a flaming plane crashed in a little town southwest of Dresden in what became East Germany. A box containing Hitler's diaries was saved from the wreckage and hidden, and the officer who saved the volumes had finally decided to sell them for publication. *Stern* magazine paid 9.3 million deutsche marks and called this "the find of the century." But as *Newsweek* noted, the find of the century turned out to be the fake of the century.

Konrad Kujau, a dealer in documents and Nazi memorabilia, had provided the diaries to reporter Gerd Heidemann, who provided them to *Stern* magazine, which sold rights to London's *Sunday Times* for a huge sum. When first accused, Kujau claimed that he could neither read nor write the kind of script in the diaries. When he confessed later, Kujau said that he had produced the first volume in 1978 as a joke. He had invented lines like "Must not forget to get tickets for the Olympic Games for Eva Braun." He had also lifted much of his content from *The Bunker*, by James P. O'Donnell.

At first, handwriting experts vouched for the diaries. South Carolina expert Ordway Hilton, the German FBI, and the former head of forensic services in Zurich all agreed that the diaries were genuine. Germany's Federal Archives explained later, "We checked the handwriting and found no reason to believe that the handwriting was forged. We did not investigate the age of the paper or ink."

The world's foremost Hitler scholar, Professor Gerhard Weinberg of the University of North Carolina, flew to Zurich and examined the diaries in a bank vault. He said that they looked genuine, and it seemed implausible to him that anyone would forge sixty-two volumes. But he was not quite sure. "There is still room—however unlikely—for suspecting that the whole thing is a hoax."

It seemed as if the world had already forgotten about the thirty-volume diary of Benito Mussolini that surfaced along with some of Mussolini's letters in Italy in 1947. Mussolini's son and an expert from Switzerland vouched for their authenticity, and London's *Sunday Times* bought the rights for a large five-figure sum. In fact, a woman named Rosa Panvini and her daughter Rosa had forged them; they were convicted and given a suspended sentence. The *Sunday Times* got no refund.

The tide gradually turned for the Hitler diaries. Historian H. Trevor Roper declared himself "100 percent certain of the diaries' authenticity." Twelve days later he publicly backtracked, and later yet he said, "I'm extremely sorry." Document expert Kenneth Rendell, hired by *Newsweek,* judged the diaries bad fakes on the basis of many mistakes in the handwriting and the cheap quality of the notebooks. Some of the ink and pencil looked wrong to him also. Chemical examination showed that the ribbon markers in the diaries contained polyester, not yet invented in Hitler's day, and the glue in the bindings was also of a more recent date. Paper expert Julius Grant found that the paper was made with bleach not yet available in Hitler's time.

Clifford Irving was not much impressed by the Hitler hoax. It doesn't take much to fool internationally renowned handwriting experts, he remarked. "We learned that back in 1972."

When Kujau was released from prison, he opened an art gallery in Stuttgard called Galerie der Falschungen—Gallery of Forgeries. He filled it with his own paintings mimicking artists like Dalí, Dürer, and Van Gogh. He explained, "People know me as a forger. That's what they want from me."

In July 1991 most of Britain was fascinated by the five-part television drama *Selling Hitler*. Kujau commented from Germany, "I was always surprised at how easy it was. People are crazy." For fun, he forged a Hitler letter authorizing him to produce the diaries. (He was six years old when Hitler purportedly wrote it.) If he is telling the truth, one customer in his art shop who read the letter said seriously,

"They shouldn't have locked poor Mr. Kujau away. He does have a written order here to write the diaries."

What possesses Kujau and all his fellow forgers? Richard Wilbur, one of America's most beloved authors and literary scholars, observes that at its simplest, hoaxing is swindling. It is done for gain. At a more complex level, it is done to make the hoaxer appear more clever and interesting than he really is. But at a loftier, wickeder level, it is done to tamper with the fabric of reality.

Wilbur recalls, "A colleague at Harvard once told me of a medievalist who, on his deathbed, confessed to his sorrowing students that he had forged such-and-such a manuscript—and then, carried away, *falsely* confessed to having faked many celebrated documents and codices. I suspect that that fellow died laughing. When hoaxers are negligent about making their swindles air-tight, I think it is because their chief motive is not gain or imposture but a heady sense of having shaken up the realm of fact a bit."

> *That God can write straight with crooked lines does not entitle creatures to write crooked lines in the book of their lives.*
>
> —Karl Rahner

# PART III:
# POWER-PLAY—YOUR MONEY
# OR YOUR MIND

# CHAPTER 5
# FLUMMOXED BY FLIM-FLAM ARTISTS

*There's one way to find out if a man is honest—ask him. If he says yes, he's a crook.*

—Groucho Marx

There are fortunes to be made in art fakes, and profit in scientific poppy-cock. When the corridors of culture contain more spuriosity than curiosity, someone has to pay for the drives, dreams, and delusions of scholarship's artful deceivers.

# DELICIOUS DECEPTIONS

*It used to be said that Camille Corot painted 800 pictures in his lifetime, of which 4,000 ended up in American collections.*

—*Time* magazine

In 1935 five different American millionaires bought copies of Leonardo da Vinci's "Mona Lisa," thinking they had the famous original that hangs in the Louvre. That is also the year in which the grandson of painter Jean François Millet was convicted of art forgery (not Mona Lisas) and explained, "You can sell anything to Americans and Englishmen. They know nothing about art; even their experts know nothing. All you have to do is to ask a fabulous price."

There was some truth in Millet's claim; according to the United States Treasury Department, at least 75 percent of the antiques imported back then were fakes. But it wasn't only Americans who were fooled; at that time there were thirty fake Van Goghs on display in European museums. Anthony Van Dyke painted only about seventy canvases, but at least 2,000 of them have been sold. Half the 500 or 600 Rembrandts in existence aren't really by Rembrandt. Nine out of ten Rodins that surface nowadays are fakes. Nine out of ten pieces of pre-Columbian pottery in Mexico today are fakes. Before he died of AIDS, artist Keith Haring used to say that his art was for the people; now it is said that his art is also by the people. The *Times* of London reports that printers using the latest laser-scanning technology are flooding the market with cut-price forgeries of posters and prints.

The world may be riddled with written forgeries, but it is absolutely swarming with art and antique forgeries. Thomas Hoving summed it up in *Connoisseur* in 1986: "In the sixteen years I worked at the Metropolitan Museum of Art, I was responsible for collecting some twenty-five thousand works and must have seen a hundred thousand more. Fully 60 percent of what I examined was not what it was said to be."

144

## Less-Than-Ancient Art

It has been said that the prevalence of fakes is the venereal disease of the art market—the punishment for combining bad judgment with excessive desire.

In 1965 more than 100 small marble figurines from the Cyclades islands of Greece suddenly became available from dealers here and there in Europe. Such objects were known to range from 3,000 to 5,000 years in age, and until 1965 they had been extremely rare. By 1967 many more were on the market, selling for up to $30,000 apiece. At that point some suspicious experts engaged the services of Josef Riederer, a Berlin professor of archaeometry. (Archaeometry employs the latest technologies such as thermoluminescence to determine the age and chemical content of art objects.)

Dr. Riederer told *Smithsonian* magazine, "Art forgery is as old as art itself, and there are famous cases of forgeries based upon forgeries. But counterfeiters are becoming more clever and ingenious from day to day. Fortunately, so are we. Our job is to keep a step ahead of them with modern science, to make detection so precise, comprehensive and reliable that the forgers' input to outsmart us becomes so costly and time-consuming that their profit margin dwindles. It's a bit like a race and, on the whole, we are winning."

Sparing no expense, Riederer eventually proved that the suspicious figurines, which cost buyers over $3 million, were fakes from an unknown forgery workshop; they could not possibly have been lying in the ground of the humid Cyclades islands for thousands of years. If the guilty parties had not greedily dumped so many into the art market at once, the Berlin testing would probably not have taken place. It has made surprisingly little difference, however; at last report, many of the figurines were still being passed off as genuine.

Later, Riederer's laboratory settled a dispute about *Flora*, a life-size wax bust of a lovely half-nude lady whose forearms are broken off. In 1909 the director of the Prussian Royal Museum in Berlin, Wilhelm von Bode, paid a high price for *Flora* because he thought she was by Leonardo da Vinci. To von Bode's irritation, a minor British sculptor named Albert Durer Lucas volunteered the fact that his father, Richard Cockle Lucas, had created *Flora* in 1846, and that she had been broken accidentally in his workshop. If so, she was sixty-three years old and British rather than 400 years old and Italian. The 1846 newspaper stuffed inside her would prove his story, he said.

Von Bode reasoned that Lucas had only been repairing *Flora* in 1846; she had to be by Leonardo. In 1910 a Berlin sculptor named Martin Schauss published an article in which he explained why *Flora* was probably created by the great Italian forger Bastianini in 1845, then repaired in England by Lucas in 1846; if so, she was sixty-four years old and Italian. But von Bode didn't budge. For more than seventy years, *Flora* held her place of honor in the Berlin museum as a work of Leonardo. Then in 1984, long after von Bode and Lucas and Schauss were gone, *Flora* was tested by Josef Riederer; she contains a chemical that did not exist before 1833. She is almost surely the work of Bastianini. "There are many examples like Flora," Riederer observes. "A lot of money and careers hang on them. There is also an ostrich mentality among curators and collectors."

## The Art Trade

Art dealers, museum curators, buyers, and purchasing agents for major collections move about in the high-stakes world of art investment and the related realms of forgery exposure and forgery cover-up. Picasso said, "People who make a trade of art are usually swindlers." Author David Sox in his book *Unmasking the Forger* says that unmasking a forger becomes an exercise in unmasking these other people as well. At best, it is unrealistic to think that all of them have perfect aesthetic judgment and high ethical standards; their integrity, competence, and dependability are bound to vary. The art trade usually attracts a colorful array of ambitious people, not saints.

In a 1986 article titled "Money and Masterpieces," *Connoisseur* magazine questioned the ethics and wisdom of the J. Paul Getty Museum in Malibu, California, which is the richest art institution in the world. Between 1973 and 1984 curator Jiri Frel accepted from about a hundred wealthy donors antiquities which he evaluated at almost $20 million. The donors all deducted Frel's official evaluations of their gifts from their taxable incomes, and Frel's evaluations were incredibly generous. For example, one donor bought a Roman bust at Christie's in London for about $1,000 in 1978, and Frel evaluated it at over $60,000 for the donor's tax accountant in 1979. It must be a pleasure to buy a $60,000 tax deduction for $1,000.

The Getty museum reportedly spends $90 million a year from the fabulous Getty Trust. Some art experts complain that it squanders a fortune on fakes. For example, in 1985 the Getty paid $7 million for a life-size Greek male nude; then it paid $7 million for *The Annunciation* by Flemish painter Dieric Bouts. Soon after that, it paid about $17 million for *Adoration of the Magi* by Mantegna. All three of these are commonly considered inauthentic, but that does not seem to decrease the profits and power of the people involved. The more masterpieces the merrier, in the art market.

In 1967, just when the $30,000 Cyclades figurines became suspect, a Rhode Island sculptor named Armand LaMontagne set an elaborate trap for some dealers and curators, to mock their expertise. He made what looked like a seventeenth-century "Brewster" chair and aged it chemically; then he gave it to a friend for the porch of his Deer Isle cottage. As LaMontagne expected, a dealer eventually spotted the chair and bought it. Before long, the chair was sold to the Henry Ford Museum in Dearborn, Michigan, for $9,500. To the delight of its maker, it was featured on the cover of the museum catalog. Then LaMontagne announced that it was a fake.

In 1988, LaMontagne's chair was a highlight of a New York show called "April Fool: Folk Art Fakes and Forgeries." That show included such items as carved walrus tusks made out of synthetic polymer and an acrylic copy of a genuine 1840 painting. It also included homemade hooked rugs by a Maine folk artist named Barbara Merry. She sells them for as little as $20, but some dealers claim that they are a century old and resell them to gullible buyers for as much as $1,500.

At about the same time that the "April Fool" art show was taking place, a New York collector named Henry Weldon was in the midst of investing about $1 million in thirteen pieces of Staffordshire pottery almost 150 years old, which he purchased from Lindsay Antiques in London. Four years later, Weldon demanded a refund from the dealer, claiming that they had sold him modern "forgeries of no value." The art and antiques squad of Scotland Yard geared up to do scientific testing on similar pieces of pottery. One of Weldon's items was an owl-shaped jug that cost him $100,000, and another was a seven-branched candelabrum that cost him $135,000. Ironically, his collection had been featured in a recent book titled *English Stoneware and Earthenware 1650–1800*, published by Sotheby's of London and selling for $200.

147

There are two reasons for extravagant art purchases by wealthy people who know little about art: greed fuels their desire for financial profit on a sure-fire investment, and vanity fuels their desire to feel socially superior. Likewise, greed and vanity are two major reasons why artists go to all the work of forging. Poverty-stricken artists often resent the sky-high prices of things old or famous. Whether a successful art forger goes public or not, he has proved something to himself about his superior talent and other people's inferior judgment.

But not all forgers fit one pattern; art authority Sir Kenneth Clark points out that some Italians forge with elaborate devotion to mischief. For example, the celebrated forger Icilio Ioni was motivated less by greed than naughtiness, impudence, and rascality: "He enjoyed the fun of fooling the experts and museum directors and would go to any lengths to achieve it." Italy was the world's premiere fake factory.

Deception is a favorite form of creativity for some people. Gore Vidal said wryly of such a person, "He will lie even when it is inconvenient: the sign of a true artist." Perhaps Vidal knew of Rudyard Kipling's verse "The Lie," in which Kipling claimed that pottery, poetry, and painting are not quite as satisfying as the art of deception:

> *There is pleasure in the wet, wet clay*
> *When the artist's hand is potting it.*
> *There is pleasure in the wet, wet lay*
> *When the poet's pad is blotting it.*
> *There is pleasure in the shine of your picture on the line*
> *At the Royal Acad-emy;*
> *But the pleasure felt in these is as chalk to Cheddar cheese*
> *When it comes to a well-made Lie.—*
> *To a quite unwreckable Lie,*
> *To a most impeccable Lie!*
> *To a water-tight, fire-proof, angle-iron,*
> *sunk-hinge, time-lock, steel-faced Lie!*

### A Colossal Lie

When poet Rudyard Kipling died in 1936, the pride of the Metropolitan Museum was some 2,500-year-old Etruscan warriors that had been made out of wet, wet clay only twenty years earlier.

David Sox recalls in *Unmasking the Forger,* "I first saw the Met's Etruscan warriors in 1958 when I was a student at Union Theological

Seminary. I remember them as star attractions in a gallery almost entirely given over to them, and also recall how school children were delighted to see so much male genitalia on open view."

There are probably many people who still recall when they first saw the terra-cotta Etruscan warriors in the Metropolitan Museum of Art. I saw them one day in June 1960, and I was so intrigued by the eight-foot-tall "colossal warrior" that I stood there spellbound and took a snapshot that I puzzled over for months. He was a powerful figure, but he had odd proportions and a peculiar modern style. I remember exclaiming to my husband, "He looks as if he was made in the 1920s! How can that be?"

Early in 1961 I stumbled across my answer while reading the news. The colossal warrior was really a colossal fake. He was a huge cartoonish version of a tiny bronze warrior in a Berlin museum.

Etruscan culture flourished from about 700 to 400 B.C. in Etruria, near Rome; Etruscan forgery flourished there after 1860. That is when a couple of Italian stonemasons were hired to restore a shattered Etruscan tomb, which then became the pride of the Louvre. Flushed with success, the stonemasons decided to make an Etruscan tomb from scratch, and an antiquities dealer sold it to the British Museum in 1873. That fake was considered the best piece of Etruscan art in the world. Next, the dealer recruited a family named Riccardi to move to an Etruscan site to work with terra-cotta relics there. They created a variety of antiques for him from the local clay.

Riccardo was the most talented of the second-generation Riccardis, and he and his lover Alfredo Fioravanti became co-leaders of the team (Riccardo was an active bisexual). Before World War I they completed two huge Etruscan warrior figures, which they broke and sold to the Metropolitan Museum of Art. Then they served in the army together. Immediately after the Armistice at the end of 1918, they started on a colossal warrior, using as their guide a photo of an exquisite Etruscan warrior that is barely five inches tall. Although the original is clothed, the forgers chose to expose the genitals on their copy; and it is alleged that Riccardo was the model for that part.

The project was a disaster. When the figure was completed up to the waist, the men realized that the ceiling was too low; they had to make him very stocky. Because they were too crowded to see what they were doing, they got the left arm too long. Then Riccardo was killed in a riding accident. His cousins and Fioravanti finished the statue themselves, broke it up, and fired the pieces. In the summer of 1919 the unsuspecting purchasing agent for the Metropolitan learned of this newly excavated statue, for which the Riccardis were demanding $40,000. The Metropolitan bought the statue in 1921, laboriously put it back together, built a new gallery, and opened their long-awaited Etruscan warrior display in 1933.

In 1936 an aged Italian stonemason boasted that over sixty years earlier he and his brother had made the tomb that was the pride of the British Museum. People took a second look and suddenly wondered how such a ridiculous tomb was ever taken seriously; the London curators were humiliated and whisked it out of sight. In 1936 there were also ominous rumors that the Metropolitan's Etruscan warriors were forged; they were said to be the work of a man in Rome named Fioravanti. But the angry Metropolitan curator who privately called them her "terra-cotta dollies" refused to investigate; after all, the warriors were greatly enhancing her prestige as an art historian.

In about 1955 a new curator at the Met came across the colossal warrior's absent phallus in a drawer and attached it for the first time, so that he was finally complete except for a missing thumb. Ironically, within months someone secretly broke off the newly replaced part and stole it. American museum visitors were never warned that scholars in Italy considered the warriors bogus. When one Italian visitor was invited to admire them in 1959, he answered, "How can I, when I know the man who made them?"

In 1960 a Met administrator reluctantly had the glaze on the warriors tested chemically and learned to his sorrow that it contained manganese dioxide, which was not used until the 1600s—at least 2,000 years too late. A new Met director sent a curator to Rome to interview Fioravanti, who signed a forgery confession before the American Consul. He proved that his confession was true by producing the missing thumb from the statue's left hand, which he had kept for forty years. The warriors were soon carted out of their spacious gallery and hidden away in the basement of the Met.

The Etruscan statues were a colossal hoax, but Fioravanti was only a minor forger; he spent most of his life driving taxis in Rome and died in 1963. Ironically, he was buried in the same cemetery as Alceo Dossena, probably the most versatile forger of all time.

## Dossena Deception

Honest art copies become art forgeries only when used to deceive. Italians are commonly credited with being the world's best art copiers, and the most versatile of them all was Alceo Dossena. His antique creations spanned about twenty centuries of history, and he made them out of terra-cotta, marble, wood, and bronze. By the time he died in 1937, over $3 million had been paid for his forgeries, equal to perhaps $60 million if he had lived more recently. Unfortunately, other people got most of the money, and they are still getting it. Many of his forgeries are still being sold and resold as ancient art to this day. (David Sox tells the whole story and provides photographs in his book *Unmasking the Forger: The Dossena Deception.*)

Dossena was an impulsive, rebellious child who grew up in Cremona, a city full of sculptures and violins. (Cremona was the home of famed violin-maker Stradivarius.) According to his nephew, when Dossena was a twelve-year-old pupil in trade school, he became angry at a teacher who did not admire the statue of Venus that he brought in to show. On his way home, he broke off the arms and buried the statue in a hole where children liked to dig. In a few days children found it and brought it into the school, where a different teacher put it on display. Dossena reportedly burst out, "You asses! I'm the one who made the statue," and he showed the broken arms to prove it. He was expelled, and eventually became an art restorer. He was a master chemist when it came to making new things look old.

In 1916 an art dealer named Fasoli saw that he could make a fortune off Dossena's imitation antiquities. Dossena produced them with amazing speed, and Fasoli sold them for up to a hundred times what he paid Dossena. Fasoli concocted stories about where these works came from. If they were church furnishings, he sometimes told purchasers they had been found in the ruins of a church destroyed by an earthquake long ago. That was true of the Mino Tomb.

In 1922 the Boston Museum of Fine Arts paid $100,000 (Fasoli had paid Dossena only $4,000) for an elaborate marble tomb dated 1430, featuring the sleeping form of the deceased Maria Caterina Savelli. The Mino Tomb was by the Florentine sculptor Mino da Fiesole (1429–84), and it was featured at the museum entrance, where people came from far and wide to admire it. As Carlson Wade noted in *Great Hoaxes and Famous Imposters*, "One often feels a combination of intimidation and adoration when looking at the rare paintings, sculpture, and sacred art objects on display within the hallowed halls of imperious and haughty museums." No one seemed to notice that the Mino Tomb was dated one year after its sculptor was born, and that the brief Latin inscription on the tomb, which was naïvely copied from a book about the Savelli family, said, "At last the above-mentioned Maria Caterina Savelli died."

Late in November 1928, after Fasoli refused to give Dossena the $7,500 that he was demanding for a piece that had brought in $150,000, Dossena did the equivalent of taking his story to *Sixty Minutes*. He sued Fasoli for back pay. When Fasoli called Dossena an imposter and a liar, Dossena announced, "Millions upon millions have been spent for ancient sculptures that I created in my atelier. The Metropolitan Museum in New York, the museums in Cleveland, Munich, Berlin and the Frick Museums have my works of art. Many marbles attributed to the ancients were created by myself. Hoaxers passed them off as authentic."

The art world was traumatized. The *New York Times* declared sedately on December 8, "The shock of the discovery in Italy ten days ago is still acute in New York art circles. While secrecy surrounds the situation, there is no effort here to minimize the seriousness of the disclosures. The Dossena works deceived not only eminent archaeologists and connoisseurs of both Europe and America, but geologists as well." Other newspapers had a field day.

People everywhere were trying to save face and to save the value of their investments. Some in the art trade attacked Dossena as "a fraud and a publicity seeker" who was only a "simple stonemason," "nothing more or less than a craftsman turned megalomaniac." The Metropolitan hid a Dossena statue in the basement and claimed that they had never had one by him. The Boston Museum of Art insisted that Dossena lied about making the Mino Tomb.

Naïve as he seemed, Dossena had taken photos of many of his works as he made them; and he had a secret chamber in his workshop where he kept chips from many of them, such as a missing toe of Maria Caterina Savelli. In 1929 he became somewhat of a celebrity, and he won his case. He lived as an artist in his own right after that, signing all his work. Ironically, it seems that since then dealers have removed his signatures from some of those honest statues and sold them as genuine antiquities.

## Meergeren to Meer

The next spectacular art forger was an unusually small Dutch painter named Hans van Meergeren, who was enough of a success in a Delft art school that he considered himself a genius. Great was his bitterness when his career in the south of France went nowhere and he had to stoop to designing Christmas cards, restoring paintings, and selling portraits to tourists to support himself. He blamed the art dealers, professors, and critics for his obscurity, and when he was middle-aged, he decided to outwit them all. He decided to forge paintings by the great Dutch painter Jan Vermeer, who had lived almost three-hundred years earlier in Delft.

Van Meergeren devoted immense time and effort to getting centuries-old canvases, scraping off most of the paint, and recreating the recipes for Vermeer's extraordinary paint colors. To get a certain shade of blue, he sent to England for powdered lapis lazuli, a semi-precious stone. He mixed his paints with oil of lily. He figured out how to harden paint by using phenol-formaldehyde resin and baking the painted canvases in a low oven. The result was a superb approximation of Vermeer's enamel-like paint surface. This meticulous technical preparation took about four years.

Shortly before the beginning of World War II, van Meergeren turned loose on the world a Vermeer painting that no one had heard of before, *The Supper at Emmaus.* Holland's leading art critic, Abraham Bredius, studied it carefully and then declared in an art magazine, "It is a wonderful moment in the life of a lover of art when he finds himself suddenly confronted with a hitherto unknown painting of a great master . . . just as it left the painter's studio! And what a picture! Neither the beautiful signature 'I.V. Meer' . . . nor the pointille on the bread which Christ is blessing, is necessary to convince us that we have here a—I am inclined to say—*the* masterpiece of Johannes Vermeer of Delft." A Rotterdam museum paid $270,000 for the painting and sold prints of it to the public.

One by one other unknown Vermeers surfaced in the next few years and received lavish praise. Because van Meergeren's Vermeers were in fact quite inferior to genuine Vermeers, there must have been people who doubted them. But the art establishment accepted them and eagerly paid almost $4 million. Van Meergeren allegedly deposited most of his new wealth in Swiss banks.

All this took place during World War II, when Holland and France were occupied by Germany. The notorious Nazi leader Hermann Goering bought Vermeer's "Christ and the Adulteress" for himself for $850,000 and sent it to his estate near Berlin. At the end of the war, Allied forces retrieved treasures for return to their rightful owners, and "Christ and the Adulteress" was returned to Holland. There investigators uncovered the fact that van Meergeren had sold it to the Nazis, and in 1945 he was hauled into court and charged with treason for selling a national treasure to the enemy.

To save himself from a possible death penalty, he finally admitted that the painting was a forgery. At that, the very art authorities who had been tricked by the Vermeer forgeries rallied to defend them in court. Abraham Bredius and other experts testified that the "Christ and the Adulteress" had to be genuine.

Van Meergeren proved them wrong by painting a similar Vermeer in front of police witnesses. (It sold for $600.) He insisted self-righteously that he had not created his forgeries for money. "I had been so belittled by the critics that I could no longer exhibit my own work. I was systematically and maliciously damaged by the critics, who don't know the first thing about painting."

The art world was in an uproar. Although the bitter-looking Van Meergeren became somewhat of a celebrity, he must have been disappointed that his original paintings were still universally unpopular. At the end of his 1947 trial for fraud, he was sentenced to one year in jail; but he died before serving his sentence, at the age of fifty-seven.

### Cheating with Keating

Like Dossena, the next famous art faker confessed voluntarily, became a celebrity, and escaped prison. He was tried for criminal deception in London in 1977, but after five weeks the case was abandoned because of concern about his physical health. Much of the public considered him a hero because he had put one over on pompous art experts; before long he wrote his life story and had his own television program, in which he taught art appreciation. He had a white beard and a sense of humor that endeared him to his audience.

Like many other art forgers, Thomas Keating had begun as an art restorer. In about 1950 he began duplicating the style of certain artists he admired and passing his pictures off as theirs. He specialized in bogus Samuel Palmers, and in 1976 he released thirteen previously unknown Palmers into the art market at once. The fact that all thirteen pictures were of Shoreham, England, caused the *London Times* to challenge their authenticity. In response, Tom Keating wrote to the paper that he had forged those Palmers and about 2,500 other pictures. He had forged Constable, Rembrandt, Degas, Gainsborough, Goya, Renoir, Turner, Toulouse-Lautrec, Modigliani, Monet, Van Gogh, and others. He refused to the end to provide the world with a useful list of his forgeries.

Keating was a study in contrasts. On one hand, he went to great lengths to make his forgeries seem authentic. He spent time shopping for old frames and canvas mountings in junk shops. For ink for his Rembrandt drawings he simmered walnuts in water for ten hours, then strained the juice through silk. He faked mildew marks by soaking paper in water and then sprinkling grains of instant coffee over it.

On the other hand, he always left clues in his pictures to show that they were fake. Sometimes he used modern paper for an old drawing or wrote on the canvas "This is a fake" with white lead paint, which would show up in an X-ray. He claimed that he forged "simply as a protest against merchants who make capital out of . . . artists, both living and dead." He said he didn't do it for money, and that he gave away more of this art than he sold.

Keating became so popular that he lived to see Christie's auction off 150 of his genuine pictures in December 1983 for about $125,000. Two months later he died of a heart attack. In September 1984 Christie's held a second Tom Keating auction and sold another 200 of his pictures for over $500,000. At the second auction there was an overflow crowd of 1000, and one painting alone, "Monet and his Family in their Houseboat," brought in about $32,000.

Now there are forged Tom Keatings on the market. The French fablist Jean de la Fontaine gave us the saying, "It is double the pleasure to deceive the deceiver." Perhaps it is double the pleasure to forge the forger.

## Caveat Emptor: Let the Buyer Beware

Dossena, van Meergeren, and Keating are considered the three most successful art forgers in our century, but the most successful art forgers of all are most likely some others we never heard of. They are the ones who never got caught.

The man alleged to be the biggest art forger in the United States in the 1980s was Anthony Gene Tetro. His home was in Claremont, California, and his art work is in homes and galleries across the United States. The art is all signed with names like Norman Rockwell, Marc Chagall, Joan Miró, Pablo Picasso, and Salvador Dalí. Tetro went too far when he forged paintings by a *living* artist. Japanese relatives of artist Hiro Yamagata spotted bogus paintings by him in a Beverly Hills gallery in 1988. Yamagata called the police—launching a year-long investigation.

In August 1989 Tetro was charged with forty-five felony counts. His defense was that he is not responsible for what dealers do with his products; he has a legal right to make and sell copies of famous artwork so long as he sells them as copies. (He later took part in a Nova program call "The Fine Art of Forgery.")

August 1989 also happened to be when art dealer Annette Couch reported to the Los Angeles police that she had been offered Renoir's "A Young Girl with Daisies" for only $3.25 million. It was literally a steal. This century-old painting of a soft, bare-shouldered young woman with flowers in her lap is conservatively valued at $5 million. Furthermore, the famous original has belonged to New York's Metropolitan Museum of Art since 1959, and it is still there.

While police investigated the matter, a Japanese businessman named Koichi Akemoto bought "A Young Girl with Daisies" at a bargain price from the prestigious Beverly Hills branch of the Upstairs Gallery chain of art stores, a subsidiary of the Forest Lawn Company. Where did Upstairs Gallery get the forgery? From a dashing, smooth-talking French-born art broker named Frank De Marigny.

"Prince Frank," as he was sometimes called, was forty-one and lived in an ocean-front condominium in Manhattan Beach. He drove a Rolls Royce and a Farrari. His home was festooned with art by Chagall, Renoir, and Monet. Yet De Marigny had used the name Frank Orval when he sold a $57,000 Japanese lithograph to the National Heritage Gallery of Fine Art in Beverly Hills. Coincidentally, that lithograph was purchased by Koichi Akemoto, the same businessman who bought the Rodin painting at Upstairs Gallery.

Josh Billings said, "Nobody really loves to be cheated, but it does seem as though everyone is anxious to see how near he could come to it."

Akemoto filed a suit against all those who wronged him, for $3 million damage. De Marigny was arrested on two counts of grand theft and five counts of forgery. The police seized 1,685 forged lithographs from various Upstairs Gallery locations. The Art Dealers Association of California lamented that this scandal might upset the trustful confidence of affluent art-buyers. One Beverly Hills art dealer who insisted on anonymity remarked that knowledgeable people from New York and Europe are used to spotting art forgeries in Southern California. "There are so many fakes in Los Angeles, especially Beverly Hills, that it's a big joke."

### Fake Photos

In his 1494 book *Ship of Fools*, Sebastian Brant said, "The world wants to be deceived." Five-hundred years later, that seems more true than ever. Most of us at least like to be fooled by a kind camera that flatters our looks or fosters our hopes.

Photography is an art form that makes accidental or intentional deceptions easy. The book about photographic deception called *Making People Disappear* shows how totalitarian regimes of all kinds have fudged photos to produce propaganda: retouching, blurring, recentering, cutting, making ellipses, and eliminating. On the other side, anti-Hitler propagandists once made him look demonically possessed by doctoring an ordinary movie film of him. They deleted certain frames, making his normal walk turn into an uncanny jig, which was said to be how he celebrated the news of his successful invasion of Poland. (At the end of the twentieth century, new computer graphics techniques make it vastly easier to tamper with photos.)

"Cameras don't lie" is as silly as "Stoves don't cook." Just as stoves are for cooking, so cameras both record and distort the truth.

Simple photographic trickery can befuddle the most intelligent people. In 1991 a blurry photo appeared in newspapers across the country and on the cover of *Newsweek* on July 29. It allegedly showed three American servicemen who had disappeared in the Vietnam War in 1966, 1969, and 1970. In the photo the three stand together, very much alive, with an extremely peculiar sign dated May 25, 1990. The article inside *Newsweek* began, "This is a story about anguish, hope and longing—and what may be a cruel hoax."

Though many saw the photo as a clumsy, pieced-together fake (there is no doubt it came from some Cambodians who have provided fake photos in the past), the families of the missing men understandably got their hopes up all over again. Some marchers used the enlarged photo on posters and had it printed on T-shirts that said, "Please help us bring them home NOW." The grown daughter of one of the three men in the picture complained bitterly about the Pentagon, "Why don't they stop trying to debunk the photo?" So it is that people are apt to cling to affirmations of what they ardently desire.

As an experiment in photo fakery, in September 1991, I superimposed a head of C. S. Lewis from about 1940 and the heads of his two literary executors from about 1975 on the three men in the Cambodian photo and changed the date on their sign to 1963; then I sent it out in a Lewis newsletter with a warning to check the July 29 *Newsweek*. At least two of my readers took it seriously. That reminded me of the obviously fake photo of the dome falling off Wisconsin's Capitol that appeared on page one of Madison's *Capital-Times* on April 1, 1933. Most shocked readers didn't notice that it looked fake until they came to the small words "April Fool" below.

Arthur Conan Doyle, author of the Sherlock Holmes detective stories, had a strong interest in the paranormal. One Sunday afternoon in 1917, cousins named Frances Griffiths and Elsie Wright, aged nine and fifteen, saw some fairies and took clear snapshots of them with their box camera. Conan Doyle believed the girls' story and presented their snapshots to the public as evidence that fairies really exist. Whether fairies exist or not, the public did not think that the snapshots were what they were purported to be.

In 1983, sixty-six years later, Elsie Wright and Frances Griffiths decided that it was time to confess what people had suspected all along. The fairies were paper dolls that the girls had propped up on the grass with pins. That explains why the fairies looked like two-dimensional fantasy art from early in this century and why one of the little figures had no wings.

Unlike the cruel 1991 prisoner-of-war photo, the English fairy photo was a bit of entertaining frivolity that did no harm aside from making fifty-eight-year-old Arthur Conan Doyle look amazingly gullible.

# WINKING AT HOODWINKERS

*A lie is an abomination unto the Lord and a very present help in trouble.*

—Adlai Stevenson

In addition to getting mixed up with the fairy-photo hoax, Arthur Conan Doyle had two other connections with fakes. In 1911 he bought a typed Sherlock Holmes story called "The Man Who Was Wanted" from one of his admirers, with the idea that he might want to draw from it someday. In 1942 his impulsive son Adrian came across the story in a trunk, pretended it was in his father's handwriting, and sold it to magazines in the United States and Britain. (No one knows if Adrian really thought that the typed story was by his father.)

A few Sherlock Holmes experts protested that this inferior story had to be forged, but they were ignored. When the well-intentioned author of the story wrote to Adrian to set the record straight, Adrian sued the elderly man for slander. Fortunately, he had kept his 1911 letters from Arthur Conan Doyle, which settled the matter. "The Man Who Was Wanted" was no longer wanted.

## The Perpetrator at Piltdown

It seems that there is a natural human urge to dig in the ground or search in old trunks for things of value, and there is a corresponding urge to plant things there deceptively. We know who dug up the Piltdown Man, but we aren't sure who planted him. First the trick was blamed upon an amateur scientist named Dawson, then upon the famous philosopher-theologian-scientist Pierre Teilhard de Chardin. Another possible perpetrator of the great Piltdown hoax was none other than Arthur Conan Doyle.

The hoax was a failure because it was too successful and lasted too long. Arthur Conan Doyle had a long-term grudge against Edwin Bay Lankester, a cocky scientist who bitterly ridiculed spiritualism. (Conan Doyle believed in both evolution and spiritualism.) From

159

1906 to 1909 Lankester had made a string of public predictions about future fossil discoveries—and the Piltdown hoax conveniently fulfilled all of them. He was completely taken in by the Piltdown Man, but was never humiliated by its fraudulence in his lifetime.

The hoax was simple. On December 18, 1912, Charles Dawson, an attorney, and Arthur Smith Woodward, the British Museum's leading paleontologist, announced to the world that they had discovered an early human fossil in a shallow gravel pit near the village of Piltdown in Sussex. This was promptly accepted as the earliest known human fossil and was the pride of British science. Even more than the fake Etruscan tomb on display in the British Museum, the Piltdown Man served as evidence of innate British superiority. The British could say, "Our Etruscan tomb is the best, and our prehistoric man is older than your prehistoric man."

Over forty years later, someone finally noticed that the Piltdown Man had a jaw from an orangutan with its teeth crudely filed down to look human. The bizarre array of animal fossils found with the Piltdown man ranged over about a half million years of prehistory, but the ape jaw was only 500 years old. In 1955 J. S. Weiner published *The Piltdown Forgery*, blaming Dawson for the hoax, but admitting the possibility that someone else had tricked him. Weiner mentioned Conan Doyle's presence on the scene, but cast no suspicion on him.

Pinning the hoax on Conan Doyle is a bit like pinning a hoax on the world's greatest fictional detective, but a *Science 83* article called "The Perpetrator at Piltdown" piled up impressive circumstantial evidence. Conan Doyle was a retired medical doctor and successful author who loved jokes. He was an expert in anatomy and took an interest in human jaws and skulls. He also took an immense interest in evolution and paleontology and had actually discovered some dinosaur fossils near his house. He lived about seven miles from the Piltdown gravel pit and visited there frequently when out walking in the neighborhood in 1912. (He also owned and drove a car.) He watched as Dawson and Woodward dug in the gravel pit looking for fossils. When they found the Piltdown Man, he expressed great interest and cheered them on.

Conan Doyle had easy access to all the odd materials used in the hoax: a rare, thick human skull; an antique orangutan jaw from the East Indies; a fossilized hippo tooth from Malta; some fossilized elephant teeth and flints from Tunisia (he visited Tunisia in 1909). The

Piltdown hoax also included Pleistocene beaver teeth just like those found in abundance next to the Sherington Golf Course where Conan Doyle liked to spend his vacations.

In 1912 Conan Doyle published a boys' fantasy titled *The Lost World*, in which a fictional geologist who strongly resembled Woodward traveled up the Amazon to an isolated plateau—which resembled the area around Piltdown so closely that they both have a spot named Battle in the same place. This plateau was the home of modern-day dinosaurs, mastodons, and ape men. (Incredible as it seems, the Pennsylvania Museum allegedly outfitted an expedition to Brazil in 1914 to locate this isolated plateau.) The entire story was told by a certain Professor Challenger, and his photo at the beginning of the story is really Arthur Conan Doyle in disguise. He was full of fun.

> "I could hardly imagine a more damning case," I remarked. "If ever circumstantial evidence pointed to a criminal it does so here."
>
> "Circumstantial evidence is a very tricky thing," answered Holmes thoughtfully; "it may seem to point very straight to one thing, but if you shift your point of view a little, you may find it pointing in an equally uncompromising manner to something entirely different." [from "The Bascomb Valley Mystery" (1891)]

Indeed, circumstantial evidence points in several different directions in the Piltdown hoax. Some articles in *Antiquity* have pointed to J. T. Hewitt, who allegedly admitted his involvement in the hoax to a friend. In 1986 *The Piltdown Inquest* pointed to Lewis Abbott, a local jeweler and fossil collector who claimed that pompous paleontologists should be punished by clever fakes. In 1989 an excellent monograph titled *The Curious Incident of the Missing Link: Arthur Conan Doyle and the Piltdown Man* by Douglas Elliott sought to exonerate Conan Doyle. In 1990 *Piltdown: A Scientific Forgery* pointed to an eminent anatomist, Sir Arthur Keith. Next, an article in *New Scientist* defended Keith and pointed convincingly to an eccentric scientist named Martin Hinton who was an authority on the Piltdown region. Hinton had reason to hoodwink Woodward, who had evidently hindered his career. When a perceptive American attacked the authenticity of the Piltdown skull in 1915, Hinton wrote to congratulate him.

And in 1935 Hinton announced in *Who's Who* that he was greatly interested in hoaxes.

Evidently Dawson-Teilhard-Hewitt-Keith-Hinton kept hoping the Piltdown hoax would be exposed. In 1914 an elephant bone carved to resemble part of a cricket bat was discovered at the Piltdown dig. In 1915 diggers at a distant site called Piltdown II discovered a tooth obviously from the jaw found back in Piltdown I. In 1935 a more modern skull was found in much older stratum in the village of Swanscombe. But no one paid attention to the additional clues, and the hoaxer had to keep his failed joke a secret to protect his reputation. Textbook after textbook taught about the Piltdown Man for over forty years. His creator had underestimated the gullibility of the scientific establishment, as most people do.

### A Mammoth Fraud

There was nothing entirely new about the Piltdown hoax; people had concocted strange creatures before and had been burying and digging up fakes for centuries. What makes the Piltdown hoax fascinating is that sensible objections to the skull were ignored, and it was accepted for so long by authorities who should have known better.

They should have recalled the famous Cardiff Giant, which was dug up just forty-three years earlier on a farm in New York. As soon as well-diggers came across a twelve-foot-tall stone giant, hundreds of thousands of people started streaming to the farm to marvel at it. Four local doctors declared it a petrified body, and a fifth doctor declared it a 300-year-old statue. A scholar at Yale Divinity School declared it an ancient Phoenician idol of the cherubim type, with feathered wings, a crescent-shaped wound on the left side, and a faint inscription. It was also identified as the body of an American Indian prophet who died centuries ago. The director of New York State Museum, a leading paleontologist, was baffled; and so was Ralph Waldo Emerson.

It turned out that George Hull, a relative of the farmer who found the giant, had spent several thousand dollars on a piece of gypsum from Iowa, a sculptor in Chicago, and transportation of the giant to the New York farm. There it lay for a year before it was discovered in 1869. Phineas T. Barnum tried to buy the giant, but Hull refused; so Barnum paid a sculptor to make a copy (purportedly of papier maché), which he falsely exhibited as the original. When George Hull took the Cardiff Giant to New York City for display, he found that Barnum had beat him to it with his hoax of a hoax. The original Cardiff Giant is on display to this day at the Farmer's Museum in Cooperstown, New York.

Twenty years after the world learned of the Cardiff Giant, the world learned of the Holly Oak pendant. This tale, as recorded by David Meltzer in *New Scientist* in July 1990, is at least as bizarre as that of the Piltdown Man. In December 1889 an archaeologist named Hilborne T. Cresson of the Peabody Museum at Harvard brought forth a shell pendant with the figure of a mammoth engraved on it; he had found it in Holly Oak, Delaware. This was marvelous archaeological news. Mammoths have been extinct in North America for over 10,000 years, and no art that old had ever been discovered in North America. This pendant could settle the old debate about whether humans were in North America 10,000 years ago, and it could put North America on a par with France, where a tusk with a figure of a mammoth carved on it had been discovered in 1864.

Cresson discovered the Holly Oak pendant early in 1864, shortly before Edouard Lartet discovered an almost identical mammoth in France; but Cresson had inexplicably waited twenty-five years to reveal it. He was a student at the School of Fine Arts and Archaeology in Paris in the 1870s, and so he must have examined Lartet's mammoth there. Back in the United States, he married into the wealthy Cresson family and took their prestigious name. He began work at the Peabody Museum in 1889, starting on shell pendants and other artifacts from Fort Ancient sites. In December he announced his spectacular Holly Oak pendant and showed it at the February 1890 meeting of the Boston Society of Natural History. The silence of the scientific community was deafening, which had to signal disbelief.

In 1891 Cresson was fired by the museum for filching artifacts from excavations. In 1894 the headline of the September 8 issue of the *Philadelphia Inquirer* blared "DR. HILBORNE CRESSON TAKES HIS OWN LIFE." The article said he "blew his brains out in a park in New York City." A note in his handwriting claimed that Secret Service detectives were following him and he believed they suspected him of counterfeiting. He was only forty-two years old.

Cresson's ignominious pendant was forgotten for eighty-five years, until it was rediscovered in a drawer in the Smithsonian and burst forth on the cover of *Science*. In May 1976 Geologist John C. Kraft and archaeologist Ronald A. Thomas of Delaware had checked the Holly Oak locale and stated that the pendant was probably 5,000 to 10,000 years old and possibly over 40,000 years old. Although they made perfunctory mention of the idea that the pendant could be an 1864 forgery, they claimed boldly,

> It is clear that the Holly Oak pendant is old and bears a carving of a woolly mammoth that was incised at the time of construction of the weathered pendant and near the time of origin of the shell. . . . Reexamination of old discoveries, coupled with the application of new concepts in sedimentology-stratigraphy and palynology, has led to an exciting new association of early man with the woolly mammoth in America. Possibly, further work will prove truly ancient [more than 40,000 years ago] presence of early man.

This sounds like a bid for a government grant!

Reaction was slow, but in 1983 Meltzer and a colleague sent a letter to *Science* explaining why their research led them to believe that the Holly Oak pendant was a fake. *Science* editors replied enigmatically that they were consulting their attorneys about "the legal ramifications" of publishing such an idea. (Did they fear that the state of Delaware would sue for libel?) For some reason it took *Science* two years to publish the letter; it appeared in January 1985, followed by a reply from Kraft that the evidence contained "nothing new or persuasive."

As Aleksandr Solzhenitsyn observed, "When the truth is discovered by someone else, it loses some of its attractiveness."

In the meantime, accelerator mass spectrometry became available, and tiny fragments of the pendant went off to Zurich for analysis. That proved that Cresson's pendant is less than 1,000 years old, the age of the Fort Ancient pendants. Because there were no mammoths in North America 1,000 years ago, it seems that Cresson stole a Fort Ancient pendant in 1889, carved a mammoth on it, and pretended that he had found it in Holly Oak when he was a teenager. When this news came out, many scientists suddenly claimed that they knew it all along; but one of the Holly Oak pendant's chief defenders shrugged that we'll never know for sure—and anyway, "Who cares?"

These are the two typical reactions from people who go along with a hoax in any field, when the whistle-blower wins the day: "We knew it all along," and "Who cares?"

## Betrayers of Truth

"Who cares?" was what many scientists were saying about the AIDS virus dispute in early 1991, according to *Newsweek*. It had been dragging on since 1985, when Luc Montagnier of the Pasteur Institute in Paris charged that Robert C. Gallo of the National Institutes of Health deliberately tried to steal credit from him for discovering the virus from which Gallo developed his blood test for AIDS. Gallo had become a scientific superstar and had been thought of as an American contender for the Nobel Prize.

At the very time when challengers of the Oak Hill pendant were waiting almost two years to get their letter into *Science*, Gallo published a landmark article there in May 1984, telling how he had identified a virus and developed a blood test for it. He included a photo of his virus. He did not mention that in 1983 Montagnier had identified more or less the same virus and sent him a sample. He also failed to mention that the photo he used in *Science* was really a photo of Montagnier's virus. Montagnier got so angry that he sued.

This entire fracas came on the heels of the 1982 publication of *Betrayers of the Truth*, a fascinating overview of scientific fraud by William Broad and Nicholas Wade. They point out that scientists have always had two goals: to understand the world, and to get credit for their work. Unfortunately, the desire for credit can eclipse the search for truth; ambition and careerism take over. The research grant system promotes this. "Science is also a race, an often furious competition in which individuals strive to be first—for without priority, discovery is bitter fruit. Under the pressure of competition, some researchers yield to the temptation of cutting corners, of improving on their data, of finagling their results, and even of outright fraud." As the authors explain, glory is the carrot, and possible denial of grant money is the stick.

In 1987 the conflict between Montagnier and Gallo was supposedly settled with a compromise in which the two researchers shared credit for the discovery. But in the fall of 1989 investigative reporter John Crewdson published a sixteen-page article in the *Chicago Tribune* making new allegations against Robert Gallo. That prompted Representative John Dingell of Michigan to pressure NIH to look into the matter. During the investigation, Gallo took the high road, scorning the cynical idea "that science is more about personalities and secrets than about solving problems." Montagnier retorted, "It's a question of Gallo's personality. . . . He doesn't know how to back down."

The NIH investigation showed that Gallo's 1984 article in *Science*, which he used in a patent application, included falsehood and fraudulence. The value of that patent to Gallo and his assistant Mikulas Popovic was $2 million apiece in royalties. Gallo allegedly cut out of the article Popovic's acknowledgment that the French were the true discoverers of the AIDS virus. Some of the experiments described in the patent application were allegedly never done, and some that were done with negative results were left out. In 1992 NIH's Office of Scientific Integrity issued a report that condemned Popovic alone for "reckless disregard for truth in science," and merely criticized Gallo for his "less than collegial" and "self-serving" manner. A panel of outside consultants judged the report too mild in its criticism of Gallo, but NIH was satisfied with it.

Thomas Jefferson's dictum "Honesty is the first chapter of the book of wisdom" must sound terribly out of date to some scientists.

Odd as it seems, the scientific establishment insists that it adequately polices itself. In *Betrayers of the Truth*, authors Broad and Wade say this self-policing is imaginary. "The external police force, it so happens, turns up bad science, outright error, and deliberate fraud by the bucketful. . . . An unending stream of falsified reports is regularly detected by even what limited police powers the FDA and EPA possess." Reports of falsified research since 1973 (the date of a notorious case in which white mice were blackened with India ink to fake a successful skin transplant) have almost all included allegations of investigative incompetence or university cover-ups.

In January 1987 *Science* magazine flatly denied that there is misrepresentation and error in research reports: "We must realize that 99.9999 percent of [scientific] reports are accurate and truthful. . . ." Yet the pages of *Science* alone refute that: in 1976 it published the woolly report on the Holly Oak pendant; in 1981 it published a report on research by Mark Spector that proved false; in 1984 it published the report by Gallo that proved false; and in 1986 it published a report from Harvard Dana-Farber that proved false.

Daniel Greenberg answered *Science*'s 99.9999 percent claim in *U.S. News and World Report*: "The claim of a failure rate of 1 per million—following a banner year for exposures and retractions, including the Harvard Dana-Farber paper in *Science*—was offered without any supporting evidence." In fact, the evidence was all on the other side. As Eugene Dong of Stanford University School of Medicine remarked wryly in 1991, "Based upon the scientific community's public statements, virtually no scientist has ever seen scientific fraud."

## Laboratory Legerdemain

Dr. Dong, an associate professor of cardiothoracic surgery and a practicing attorney, expressed his concern in *The Chronicle of Higher Education* on October 19, 1991: "After 20 years of backing and filling, the scientific community is facing the day of reckoning for its failure to address the research-fraud issue." Because research is federally funded, Dong said, federal anti-fraud statutes will probably be invoked in the future against dishonest researchers, as they should be.

To begin with, scientists carelessly assume that published data is accurate and do not analyze it with a view to uncovering intentional misrepresentation. Furthermore, when universities conduct investigations of alleged misconduct, they notify the accused in advance; as a result, laboratory data is quickly lost or destroyed. Then the accused is judged guilty of mere sloppiness, not fraud.

Dong believes that universities and institutions such as NIH should not be expected to investigate and punish those alleged to have violated United States civil and criminal laws. That is the job of the Department of Justice and another agency. When the day comes that universities face serious financial penalties for laboratory fraud, they will pressure their employees not to cheat the government with fake or fudged research.

Robert Gallo was only a potential Nobel Laureate, but David Baltimore was a real one. He headed a medical research laboratory at MIT in 1986, when he co-authored with Dr. Thereza Imanishi-Kari a paper for the journal *Cell* about an amazing scientific breakthrough: transplanted genes had produced new antibodies in mice. This might have led to a cure for some auto-immune diseases—but the data was faked. The government had paid for fraudulent research, then paid to have it published.

One would think that by 1986 all scientists would have read *Betrayers of the Truth*. Broad and Wade gave some practical suggestions that would end "laboratory legerdemain," including the inherently dishonest practice of lab chiefs signing their names to work in which they have been only peripherally involved, if at all.

> It would . . . spare the public the ludicrous spectacle of lab chiefs who hog credit for everything that goes well but disclaim responsibility when fraud is discovered. If a lab chief is not close enough to a research project to know whether the data is being falsified, he should not put his name on the paper. For the papers he does sign, he should take full responsibility. To most nonscientists, such principles probably seem too obvious to be worth stating.

Evidently, they were not obvious to Baltimore even after they were stated this urgently in 1982.

Dr. Margot O'Toole was a young postdoctorate research fellow in Baltimore's laboratory, and when she challenged the co-authored paper, she suddenly found herself an outcast in the scientific community. She lost her job and her home, and her husband's career was threatened. She was accused of being over-emotional because she nursed her baby. What hurt her most, she said, was being called a bad scientist when she stood up for truth.

Baltimore portrayed attacks on the paper as attacks on science itself: "Uninformed or malinformed outsiders cannot effectively review the progress of scientific activity." Superficial investigations by MIT, NIH, and Tufts University all failed to find fault with the paper, but O'Toole didn't give up. Her case came to the attention of Representative John Dingle, who had the Secret Service analyze Imanishi-Kari's lab notes. At that point Baltimore sent out a letter to 400 researchers warning that this kind of governmental interference could cripple American science. "My great fear is that this investigation, because of its intimidating nature, could undermine scientific collaboration." This alarm raised a storm of protest.

In spite of all the protest, the Secret Service decided that Imanishi-Kari's 1984–85 lab notes had been fabricated in 1986, and that turned the tide. The NIH finally investigated more thoroughly and condemned the paper. In May 1991 Baltimore apologized for what he characterized as "an excess of trust" in his collaborator. It had taken five years and five separate investigations to partially settle that case; the cost in wasted time and resources was astronomical. In 1992, David Baltimore indicated that he wanted to withdraw his 1991 apology. Meanwhile, high-placed lab chiefs are still routinely taking credit for work that they didn't do and didn't check.

## Burt and Bettelheim

Is nothing sacred? It turns out that the two most famous and influential child psychologists of the twentieth century were frauds.

Sir Cyril Burt was born in 1883 and was considered the most prestigious, powerful, and influential psychologist since the American genius William James. He held the chair of psychology at London's University College, was knighted by King George VI, and received the Thorndike award from the American Psychological Association. Most of Burt's career was based upon his statistical studies of the intelligence of identical twins, showing that poverty was due to inferior intelligence of the working class. In the 1940s Burt was involved in setting up the old three-track British school system that segregated students on the basis of an IQ test they took at age eleven.

Burt was a dazzling public speaker with enormous charm. In 1960 he gave one of his spellbinding performances at a symposium in London. After the speech, the eminent geneticist L. S. Penrose reportedly remarked, "I don't believe a word the old rogue says, but, by God, I admire the way he says it."

When Burt died in 1971 at the age of eighty-eight, Arthur Jensen of Stanford University paid this heartfelt tribute: "Everything about the man—his fine, sturdy appearance; his aura of vitality; his urbane manner; his unflagging enthusiasm for research, analysis and criticism; . . . and, of course, especially his notably sharp intellect and vast erudition—all together leave a total impression of immense quality, a born nobleman."

In *Betrayers of the Truth,* Broad and Wade point out that science is in one sense a celebrity system in which the scientific elite control the allocation of rewards. The elite receive undue prominence, and their work is usually immune to scrutiny.

A year after Burt's death, Princeton psychologist Leon Kamin began to scrutinize his statistics and found major flaws. For one thing, in three different studies of different numbers of identical twins, Burt reported the same statistical correlation of IQ scores to the third decimal point, which is incredible. There were similar flaws in Burt's reports dating back as far as 1909. Arthur Jensen insisted that if Burt had been trying to fake his data he would have done a better job of it.

In 1976 London's *Sunday Times* reported the shocking fact that Burt's two field investigators and co-authors of his studies, Margaret Howard and J. Conway, were nonexistent. These two phantom experts had often signed reviews praising Burt and attacking his enemies in the British *Journal of Statistical Psychology* during the fifteen years when Burt was its editor. Burt's housekeeper admitted to the *Sunday Times* that she knew he used pseudonyms.

It seems clear that Burt had solemnly reported nonexistent tests and studies and had signed fictitious names to articles he published. There is no way for researchers to discover which parts of his life work might be valid because he often referred to unpublished reports that can't be found, and he carelessly stuffed whatever papers he kept into six chests instead of filing them. These papers were all burned after his death. According to *Science* magazine, this forgery may rank with that of the Piltdown man.

At first the Harvard psychologist Richard Herrnstein found the suggestion of fraud outrageous: "I think it's a crime to cast doubt over a man's career. Burt was a towering figure of twentieth century psychology." But as he worked on Burt's biography, he came to realize that Burt had lied. Not all of Burt's professional colleagues had been so completely fooled. Philip Vernon of the University of Calgary stated in *Time*, "There were certainly grave doubts, although nobody dared to put them into print because Burt was so powerful." Professors Anne and Alan Clarke told *Newsweek*, "People had grave doubts long ago, but Burt was a fearsome figure. He was an autocrat of the old school, wrapped in a most charming style."

In 1976, the very year when the *Sunday Times* exposed the fraudulence of Sir Cyril Burt, Bruno Bettelheim published his best-selling book *The Uses of Enchantment: The Meaning and Importance of Fairy Tales*, written with a grant from the Spenser Foundation. Bettelheim had made himself famous as the foremost authority on childhood autism, and he ran Chicago's prestigious Orthogenic School for emotionally disturbed children.

Bettelheim claimed to pride himself on getting the authentic version of each fairy tale he psychoanalyzed, assuming that there is profound folk wisdom in the exact details that developed "through the centuries (if not the millennia) during which, in their retelling, fairy tales became ever more refined." In light of the fact that he focussed largely upon stories from the Brothers Grimm, which were radically "refined" and faked at one fell swoop in the 1800s, the authenticity of the ages evaporates.

But the authenticity of Bettelheim is evaporating also. After his death in 1990 a professor of anthropology at the University of California at Berkeley sadly announced that *The Uses of Enchantment* was copied from a 1963 book titled *A Psychiatric Study of Fairy Tales*. Bettelheim discussed the same folk tales in the same order and in the same words, "not just a matter of occasional borrowings of random passages, but a wholesale borrowing of key ideas."

After his death various adults who had lived in his Orthogenic School revealed that he was an impulsive child-abuser and that they lived in terror of him. He had claimed, "As an educator and therapist of severely disturbed children, my main task was to restore meaning to their lives." To the contrary, some of them claimed, he misdiagnosed normal children as mentally disturbed in order to claim later that he had cured them. He did not cure the really ill ones.

Bettelheim dishonestly claimed that autistic children recovered under his care. He convinced desperate parents of the falsehood that autism was a psychological condition caused by bad mothering, then accepted large amounts of money from them for help that never materialized. All that vulnerable parents got for trusting him was false guilt and true grief; yet he was never exposed publicly in his lifetime. As autism expert Bernard Rimland observed grimly, "He will not be missed."

## Mind over Matter

J. Fontesque has never been missed either, but he did no harm. In 1936 *Who's Who in San Diego* included his profile: he was the author of numerous articles, a member of the California Mycological Society, and President of the International Board of Hygiene. *Who's Who in San Diego* didn't mention that he was nonexistent.

In the 1920s a group of San Diego friends, including Dr. Rawson Pickard of La Jolla, decided to call themselves the International Board of Hygiene, and Pickard adopted the name J. Fontesque. He sent an

171

impressive letter about the Board of Hygiene to the League of Nations, written in French on expensive engraved stationery. The group declared a certain Mexican beer "totally non-fattening," and the brewery then advertised it in San Diego as calorie free. Fontesque published occasional scientific articles on a wide array of subjects for many years, thanks to various members of the Board.

It's one thing to fool *Who's Who in San Diego*, but it's another to fool *Who's Who in America*. When Rutherford Aris of Minneapolis received a letter calling him Aris Rutherford and asking him for biographical data, he answered that he was already listed correctly and that someone had simply reversed his names. The editors ignored this explanation and sent him a form letter that warned, "The editors will have no alternative, in the absence of your good assistance, but to compile data from whatever sources are available." That did it; Mr. Aris sent in a preposterous biography for Mr. Rutherford.

The fictional Mr. Rutherford was a whiskey expert who was born in Strath Spey, Scotland; educated at Glenlivet Institution for Distillation Engineering; and once served as Professor of Distillation Practice at the Technical Institute of the Aegean in Corinth. His mother's maiden name was Ephygeneia Aristeides. He was a member of the Hellenophilic Club and a Trustee of the Scottish-Greek Friendship Trust. He had published two books on whiskey manufacture and another titled *American Football: A Guide for Interested Scots*. In future years Mr. Aris intended to have Mr. Rutherford publish new books explaining baseball for Englishmen, basketball for the Welsh, and ice hockey for the Irish. Unfortunately, the *Minneapolis Star* exposed the hoax, and Mr. Rutherford was removed from the next edition of *Who's Who in America*.

Unlike J. Fontesque and Aris Rutherford, David Starr Jordan was a real scientist, well-known in his day. In the September 1896 issue of *Popular Science Monthly*, he published a satire ridiculing the popular idea that the mind can directly control matter, and he illustrated it with a fake photo. (This magazine was for scientists and people with a serious interest in science, not for the general public.)

Dr. Jordan explained that he had succeeded in photographing the combined images of a cat in seven people's minds. To do so, he had used a sympsychograph. The key was a lens with curved facets, which he described in detail. Each of the seven facets had insulated tubing connected to the eye of a person who was concentrating upon a cat. Electric impulses were transferred from the brain to the retina and through the eye into the tube, then to the lens. From the lens the images converged upon a sensitive plate, just as light is focused in ordinary photography. The image on the photographic plate was the "innate idea of the mind or ego itself . . . the image of ultimate feline reality."

Jordan concluded, "The photograph assumed to have resulted from this process is very striking—a comfortable cat at rest, with various shadowy feline faces in the background." He added that his next project would be to photograph "the cat's idea of man."

Jordan's air of authority made the satire fall flat. He reported in his autobiography that a surprising number of people took the thing seriously because of all the technical details he included. "One clergyman even went so far as to announce a series of six discourses on 'The Lesson of the Sympsychograph,' while many others said they welcomed the discovery as verifying what they had long believed."

# CHEATING IN THE SCHOOL OF LIFE

*In this world there are clever people without wisdom.*

—Celtic Proverb

The world of learning is full of lapses, lunacy, and larceny; and it often seems that the higher one goes in academia, the more malarkey one finds. At every level of schooling, the struggle against malarkey is apt to backfire; reformers are often charged with bigotry, ignorance, or professional jealousy.

At the bottom, some teachers think that the biggest fraud for little children in American schools today is the idealistic-sounding bilingual education program. English is by far the hardest and most valuable major language there is; the older children get, the harder it is for them to master it. Yet instead of helping children from poor Spanish-speaking homes to become as fluent as possible in English as fast as possible, while nurturing their proper love for Spanish, the drawn-out "bilingual" program hinders them from achieving early excellence in English. They will never catch up.

Another area of controversy in education is the conflict between evolutionism and creationism. When there are skirmishes on this front, reporters tend to assume that anyone who opposes Darwinism must believe in a flat earth: it is a battle between religious dogma and scientific fact. But that is malarkey; it is usually a battle between religious dogma and cultural dogma masquerading as science. One does not have to be a fundamentalist to see that popular Evolutionism (in contrast to evolution) is as intellectually bankrupt as Marxism; C. S. Lewis pointed that out long ago in his essay "The Funeral of a Great Myth." (The American Scientific Affiliation provides helpful guidelines for keeping schools fair and honest on this subject.)

The graduate-level subject that is most apt to raise charges of fraud today is Deconstruction, which was the most elite source of esoteric wisdom in 1980. Berkeley philosophy professor John Searle says, "Deconstruction has rather obvious and manifest intellectual weaknesses. It should be fairly obvious to the careful reader that the emperor has no clothes." Jacques Derrida, the founder, was lured from Yale to the University of California at Irvine in the mid-1980s with an extraordinary offer: $30,000 for every five-week quarter he teaches. He reportedly opens every lecture by saying, "Oh my friends, there is no friend," and part of what he teaches is that no one can know what words mean. According to Cambridge philosopher Hugh Mellor, Derrida "has to write more and more obscurely to disguise the fact that he has nothing to say." Whether Deconstruction is a fraud or not, its valiant co-founder Paul De Man certainly was. His big secret leaked out in 1987: he had aided the Nazis during World War II.

## Backhouse: A Quiet Scholar

The greatest academic fraud of all time was Sir Edmund Trelawny Backhouse. There is still a marble tablet at the great Bodleian Library in Oxford commemorating him along with some of its other greatest benefactors such as Sir Thomas Bodley, Oliver Cromwell, and the Rockefeller Foundation. For all his life and thirty years after, Backhouse maintained a reputation for serious scholarship. He spent his old age in Peking, appearing as an absent-minded professor with a long white beard, dressed in a long white silk robe.

Ironically, two years before he died, he wrote, "I have ever been veracious." He must have been chuckling wickedly.

Edmund Backhouse was born in a well-to-do English family in 1873; two of his brothers eventually became British Admirals. Everyone who met Backhouse was won over by his courtesy, charm, and professed regard for truth. He was a genius at languages, but he became an ongoing problem to his family; he dropped out of college, bought valuable jewels on credit for actresses, and never paid his debts. He led a secret life full of outrageous fraudulence, thievery, and debauchery; he faked illnesses, and he occasionally disappeared. He had just the gifts for becoming an international confidence artist.

He somehow got to China in 1898 and became a successful looter and crook, selling imaginary battleships to gullible officials. He was or claimed to be a professor at the University of Peking. He wrote the exciting diary of a Chinese aristocrat who lived through the Boxer rebellion; then he pretended that he had discovered it in 1900 and saved it from a fire. In 1910 he used that diary as the basis of the immensely popular history *China under the Empress Dowager,* which he co-authored with a *London Times* journalist.

During the havoc of the revolution in China, Westerners were busy packing treasures off to their homelands. So it was that in 1913 Backhouse sent to Oxford twenty-nine crates full of more than 27,000 manuscripts, weighing 4.5 tons. (One wonders if he stole them.) He meant to move to Oxford and store the manuscripts at the Bodleian for his own research there; but transportation charges were so high that he donated them to the Bodleian instead, and the Bodleian paid the charges. This gave Oxford the greatest collection of Chinese material in all of Europe and caused librarians to advance Backhouse a great deal of money to increase the collection. He was such an academic celebrity that he requested an honorary doctorate. He was offered a professorship in London which he accepted, then one in Oxford. People overlooked the fact that his 1914 book *Annals and Memoirs of the Court of Peking* was surprisingly licentious.

Eventually the Bodleian discovered that it had bought clumsy forgeries from him. Loyal to the end, authorities decided that he had no doubt been tricked by some clever Chinese—although he stubbornly insisted that the forgeries were genuine. In 1915 Backhouse became a British secret agent and at great expense to England obtained 200,000 nonexistent rifles for the Foreign Office. In 1916 and 1917 he swindled a New York company out of a fortune by forging a nonexistent contract with the Chinese prime minister. He stole fortune after fortune, but his embarrassed victims never publicized what happened. To his public he was always a quiet, humble scholar.

In 1973 historian Sir Hugh Trevor-Roper was asked to evaluate two volumes of memoirs that Backhouse meant to have published. To Trevor-Roper's amazement, the "memoirs" were incredibly obscene pornographic fiction. This led him to investigate Backhouse and to write *Hermit of Peking: The Hidden Life of Sir Edmund Backhouse.* Most of Backhouse's life is still hidden, but even at that he is clearly one of the greatest rogues of history.

## Kawari and Kent State

About sixty years after the University of Oxford became enamored with Edmund Backhouse, it became enamored with Issa Al-

Kawari, the most influential non-royal politician in Qatar (one of the tiniest Gulf States). He enrolled in the doctoral program at Exeter College in 1976 and said he would write a thesis on "Mineral Resources in the Arab-Islam Empire."

By 1979 Kawari had not produced any work on his thesis, but Qatar was producing what eventually amounted to ú60,000 in donations to a privately-funded Centre for Arab Gulf Studies at Exeter. This center was the brainchild of Professor Muhammed Shaban, an Egyptian academic entrepreneur, and it had close ties to the British Foreign Office. High-ranking diplomat Brian Pridham of the Foreign Office was its Director. As a thriving center for Arabic studies, the Centre had received ú3.5 million in gifts from the Gulf States.

Along the way, Kawari produced a new subject for his thesis: "Public Administration in Qatar," but no more. In 1983 Professor Shaban advised Kawari that he was entering his eighth year and that it would be difficult to get any more extensions. Nothing happened. In 1985 Dr. Ian Netton, head of Islamic studies, strongly recommended that Kawari be granted only one more year of "research" time. That did the trick. In six months the Centre received a lengthy thesis from Kawari titled "The Exploitation of Oil in Qatar."

The Centre's Professor Aziz al-Azmeh, from Syria, read Kawari's thesis and discovered to his astonishment that it was essentially his own work. Six years earlier he had been commissioned by Kawari to produce this report for the Qatar government. Azmeh had assembled the material and then paid Graham Benton, a British journalist, £1000 to write the article for him. Now it had surfaced as Kawari's thesis.

Azmeh reported the plagiarism and suggested that Kawari's candidacy for a doctorate should be terminated. In answer, an examining panel headed by Shaban recommended Kawari for a Ph.D. Shaban then held a reception for Kawari and introduced him to Director Pridham so they could talk about Kawari's role in the Centre's future. When Azmeh and Netton appealed to Exeter for academic discipline, the Dean answered that Exeter's interests could be adversely affected if the plagiarism charge were proved. Director Pridham declared, "The implications of this accusation for the university's interests in the Gulf are dreadful."

Azmeh filed a written complaint, and an administrator named Yates scheduled a formal inquiry. At that point Kawari threatened to sue the university if it did not grant him his degree. Then Yates and

Pridham suddenly traveled to Qatar as Kawari's guests and returned with a new research contract funded by Qatar.

On December 4, 1988, an *Observer* article about the affair concluded, "The Qatar Minister got his Ph.D. and Exeter continues to get its Arab funding. The only unhappy people were those who tried to bring the issue to light."

This kind of thing can happen anywhere. In his book *Ripoff,* Steve Allen said that in 1978 trustees of Kent State University were wondering what to do about the doctoral degree that Andres Bermudez of Puerto Rico had received from their business department. Investigation showed that he had "received preferential treatment in the form of improper waivers, substitutions, and transfer credits in the course of his academic career at Kent State." Much of his doctoral dissertation was outright plagiarism. What had he done right? He had paid the expenses for ten Kent State business professors to visit Puerto Rico, and he had given them presents there.

## Castaneda's Conjuring

The scholarly careers of Dr. Issa Al-Kawari and Dr. Andres Bermudez were normal when compared to the scholarly career of Dr. Carlos Castaneda. His graduate studies at the University of California are one of the most preposterous hoaxes of all time. While witching his way to a Ph.D., he sold 4 million books and became a famous cult figure. One of his academic defenders said that he was "a fine, gentle, kindly young man," attacked only because of envy.

Carlos Castaneda was born in Brazil in 1935, the son of a literature professor. When he was six years old, his mother died and he moved to his grandparents' chicken farm. His uncle was Oswaldo Aranha, who was both President of the United Nations General Assembly and ambassador to the United States. Carlos grew up speaking Italian and Portuguese, attended boarding school in Buenos Aires, graduated from Hollywood High School, studied art in Italy, and served in wartime in the United States Army in Spain. In the summer of 1960, when he was an anthropology student at UCLA, he made several trips to the Sonora Desert to collect information on medicinal plants used by Indians there.

Coincidentally, another Carlos Castaneda was born in Peru in 1925, the son of a well-to-do jewelry-store owner. He grew up with his parents in the Andean city of Cajamarca, speaking Spanish. He was in no way related to Oswaldo Aranha. He was known for gambling and telling tall tales. In 1948, at the age of twenty-two, he finished high school in Lima and entered art school there. His mother died in 1950. He married in 1951, and then deserted his wife and baby and moved to the United States. In 1956 he studied creative writing at Los Angeles City College and married again, but never lived with his second wife. He entered UCLA in 1959, when the Piltdown Forgery and the story of Ferdinand Demara, The Great Imposter, were popular. In 1962 the Anthropology Department gave him some money to help him do his field work.

The Brazilian Castaneda was the famous one, though he was entirely fictitious; the Peruvian Castaneda was the real one. His 1968 book *The Teachings of Don Juan: A Yaqui Way of Knowledge* and the four that followed it recounted Castaneda's years of experimentation with Yaqui Indian religion and hallucinogenic drugs under the tutelage of Don Juan, a desert shaman who took a liking to him and taught him sorcery.

Aside from sorcery, Castaneda claims to have done many things that are humanly impossible. Without mentioning how he could have done it, Castaneda claims to have transcribed verbatim Don Juan's Spanish monologues at lightning speed, no matter where they were or what they were doing. (Linguists observe that many of Castaneda's English translations of those phantom Spanish monologues can't possibly be translations from Spanish.) Late one day Don Juan told Castaneda to catch two lizards (with no equipment) and then to use the fiber of a century plant and thorn of a prickly pear to sew shut the eyes of one lizard and the mouth of the other without damaging them. Castaneda did all this promptly, with no trouble—in twilight. He didn't explain how he turned cactus fiber into thread, how he turned a thorn into a slender needle, or how he held two lizards still while stitching their eyelids and lips shut. Readers took it all on faith.

It is said that Castaneda's only real sorcery was turning the University of California into an ass. No one but Castaneda ever saw Don Juan. Castaneda had no corroborating photos, tape recordings, or even any field notes. In his nine years of alleged desert research with a Yaqui Indian, he learned nothing about the region's plants and animals and didn't learn one Indian name for any of them. He claimed to climb trees that can't be climbed and to stalk animals that can't be

POWER-PLAY—YOUR MONEY OR YOUR MIND

stalked. He casually referred to hiking for hours in 100 degree heat. He said he enjoyed being drenched by warm winter rains in a desert where winter rains are icy cold. He could provide no samples of the hallucinogenic mushrooms that he supposedly used, and indeed there are none in that region. Worst of all, he obviously knew nothing at all about Yaqui Indian beliefs and culture

Charles Caleb Colton once said, "The more gross the fraud, the more glibly will it go down, and the more greedily be swallowed, since folly will always find faith." In spite of everything, Castaneda's first book was issued by the University of California Press in 1968 with this announcement: "It has been assumed that the West has produced no way of spiritual knowledge comparable to the great systems of the East. The present book is accordingly nothing less than a revelation." An eminent reviewer in *American Anthropologist* said it "should attain a solid place in the literature of both hallucinogenic drugs and the field behavior of anthropologists."

Castaneda cranked out one wildly popular Don Juan book after another and contradicted himself right and left. The Anthropology Department at UCLA granted him a doctorate in 1973 for his third book, *Journey to Ixtlan*, under another title. Professors knew better than to offend the members of his doctoral committee, but some of them must have wondered, "Does a daydream count now as an informant? Does a fantasy count as a field report?" In *The Decline of the West*, philosopher Oswald Spengler said that fraud by scholars is one of the signs of a decadent civilization.

In 1976 Richard de Mille completed some masterful sleuthing and published *Castaneda's Journey*. He kept digging, and in 1980 he published *The Don Juan Papers*. Among many other things, he reveals that UCLA's Professor Goldschmidt was Castaneda's Department Chairman and the ranking anthropologist on the editorial committee of University of California Press. His foreword to Castaneda's first book is the reason it was taken seriously. At the end of 1978, in the face of overwhelming evidence of fraud, Goldschmidt said, "We possess no information whatever that would support the charges that have been made. . . . I am not going to say mea culpa." The members of Castaneda's committee refused to give an inch.

De Mille suspects that a small group of dissident culturologists at UCLA arranged for publication of Castaneda's first book as an inside joke and an affront to their opponents. Because of the way it was promoted and its appeal to the youth and drug culture, the book caught on beyond their wildest hopes or fears, turning their picaresque graduate student into a celebrity scholar.

Though he had done nothing that would ordinarily merit such advancement, the Dreaming Dissertator made no secret of his aspiration to doctorhood. The pranksters had three choices. They could repudiate *The Teachings*, claiming Castaneda had deceived them, which would make them look like fools. They could boldly admit their prank, which would set off an endless professional wrangle, wherein they would suffer sorely, and which might provoke administrative reprisals. Or they could stonewall, thumbing their respective noses at critics, handing the prodigy his scroll, and closing the village gate behind him. Of three bad choices, the last was least.

De Mille has analyzed Castaneda's appeal. His book told young people what they wanted to hear, that their 1960s idealism and drug use were akin to an ancient and noble culture. In person Castaneda was usually charming and full of stories. He spoke softly, in a soothing way. He often acted a bit fragile, naïve, confused, or vulnerable; and he told women tales that made them want to comfort him. He appealed to older men by playing son to them, and to young men he told of brave adventures.

De Mille theorizes,

The mortal yearning for Paradise is very strong indeed, and anyone who promises to lead us there is trusted. For the born-again the promised land is Beulah, for Marxists a classless society, for futurists like Timothy Leary a homey mechanical doughnut in the sky. For a handful of professors and thousands of pseudo-anthropology fans, Paradise is a balmy purple desert where one can have endless private metaphysical conversations with a mystical old Indian named Don Juan.

### Eyewash in Academia

There is more rigmarole in research and resumes than an honest person would ever suspect. Samuel Johnson explained, "We are

**181**

inclined to believe those whom we do not know because they have never deceived us."

Most well-educated Americans believe that Eskimos have many words for snow in its various forms instead of one general word for it. This fact has been taught in psychology books since about 1958, when amateur linguist Benjamin Lee Whorf first pointed it out. In 1991 anthropologist Laura Martin co-authored *The Great Eskimo Vocabulary Hoax*, a book that traces the evolution of this modern myth. Although Whorf implied that the Eskimos have seven words for snow, most references now claim that they have seventeen to twenty-three and the *New York Times* once set the number at a hundred. In fact, Eskimos have about a dozen words for snow, equivalent to our own ten terms such as blizzard, slush, and avalanche. Eskimos do not perceive snow differently from other people. When Martin broke this news to her colleagues, she was disappointed by their common response: "Who cares?" Many seemed to prefer the eyewash to the facts.

In 1984 the editor-in-chief of the *Christian Science Monitor* announced a study of National Merit scholars showing that they come from a variety of ethnic, economic, and religious backgrounds, but they have one thing in common: They all come from families that sit down to dinner together every night. This heartwarming news spread far and wide; then someone tried to find out about the study and learned that there was none. It had been a false rumor. The *Monitor* apologized, but expressed hope that it would prove true after all.

Every year many high school students receive a letter in the mail announcing that an organization like Who's Who among American High School Students has selected them to appear in a reference book recognizing the best and brightest students in the nation. Actually, there is no selection process; each name appears in tiny print along with as many as 350,000 others. The aim of the project is to extract the price of the book from flattered students and their parents. Jonathan Swift said cynically, "Happiness is the perpetual possession of the well deceived."

In 1987 the son of France's wealthy Baron Guy de Rothschild enrolled as a part-time student at Duke University and joined a fraternity. He was a good friend of the Kennedys and various Hollywood celebrities, and he spent $200 a month sending bouquets to high-society friends. He coached a swimming team and had a wonderful time. After two years, his fraternity asked him to prove his identity, and he disappeared—owing college friends well over $14,000. He was really Mario Cortez of El Paso, who had changed his name to Rothschild. He couldn't speak French.

Frank McKinney Hubbard, an American newspaper humorist, was correct when he said, "It would be a swell world if everybody was as pleasant as the fellow who's trying to skin you."

According to Vancouver columnist Allan Fotheringham, a quiet professor named Dimitri Conomos was hired at the University of British Columbia in 1975 on the strength of his master's degree in music from the University of Sydney, Australia, and his doctorate in music from Oxford. Between 1976 and 1988 he received six Ottowa research grants worth a total of $175,732, to enable him to study the history of Serbian and Moldavian music in the fifteenth and sixteenth centuries. In 1989 news arrived that no one at the University of Sydney or Oxford had ever heard of him, and he disappeared. If he knew anything about old Serbian and Moldavian music, he took it with him.

Samuel Mercer (1879–1969) was born in Bay Roberts, Newfoundland, on May 10, 1879. He eventually became an Episcopal priest, held twelve degrees, published twenty-nine books, and spoke fifteen languages; but he lied about his origin. When he entered Harvard University in 1905, he had expanded his name to Samuel Alfred Browne Mercer. Five years later, when he entered the University of Munich, he changed both the year and country of his birth: "Ich bin am 10 Mai 1880 in Bristol, England geboren." In his autobiography Mercer referred to his birth in 1880, "the year in which Gaston Maspero, the famous French Egyptologist, discovered the inscriptions in the five Sakkara pyramids in Egypt. . . ." A fitting coincidence, because Mercer had spent six years translating those hieroglyphics into English. But the 1880 date was doubly false: Mercer was born in 1879, and Maspero made his discovery in 1881.

### Drives, Dreams and Delusions

In Steve Allen's book *Ripoff: A Look at Corruption in America,* he tells of the company named Term Papers, Unlimited, which sold about $1.8 million worth of fake scholarship in its first year, with franchises opening in fifty cities. A freshman at the Massachusetts

**183**

Institute of Technology bought an essay from this company and turned it in to his English professor. The title was "Why I Would Not Use a Professional Term-Paper Writing Service."

It is hard to satirize the gall that goes with sleazy scholarship, but columnist Jerry Kobrin did. When three separate leaders in Orange County, California, were caught faking their academic degrees in 1990, Kobrin said he saw nothing wrong with what they had done. In fact, he explained modestly, he had been an authority on this kind of academic enhancement ever since he successfully defended the practice back in 1946 in a much-acclaimed Ph.D. dissertation that he wrote while he was attending Harvard Divinity School.

Helping someone write a Ph.D. thesis is being an accessory to fraud in Germany, and the customer risks losing his degree and going to jail for up to five years. But with about 17,000 Ph.D. theses submitted every year, professors feel absolutely helpless about making sure that students do their own work. The Institute of German-American Career Consultants charges about $17,000 for a 200-page thesis written to order in eight to ten months. Typical subject areas are medicine, law, business, economics, and political science.

Achim Schwarze says that although he dropped out of school at sixteen, he feels he deserves to be called Dr. Dr. Dr. Dr. Dr. Schwarz because he has earned five Ph.D.s with theses that he illegally wrote for graduate students. He feels he could write a Ph.D. thesis on any topic now, but he claims to have quit in favor of writing books. When he wrote theses, his pattern was fifteen pages defining the subject, ten showing what it is not, fifteen on methods, thirty on how others have seen it and how the writer sees it, thirty on how it might have been seen, thirty on what the author knows now, and ten on outlook and bibliography. He adds some quotations from the published work of the graduate student's thesis supervisor if at all possible. He charges about $27,000 for 180 pages.

Unlike ordinary academic ghostwriters, Dr. Frank Gratz is a "dissertation consultant" for business executives who need Ph.D.s for advancement and salary increases; he helps ten businessmen a year and charges about $33,000 each. He makes all the arrangements for them and also trains them for their oral exams, but claims that he does not break the law by actually writing their theses.

Dr. Carlo Otto Gantert actually advertises an international ghostwriting bureau, and he also sells seven different Ph.D. titles from a bona fide church-related university college for $14,000 or more. The entire process from enrollment to graduation takes only a few weeks, but if one wants high grades one has to pay $3,500 to $7,000 extra. Part of the tuition is tax-deductible.

For people who can't afford to send $20,000 to Dr. Gantert for good grades and a German college degree, there are bargain-basement American diploma mills like Marmaduke University and Pacific Western University. The Universal Life Church organization of Modesto, California, offers a Doctor of Philosophy in Religion accredited by the "International Accrediting Association." Candidates must study a booklet and answer correctly fifteen of the twenty questions that come with it. The cost for this course and the official Doctor of Philosophy certificate is $100.

What practical good is a diploma-mill degree? In 1980 Srully Blotnick, Ph.D., began publishing his popular business column "Insights" in *Forbes* magazine. This led to his publishing *The Corporate Steeplechase* and four other best-selling books, appearing frequently on television talk shows, and being widely quoted as an expert on corporate culture and male-female relationships. He constantly drew upon the valuable statistics that he had gleaned from monitoring thousands of families for over twenty years. He made a small fortune from all this.

In July 1987 a reporter for the *New York Daily News* discovered that Blotnick's Ph.D. was from a diploma mill; there had been no twenty-year study of thousands of families. Six months before the exposé, *Forbes* had removed the Ph.D. from Blotnick's title, but continued to call him a "business psychologist" although he was not a licensed psychologist. When the hoax was exposed, *Forbes* cancelled Blotnick's column; but in 1988 Penguin Books went right ahead and published his latest book—appropriately titled *Ambitious Men: Their Drives, Dreams and Delusions*.

*Every crowd has a silver lining.*

—P.T. Barnum

# CHAPTER 6
# SWINDLERS, HOAXERS, SHAMS, AND SCAMS

*Those who know Louisiana towns say it's just a short drive between Plain Dealing and Swindleville.*

—L. M. Boyd

The kingdom of criminal deception includes realms of roguery that look like panoramas of paradise. Its lords and ladies rule by betrayal, although they sometimes wear the faces of angels. In this moral no-man's-land, religion is just another lie.

# STEAL MY WALLET, NOT MY HEART

*Sin has many tools, but a lie is the handle that fits them all.*
—Oliver Wendell Holmes

Being defrauded is like being burglarized in the brain as well as the billfold. Fraud not only leaves us poorer, but it leaves someone's dirty fingerprints on the windowsill of the mind.

One year when postal rates were lower, an Englishman sent letters to many football fans who were potential gamblers, announcing that he had a foolproof way of predicting who would win. To demonstrate, he predicted the winner of the upcoming game. He sent the same letter to many other fans, predicting that the other team would win; and he sent to many others predicting a tie. One week later he followed up with a new set of letters to the group for which his first prediction had happened to come true. Each week he sent out new predictions to a rapidly shrinking list of names and addresses.

In six weeks he was down to a handful of people who had watched him predict correctly the winners of five games in a row. If they had ventured money on his tips, they would have profited handsomely. At that point he invited them to invest money in a project of his, and more than one gladly sent him very large amounts. After all, the man had proved himself a genius week after week.

They gambled on his integrity and lost, but he gambled on his luck and lost. He eventually ended up in prison for fraud.

## Making It in America

Discovering a friendly young genius is one of life's happy thrills. It's a chance to hitch your wagon to a star.

In 1984 Barry Minkow graduated from Grover Cleveland High School, where he was voted class clown and most likely to succeed—both for good reasons. Although his parents were distinctly unsuccessful, at the age of fifteen Barry founded a carpet-cleaning business; and although he was not a gifted student, he was soon earning more

188

money than his school principal. Barry idolized Ronald Reagan; Donald Trump was the hero of the day. Ivan F. Boesky expressed the temper of the times when he demanded, "What good is the moon, if you can't buy it and sell it?"

Shortly after graduation, Barry hired a public relations firm for $1,500 per month, which put him on radio and produced a glossy press kit. Then the firm put him on TV shows and produced his book *Making It in America*. The cover exclaimed "18 Years Old and a Million Dollars," and Barry handed out autographed copies wherever he went. In the book he praised his brand of positive thinking and the glories of free enterprise. In March 1985, Barry received a formal certificate of commendation from Mayor Tom Bradley of Los Angeles, which began:

> Whereas Barry Minkow of Los Angeles has set a fine entrepreneurial example by obtaining the status of a millionaire by the age of eighteen years old, and whereas Barry Minkow at the age of nine years old began cleaning carpets and it was a trade he fully mastered by the age of fifteen, when he ventured into his own entity, and whereas ZZZZ Best Carpet Cleaning, Inc., began as a small home-garage business run by Barry with one employee and $6,200 in the bank, and has grown to become one of the most reputable and reliable carpet cleaning services throughout Southern California.

Barry told investors, "I own 100 percent of the fastest-growing carpet-cleaning business in California. We're in the process of opening our San Diego location—our fourth in two years. A $1.5 million restoration job in San Diego is just waiting for the capital." Insurance restoration jobs for accidents such as interior flooding were his specialty; he made so much profit on them that he could pay high rates on his loans without blinking. Some early investors got 52 percent annual interest at first.

To older men Barry gave not only respect and intense attention, but something akin to adulation. To older women, Barry was a fun-loving, flirtatious friend, a bundle of mischief and vitality. To people his own age, Barry was dynamic, hip, humorous, and full of action. To the Bank of Granada Hills, he was their biggest depositor, their biggest borrower, and their most famous customer. (They watched him

189

pull up while talking on the phone in his Ferrari, followed by his right-hand man in a Mercedes. They loved him.) When he was nineteen, Barry bought a $700,000 house, hired servants, and installed his seventeen-year-old primary girlfriend as lady of the manor. Although he entertained lavishly, he did not drink; and after President Reagan announced a war on drugs, Barry came out with anti-drug publicity—"Millionaire Pledges War on Drugs"—and photos captioned "My Act Is Clean. How's Yours?" (He did not count his steroids as drugs.)

At the beginning of 1986 Barry's company went public, and his PR team waged a successful media blitz; he was featured on TV programs and in newspapers and magazines across the country. Interviewers were delighted with him. In December ZZZZ Best raised $15 million in a public offering of its stock. Barry was invited to appear on the *Johnny Carson Show,* but underwriters told him that would offend the Securities and Exchange Commission. On December 20, Barry hosted a lavish black-tie Christmas dinner party for over 800 people in the Grand Ballroom of the Bonaventure Hotel in downtown Los Angeles, with gifts and awards for many of the guests. As master of ceremonies, he was marvelous. His guests adored him.

In March 1987, *USA Today* reported that Barry had been named one of America's 100 top young entrepreneurs. His old high school declared a "Barry Minkow Day." He bought himself a new $130,000 Ferrari for his twenty-first birthday and expressed an interest in buying the Seattle Mariners. Then Drexel Burnham Lambert decided to buy KeyServ, the Sears carpet-cleaning concession, in order to merge it with ZZZZ Best.

In April the stock in his company rocketed 332 percent, to $18 per share, and he was said to be worth $100 million. He appeared on the *Oprah Winfrey Show* in a segment called "Young and Rich," and said among other things, "I'm really not into the material things. . . . $90 million is nothing. . . . Five to ten billion is the kind of range I want to move up to."

After the *Oprah Winfrey Show,* Barry hosted a conference called "The Sky's the Limit" at the Century Plaza Hotel for about a thousand ZZZZ Best and KeyServ employees from across the country. He held candlelight dinners for them, gave inspirational speeches, enjoyed standing ovations, and spoke about his dream of becoming President of the United States. The conference cost $1 million. About a week later, Barry issued a press release that said, "ZZZZ Best . . . has entered into contracts for approximately $25.7 million of new insurance restoration work during the past 30 days. . . ." This information was more good news for all who basked in Barry's glow.

### Faking It in America

According to *The Unreality Industry* by Ian I. Mitroff and Warren Bennis,

> Unreality is big business. It is manufactured and sold on a gigantic scale. It has intruded itself into every aspect of our lives. For example, by some estimates, public relations, i.e., the deliberate manufacturing of slanted information, accounts for up to 70 percent of what passes for news and information in our society. The end consequence is a society less and less able to face its true problems directly, honestly, and intelligently.

On May 22, 1987, a reporter revealed in the *Los Angeles Times* that in 1986 Barry had committed credit-card fraud. At that, his huge pyramid started to crack, and it collapsed fast. He had been running a variation of the old Ponzi scheme, named after Charles Ponzi's postal-coupon racket in the early 1900s. Funds from the second crop of investors were used to pay high profits to the first investors. When there were no longer any new investors after the bad news in the *Los Angeles Times*, it was all over.

Barry had titled the story of his success *Making It in America*, and in 1989 Joe Domanick titled a fascinating book about Barry Minkow *Faking It in America*. Just before his twenty-third birthday, Barry was sentenced to twenty-five years in prison and $26 million in restitution. He finally got mentioned on the *Johnny Carson Show*—as a joke.

Barry Minkow is one of the world's best examples of the truth spoken by journalist D. R. Segal: "Chutzpah is the oil and fuel of the great shams and larcenies of life. Done with an air of unassailable confidence, almost any bold, dumb, or dangerous act can be carried off with impunity."

Barry's legitimate "switch and bait" carpet-cleaning business was never a financial success, and so he used it as a front for fraud. At age sixteen he repeatedly filed false claims with State Farm Insurance for nonexistent burglaries of fantastically expensive nonexistent equipment. He lied to get loans. Later he used customers' credit-card numbers for false billings and used their money for months on end, shifting it from one bank or private investor to another to give the impression that he had plenty of collateral.

Adolf Hitler said, "The great masses of people will more easily fall prey to a great lie than a small one." Barry was in no way a Nazi, but his close friend and helper Tom Padgett was. (They kept that fact a secret.) Tom pretended to head a nonexistent company that awarded restoration jobs to Barry. The restoration jobs were all false; ZZZZ Best never restored one building.

Once when Barry almost got caught, he flew to Denver to arrange to rent part of an unfinished San Diego building that he had lied about, then paid $1.5 million to have the building finished in eleven days by contractors who worked around the clock. A gullible inspector noted with satisfaction that the "repaired" building didn't look as if it had ever been water-damaged. (Of course not; it hadn't.) Barry once installed telephones and hired a crew of teenagers to pretend to be taking orders from hundreds of customers; in fact they were calling each other and jotting down nonsense. Once he hired men in suits to staff empty desks in an artificial office with empty file cabinets. His right-hand man, Mark Morze, produced blizzards of forged contracts, business letters, orders, bills, checks, and financial records. (For his efforts, Morze was paid upward of $3 million, much of which he squandered in Las Vegas.)

Some private investors lost their life savings to Barry Minkow because they liked him so much. In his last two years of business, he also managed to defraud the general public of about $70 million. For example, Union Bank lost $7 million, Swiss banks lost $4 million, First Interstate Bank lost $2 million, stock purchasers lost far more than $15 million, and creditors such as his advertising agency, American Express, and Pacific Bell lost hundreds of thousands. No one can tell where all the money went.

Barry the Boy Wonder was the quintessential confidence artist, endowed with high energy and an actor's ability to improvise instantly in order to use people. First, he knew the trick of selling himself, "the American boy genius," instead of his product. Second, he knew the trick of sensing and becoming whatever a given person wanted him to be. Third, he exuded a contagious enthusiasm for life.

And to these three he added the irresistible combination of wealth and generosity. As a result, at every level people overlooked things for him, gambled on him, and bent rules for him.

## Rogues' Gallery

We have a helpful list of "Ten Commandments for Con Men" by one of the great international charlatans of our century, "Count" Victor Lustig, who had twenty-five aliases. The Count's most unusual scam was selling the Eiffel Tower. Having read in Paris that upkeep on the Eiffel Tower was expensive for the French government, he forged some official government stationery and as a government official called five wealthy European scrap merchants to a secret conference to select a buyer. He took each man on a tour of the Tower, selected the best victim, and accepted an illegal bribe as well as official payment to the French government. Then he fled the country, and his victim was too ashamed to report his loss. One year later the Count returned and sold the Eiffel Tower again the same way. The second victim reported the crime, so there wasn't a third victim.

The Count's Ten Commandments:

1. Be a patient listener (it is this, not fast talking, that gets a con-man his coups).
2. Never look bored.
3. Wait for the other person to reveal any political opinions, then agree with them.
4. Let the other person reveal religious views, then have the same ones.
5. Hint at sex talk, but don't follow it up unless the other fellow shows a strong interest.
6. Never discuss illness, unless some special concern is shown.
7. Never pry into a person's personal circumstances (they'll tell you all eventually).
8. Never boast. Just let your importance be quietly obvious. [The rule against boasting does not always apply in the United States today.]
9. Never be untidy.
10. Never get drunk.

Every newspaper is apt to have stories about minor charlatans, because they are always active everywhere; but the stories of great past masters of fraud like the Count are classics.

Jonathan Wild (1682–1725) aided burglary victims in London a century before there were any public police. It was a crime to buy and sell stolen goods then, and thieves could not get a fair price for their loot from pawnbrokers. Wild, who became acquainted with the criminal world while he was in prison for debt, opened a London tavern for criminals and then formed an agency to aid burglary victims, along with a secret corporation of burglars. Thieves brought their loot to his warehouse, and victims hired him to seek their lost possessions in the London underworld. He demanded a large reward if he restored the stolen goods, as he usually did. This way the burglars were much better paid than ever before, their victims were grateful to be able to buy back lost treasures, and Wild got rich. In the end, he had so much extra unclaimed loot that he bought a ship and exported it to Europe; but some criminals turned him in, and he was tried and hanged. In those days graverobbers sold cadavers to surgery students; fittingly, Jonathan Wild's own body was stolen from his grave.

Charles Price of London (1727–83) was like a one-man band of thieves because he was a superbly inventive actor. He had an entire wardrobe of complex disguises and could appear to be many different kinds and sizes of people. When he forged documents, he not only printed them, but even made the right kind of paper for them. Some of his audacious frauds would have made superb stage plays because they had elaborate comic plots in which he played multiple roles. He was author, director, property manager, make-up artist, wardrobe manager, and all the actors.

"Count Alessandro Cagliostro" (1743–95) was such a genius at duping and robbing sensible people by playing upon their hopes and ambitions that the historian Thomas Carlyle called him "the king of liars." His uncle paid for his education in a monastery, but when he was twenty he was thrown out; so he robbed his uncle and went traveling. He picked up lore in Egypt and the Middle East and became an absolute spellbinder. At the height of his career, he and the Roman beauty Lorenza Feliciani toured Europe like royalty, entertaining with a display of occult knowledge, magic tricks, chemical marvels, medicine, and mystic powers. Their crowning success was an ancient religious cult that they invented, which included traveling seances and sex orgies. Cagliostro's downfall came when he got involved with the theft of Queen Marie Antionette's diamond necklace.

Joseph Weil (1877–1937) claimed that he garnered $8 million by the time he retired from fraud in 1934. He was handsome, charming, and well-dressed. Once he sold a Detroit industrialist pills that would turn water into gasoline. He used to sell stock in a nonexistent gold mine by coming into town and planting copies of a fake newspaper in the library; then he would cinch a sales spiel to a prospective investor by inviting him to read a news article about his gold mine in the local library. His most famous stunt was renting an empty bank building, staffing it with his friends, and opening it for business under a fake name. The "bank" would accept large initial deposits, then disappear overnight with the money.

Dr. Emil Savundra (1923–76) was an international swindler and forger who didn't do things half-way; he awarded himself three doctorates and parked at his mansion a Rolls-Royce, two Aston Martins, and a Jaguar. One of his first successful scams was selling $1 million of nonexistent oil to Communist China. In 1963 he founded FAM, a British auto-insurance company that swept the country by offering lower rates to customers and higher commissions to agents. He spirited the premiums out of Britain, and when he let his company collapse in 1966 it was £3 million in debt, leaving 400,000 motorists uninsured and 43,000 policy holder's claims unfilled. In 1967 he brazenly returned to England to appear on television with David Frost, and referred to his angry policy holders as peasants. He was arrested and tried and spent six years in London's Wormwood Scrubbs prison, where inmates had a song about him:

> *Oh, Doctor Savundra, I know who you are;*
> *I know where I'd like you, under my car.*

## Communist Counterfeits

To much of the world, Communism itself looks like a gigantic fraud, and its founder Karl Marx (1818–83) appears to have been a great hypocrite. Economically, he was an irresponsible spendthrift, and other people always had to pay his bills. Aside from a few forays into journalism, which he pursued more for an outlet than for an income, he never took a job. Instead of being a true friend to the working class, he avoided all of them except his wife's maid Helen

195

Demuth, who cooked, scrubbed, and managed the family budget, but got no salary at all. On June 23, 1851, she gave birth to Marx's son Henry Frederick Demuth, and Marx forced her to place the baby with a humble foster family. He denied his relationship to Henry, who was his only living son and looked like him. Henry was allowed to visit his mother in Marx's kitchen, but he had to use the back door. He was a decent working-class boy, but Karl Marx, self-proclaimed champion of the working class, never spoke to him.

Karl Marx not only acted prejudiced against real working-class people, but he also acted prejudiced against females and blacks. He absolutely refused his bright, ambitious daughters Laura, Jenny, and Eleanor a chance at the decent educations and careers they longed for. He forced them to stew at home like idle upper-middle-class ladies, dabbling in piano and painting. When Laura married a man from Cuba with some Negro blood, Marx called him "The Gorilla."

Needless to say, Marx's megalomania can be matched by that of many other influential leaders, and there are rotters with popular appeal in most movements. We all tend to idealize, sentimentalize, or canonize a few heroes and martyrs. That is why Kim Philby has been idealized by anti-Communists, and Lillian Hellman has been idealized by Communists. Both were superb liars.

Kim Philby was born into English wealth and privilege. While studying at Cambridge in 1933, he secretly joined the Soviet Intelligence Service and pretended to become an ardent anti-Communist. Thus in 1940 he was recruited into the British Secret Intelligence Service (SIS) and spied there for the Soviet Union. Near the end of the war, he suggested formation of a new SIS Soviet section with himself as head. He used this position to thwart all British efforts against the Soviet Union and Eastern Europe. He was then promoted to representing SIS in Washington, where he spied on America for the Soviets. He was instrumental in warning two fellow spies, Donald MacLean and Guy Burgess, when they were about to be arrested—thus allowing them to escape to Russia.

Philby looked like the most likely candidate to be the next head of the SIS. But as the result of an Israeli Intelligence tip-off, the head of CIA counter-intelligence became suspicious of him, and in 1955 he was retired. Many people were outraged that he was suspected of treason. They trusted his family background, his exclusive London club memberships, and his SIS record.

In 1963 Philby defected to Russia and wrote a book about his secret career. A few months before he died in 1988, he granted an interview in which he reviewed his life as a spy and said he had no remorse for any of his activities or their consequences. To this day, however, some people refuse to believe either the public SIS records or his confession. No proof can ever be enough to disillusion them about Kim Philby's fine character and loyalty.

Communist Kim Philby pretended to be a typical upper-crust right-winger, but Communist Lillian Hellman (1905–84) pretended to be a liberal humanitarian. After a career as a successful playwright, in 1973 she published *Pentimento*, her second book of memoirs. It was enhanced by her toughness and honesty, as well as the detailed dialogue preserved in the diary she had kept since childhood. Her most famous revelation was her memorable friendship with Julia.

Julia was a school-girl friend of Hellman's who became an ardent socialist and eventually sacrificed her life in the struggle against Nazism. She persuaded Hellman to help her in the dangerous work of freeing prisoners of the Nazis. In 1977 Hellman's dramatic story of heroic Julia and heroic Lillian Hellman appeared in the award-winning Hollywood film *Julia*, which the public loved.

In fact, an American-born woman named Muriel Buttinger had been studying psychiatry in Vienna before the war and working against the Nazis. She returned to the U.S. in 1939 and settled in New Jersey. Hellman never met Muriel but heard all about her from a mutual acquaintance. When *Pentimento* came out in 1973, Muriel read it and wrote pleasantly to Hellman as a stranger, pointing out how much Julia resembled herself; but Hellman never answered.

In 1980 author Mary McCarthy impugned Lillian Hellman's honesty on *The Dick Cavett Show* and was promptly sued for $2,225,000 by Hellman's powerful lawyers. (Hellman was a multi-millionaire and enhanced her wealth with many lawsuits.) Concerned people began to do detective work for Mary McCarthy. Muriel herself decided that Hellman had used her story, which Yale University published in 1983 as *Code Name Mary*. Mounting evidence proved in 1984 that Hellman's bosom friend Julia was a piece of fiction based upon the life of Muriel, the woman whose letter Hellman ignored.

According to Paul Johnson's essay "Lies, Damned Lies, and Lillian Hellman" in his book *Intellectuals*, the Julia episode was one of the least obnoxious events in Hellman's lifetime full of fierce bullying, crafty deceptions, fraud, cruelty, and exploitation. Johnson says, "In spite of all the revelations and exposures, the nailing of so many falsehoods, the Lillian Hellman myth industry continued serenely on its course." She was a master of public relations, and she is still widely admired for her purported integrity and humanitarianism.

## Dignity and Documents

The public tends to expect integrity and humanitarianism from major antiquarian booksellers, because of the lofty respectability of their wares. As historian Barbara Tuchman said, "Without books, history is silent, literature dumb, science crippled, thought and speculation at a standstill. Without books, the development of civilization would have been impossible.... They are companions, teachers, magicians, bankers of the treasures of the mind."

The dignified Antiquarian Booksellers Association of America was embarrassed in 1989 when its ex-president and past security officer—John Jenkins of the Jenkins Book Company—was found in the Colorado River with a bullet in the back of his head. He had been the biggest man in the Texas books and documents trade.

Until John Jenkins came along, C. Dorman David had been the biggest bookman in Texas; then they joined forces. Between 1964 and 1972, when his heroin habit was most severe, David created many facsimiles of historic Texas documents supposedly intended for a collection to be called "Great Moments in Texas History." At that time, Jenkins was trying to provide his oil-rich customers with enough documents for their collections and their tax-deductible donations to institutions. The Texas Rangers eventually raided David's bookstore and seized many documents that had been stolen from the Texas State Library, which he had evidently used to make copies. (He said he had not stolen them, so he was not charged.)

Insiders knew that Jenkins was a tough tycoon and a high-stakes poker player. His business suffered huge insured fires in 1985, 1986, and 1987; and after the third fire, it turned out that four of the fire-damaged documents were bogus. In 1989 he was being investigated for arson and threatened with foreclosures; rumor has it that he owed Nevada mobsters $1,750,000. Then he died violently.

Jenkins has been likened to Thomas J. Wise, and his bogus Texas pamphlets are likened to Wise's bogus Victorian pamphlets. Thomas

Taylor, one of Texas's top forgery detectors, said in 1989 that he had already identified more than fifty forgeries of thirteen historical documents scattered through major libraries, museums and private collections in Texas—all "surfaced" since 1970. The timid Antiquarian Booksellers Association of America couldn't decide upon any position, much less a course of action, and so Taylor resigned from the Association in protest. As William James pointed out, "When you have to make a choice and don't make it, that is in itself a choice."

### Faith in the Good Doctor

Murder ended the careers of both John Jenkins and Dale Cavaness, but in neither case did most of their associates respond as if they understood. Dr. John Dale Cavaness was a native of the poverty-stricken coal town Eldorado in a section of southern Illinois called Little Egypt, where people considered him a genius. Darcy O'Brien's 1989 book *Murder in Little Egypt* tells how blindly devoted the public can be to a generous, humorous, and ingratiating man with talent and power.

Dr. Dale, as people called him, struck most patients as the most convivial and attentive of doctors. His "downhome" joshing, coupled with his quick mind, soon made him rich and popular. He was amazingly lax about collecting overdue bills, and he often cheated on medical claims for his patients' benefit. Local citizens saw him as a folksy sort of god. Few knew about his violently volcanic temper or the fact that he had been caught once selling liquid morphine and Demerol to a convicted felon; but it wouldn't have mattered. People loved him no matter what he did.

Dale's most constant recreation other than alcohol and amphetamines was hunting. He had a large gun collection and an array of trophies, including a rare snowy owl. After the great bird fell with a superficial wound and revived, Dale choked it, tried to smother it, and finally bashed its head in. Then he claimed that he had shot it by accident. Once when his champion bull worth $10,000 balked at walking up a ramp, Dale said, "You're hamburger," and shot it dead. After miring his brand new Ford truck in mud, he got onto a nearby bulldozer and demolished it.

When he was blind drunk on Scotch one evening in 1971, he crashed a borrowed pickup headlong into another car, killing a young father and ten-month-old baby and permanently disabling the mother. He shrugged it off with the remark, "Everybody's got to die sometime," and plea-bargained down to a mere $1000 fine for drunk driving.

Dale avoided, disliked, and tormented his sons, who feared and adored him. In 1977 the oldest son, Mark, was shot outside Eldorado and devoured by wild animals. In 1984 the third son, Sean, was shot on a lonely road outside St. Louis. Both were twenty-two when they died; and both had been secretly insured by their father, who was their beneficiary. Although he claimed he had not been near Sean for weeks, Dale had been seen with him just before the crime and still had the gun that killed him. He was charged with murder.

Eldorado was outraged about the arrest. People of modest means donated $36,000 to hire the best defense lawyer in St. Louis for this "innocent, persecuted man." Those who knew better, such as his ex-bookkeeper, didn't dare to speak up. One stunned but realistic friend tried in vain to reconcile all their past good times with the terrible truth. Dr. Dale was convicted, went to prison, and committed suicide; but over half the citizens of Eldorado held to their devout belief that he was an innocent victim and that those who accused him and testified against him were corrupt and inhumane villains.

American author Elbert Hubbard said it best: "Genius may have its limitations, but stupidity is not thus handicapped."

# THE GARDEN OF EDEN
# ALL OVER AGAIN

*Wonders are willingly told and willingly believed.*

—Samuel Johnson

Everyone is born homesick for heaven, and this longing takes many forms. People hanker for the world as it should be—in an ancient golden age, the good old days of yesteryear, an island paradise, an economic Utopia, or the world to come. The land of Shangri-La beckons from fiction in styles to suit every taste; and it also beckons from fiction parading as fact. So it was that in the 1930s some Americans visited Russia and returned to tell how wonderful life was there under Stalin; just what believers in Marxist theory were longing to hear.

## Paradise Found

Whether our pocket of paradise on earth features a command economy or holy ground and sacred groves, it gives us joy to think of it. As Richard de Mille observed when analyzing Don Juan's popularity, Castaneda returned with good news from a magic world that everyone has dreamed of visiting. "The mortal yearning for paradise is very strong, and anyone who promises to lead us there is trusted."

In 1980 a warm-hearted film titled *The Gods Must Be Crazy* burst upon the world, delighting viewers. In accord with decades of anthropological opinion, the film portrayed the !Kung San bushmen of the Kalahari Desert (the exclamation point stands for a clicking sound in their language) in southern Africa as an unspoiled tribe where natural human goodness and innocence still flourished. These people lived at peace with one another in small cooperative groups, without any desire for wealth or status. The land yielded generously all that was needed. Parents nurtured their children lovingly and joyfully, with almost no physical punishment. The !Kung had no hostility and aggression because no one had ever taught them to be hostile and aggressive.

Further research has spoiled this !Kung Garden of Eden scenario. Whatever the virtues of !Kung life, half their children die of disease, husbands often strike their wives, and the murder rate is surprisingly high. That is the trouble with research; facts spoil many ideas that we cherish.

When facts reveal that our hope has been betrayed, we do best to admit it. Arthur Koestler did so when he wrote a book about his disappointment in Soviet Communism titled *The God that Failed.* Alexander Pope explained 200 years earlier, "A man should never be ashamed to own he has been in the wrong, which is but saying, in other words, that he is wiser today than he was yesterday."

### Paradise of Adolescent Love

In the very middle of the Roaring Twenties, Margaret Mead set out for paradise. Her anthropology professor had urged her to seek an American Indian tribe where adolescence was smooth and easy, in order to bolster his claim that society, not biology, determines behavior. But Mead wanted something more exotic. She got a half hour of fieldwork training from her professor, then sailed to Samoa, where she stayed in a Pago Pago hotel and learned a smattering of the language. After that she moved into an American home and made daily visits to villages, where she asked girls about their sex lives. In nine months she returned to New York and wrote her report: *Coming of Age in Samoa.* It told the tale her professor wanted, in glowing terms. She also tossed in a bit of sermonizing against repressive Victorian attitudes in our own society. (That is called preaching to the choir.)

In the lush beauty of Samoa, stress-free adolescents made love to each other casually, freely, and frequently. In that tranquil culture there was no possessiveness, no competition, no conflicts, no impotence, no frigidity, no strife, no delinquency, and no rape. When this book was published in 1928, it became a best-seller. (When I entered college in 1952, it was still required reading.) It seemed to grant scientific status to the idea that casual sex and lots of it, in an easy-going society, is what makes people healthy and happy. Stormy adolescence is a result of culture, not chemistry.

Shortly after Mead died of cancer in 1983, an Australian anthropologist named Derek Freeman published *Margaret Mead and Samoa: The Making and Unmaking of an Anthropological Myth*. Freeman lived with Samoans for six years and studied them off and on for forty years; he is the world's foremost authority on them. Educated Samoans had complained to him for decades about Mead's book. He points out that Mead was only twenty-three when she went to Samoa, and very naïve. She asked leading questions and believed what amused girls politely answered. She wanted to see teenage tranquility, and so she did; but in reality Samoan adolescents were every bit as rebellious as those elsewhere. Samoans are competitive. For the incidence of rape in 1925–26, Mead should have read all the rape cases in the *Samoan Times*; rape was twice as common in Samoa as in the United States. Freeman says that since Mead's facts were wrong, "her assertion in *Coming of Age in Samoa* of the absolute sovereignty of culture over biology is clearly invalid."

## Paradise of Dreams

If it wasn't sex in Samoa that provided paradise on earth, it was dreaming in Malaya. Kilton Stewart is widely revered as a great anthropologist from Utah who discovered the dream-centered culture of the Temiar branch of the Senoi tribe in the rain forest of the Malay Peninsula. Directed by dreams discussed at the breakfast table, this Edenic tribe is free of all the ills that plague the rest of the world. They have no crime, no cruelty, no drugs, no divorce, and no war. All is peace, health, harmony, and joy. Stewart told how we can learn from the Senoi in his delightful 1950 essay "Dream Theory in Malaya." His widow Clara Stewart Flagg leads Senoi dreamwork seminars in Los Angeles to this very day.

In her 1991 advertisement, Clara Flagg claims,

> The Senoi of Malaya make their dreams the major focus of their intellectual and social interest, and have solved the problem of violent crime and destructive economic conflict, and largely eliminated insanity, neurosis, and psychogenic illness. This dream policy promoted better health among the Senoi than was found in the other groups and, at the same time, enabled the energy released in the dream to produce music, poetry, mechanical inventions, and novel

solutions to social problems; this energy also becomes the hub of social leadership.

People can read about Senoi dream therapy in books that popularized it in the 1970s, such as Charles Tart's *Altered States of Consciousness* (1969), Richard Ornstein's *Psychology of Consciousness* (1972), Ann Faraday's *Dream Power* (1972), Sol Gordon's *Psychology for You* (1972), Theodore Roszak's *Where the Wasteland Ends* (1973), Marilyn Ferguson's *The Brain Revolution* (1973), and Patricia Garfield's *Creative Dreaming* (1974). One can also read Stanley Krippner's account in the June 1970 issue of *Psychology Today* and Rosalind Diamond Cartwright's account in the December 1978 issue of the same journal. All these authors believed Stewart.

In 1978 two British filmmakers went to Malaysia to film a documentary about the Senoi dream culture, and to their dismay the Senoi denied the whole story. The pair went home and consulted anthropologist Richard Benjamin of Cambridge, an authority on the Senoi, and he explained that there is not one shred of evidence for the dream-centered culture that Stewart described.

When I read that, I managed to contact Kilton Stewart's sister, Ida Stewart Coppolino, a California education professor retired to Provo, Utah. On the telephone Dr. Coppolino reminisced about her extremely adventuresome brother sixteen years her senior. He was a great raconteur, she said, highly entertaining and persuasive. He was a lapsed Mormon and certainly no saint, no writer, no scientist, and no anthropologist. He was, she said, a highly intuitive and effective New York therapist with a degree in psychology from the University of Utah. Dr. Coppolino kindly loaned me her personal copy of Stewart's 1947 thesis about the Senoi.

His badly written thesis contradicts the claims in the well-written 1950 essay and does not seem to be written by the same person. Stewart's one published book, *Pygmies and Dream Giants* (Harper & Row, 1954), does not mention the Senoi or any dream theory. A posthumous book by the reckless young British anthropologist who was Stewart's host in Malaya, *In Search of the Dream People* by Patrick Noone, contradicts some of Stewart's most important claims and doesn't mention the others.

It is obvious that someone with a flair for writing concocted a charming anthropological fable about the blissful Senoi in order to interest people in Stewart's dream techniques. Most of the people who have tried Senoi dream theory are blissful Californians. They not only got to try some interesting dream work, but they got to think that they were tapping into the wisdom of a rain-forest paradise.

C. S. Lewis was interested in dreams. He remarked once, "Everything is a real something. What pretends to be a crocodile may be a (real) dream; but what pretends at the breakfast table to be a dream may be a (real) lie."

### Paradise of Radiant Health

If it wasn't dreaming in Malaya that provided paradise on earth, it was pure food and air in the Hunza Valley. The Hunzakuts are a people of unknown origin living in an isolated valley in Pakistan. They look more Mediterranean than Asian, and their language is not related to any other language on earth. These people were first contacted by British troops in 1891; after that, rumors spread about a healthful paradise in the Karakoram mountains. James Hilton's 1933 novel about Shangri-La, *Lost Horizons,* describes just such a valley of prolonged youth, and many people think Hilton was describing Hunza.

"It really is Shangri-La," the valley's ruler says. "But in the past, when it was more isolated, people were even more happy and healthy."

The valley with 16,000 residents is irrigated throughout by canals full of glacier water producing green terraces of wheat, corn, apples, pears, peaches, walnuts, mulberries, grapes, and pumpkins. In the 1940s travelers began reporting that this "valley of eternal youth" had many healthy people 140 years old, and *Life* magazine ran a story on them titled "The Happy Land of Just Enough."

In 1971 *National Geographic* sent Dr. Alexander Leaf of Harvard to investigate, and in his article "Every Day Is a Gift When You Are Over 100," he reported that there are three bastions of longevity: Pakistan's Hunza Valley, a spot in the Ecuadoran Andes, and a spot in the Caucasus Mountains of Soviet Georgia. Leaf's latter two bastions eventually proved false, but the Hunza claim is still popular in books and articles. Therefore editor John Tierney of *In Health* magazine went to Pakistan to investigate. In July 1990 he published "The Three Secrets of Shangri-La."

1. The first "secret" is for strong old men to forget about all the dead women and children. Infant and female mortality are very high there; and malaria, bronchitis, dysentery, tuberculosis, rickets, sore eyes, and iodine deficiency are common.

2. The second "secret" is for people to go hungry. Winter rationing and spring famine used to keep Hunza people severely underfed, and dramatic caloric restriction (short of outright starvation) definitely prolongs life.

3. The third "secret" is for people to forget their true age. As soon as birth certificates become common, claims of extreme age drop sharply. (Incidentally, about a third of the people who claimed to be 100 or more in the last United States census were not that old, according to Social Security records. As Lucille Ball once advised, "The secret of staying young is to live honestly, eat slowly, and lie about your age.)

John Tierney interviewed Ahmad Ullah Baig, cousin of a wrinkled centenarian who appeared in *National Geographic* in 1971 and again in 1975. Baig said of his cousin, "When foreigners came, sometimes he would say his age was higher, sometimes lower. He would lie. I don't know if he knew his right age. But I know he was only two or three years older than me, because my parents told me that." Thus the 102-year-old man was between 76 and 85. Tierney asked Baig why his cousin had lied, and Baig laughed. "He wanted money. The foreigners usually gave him a gift after they spoke to him, and he hoped that the older he said he was, the more money he would get." It worked.

### Stone-Age Paradise

If it wasn't pure food and air in the Hunza Valley that provided paradise on earth, it was stone-age simplicity in Mindanao. In 1971 Manuel Elizalde, Harvard-educated son of a Filipino millionaire, said of poor Filipino tribespeople, "I love these people. I would die for them." His was an anthropological dream come true; as Ferdinand Marcos's Cabinet Secretary for National Minorities, he discovered and protected the world's only surviving stone-age tribe, in the rain forest of Mindanao.

Elizalde was a notorious playboy who had his own ideas of how to protect minorities; he reportedly kept a harem in the city made up of young girls he had gathered from the tribes in his care. But he was presented to the reading public as an altruistic humanitarian.

*National Geographic* rhapsodized about President Marcos and Elizalde in both the August and December issues of 1971, then featured the stone-age Tasaday (ta-SA-dye) tribe in August 1972. Senior Editor Kenneth MacLeish's article begins, "In naked innocence, a Tasaday boy toys with a bright bloom plucked from the wilds of a primeval Eden. . . . [The Tasaday are] perhaps the simplest of living humans . . . gentle and affectionate. . . . Our friends have given me a new measure for man."

As a Hawaiian professor observed wryly, the Tasaday were "paleohippies"—bound to appeal to our 1960s counterculture movement, which made much of idealized notions of primitive society. The Tasaday were appealing because they lived communally, had no possessions or rules, and ate natural foods.

NBC paid a million-peso fee to do a television documentary and said of the Tasaday, "They are wholly unaggressive, with no words for weapons, hostility or war." Their word "Chee" means "Wow! Oh boy!" Their word "Oh-ho" means "Yessir." These laughing, hugging, "leisure-intensive" people lived in ancestral caves, went naked or wore orchid leaves, ate roots and tadpoles, made stone axes, and swung on vines. They had no pottery, cloth, metal, arts, crafts, bows and arrows, religion, agriculture, or knowledge of the outside world. They had never yet noticed the moon in the sky at night, but were willing to go up in a helicopter right away.

The Marcos government set aside 46,300 acres of rain forest as a Tasaday preserve. Some suspect that Marcos did this to steal the local mahogany. After all, there were only twenty-six people in the entire tribe, and we are told that they and their ancestors never took the three-hour walk needed to get to a nearby farming village. Do such sedentary people need over 1,780 acres per person?

There have always been doubters, but they were muzzled. (Zeus Salazar, a Manilla professor who scoffed at the claims, has been harassed with legal threats.) Elizalde carefully restricted access to the Tasaday, then cut off the area entirely in 1974. In 1975 Harcourt published journalist John Nance's book *The Gentle Tasaday: A Stone Age People in the Philippine Rain Forest*, with a foreword by Charles A. Lindbergh that said grandly, "There is a wisdom of the past to which primitive man is close, and from which modern man can learn the requisites of his survival." In 1988 Harcourt reissued *The Gentle Tasaday* as a $12.95 paperback.

According to the *Manchester Guardian*, when Marcos fell in 1986 Elizalde fled the country with $55 million. A Swiss journalist visited the Tasaday area then and announced in Zurich that the story was a hoax. Soon Judith Moses produced an ABC documentary, *The Tribe That Never Was*, but it made little impact. Her "Tasaday" informers told her that they speak the area's Manobo language, and that Tasaday is the name of a mountain, not the name of a tribe.

In 1988 an English documentary showed the "Tasaday" people living in the local village, clothed and smoking cigarettes. The boy named Lobo, featured in *Gentle Tasaday* and on the cover of *National Geographic*, had become a bitter man who admitted that he was never named Lobo. He spoke for the tribe: "Elizalde promised us things, so we changed our names and did whatever he wanted. He sent ahead messengers to tell us to take off our clothes and go to the caves. We did as we were told, but just look at us. Look around and see if we got any help. We got nothing."

Mariano Mondragaon, a lawyer who has lived in the Tasaday area for fifty years, says, "There is no Tasaday tribe. It is a concoction of Elizalde. Some of them are my in-laws." Clay Johnston of the Summer Institute of Linguistics in Dallas studied Manobo in Mindanao for ten years and says the ancient Tasaday language is just an ordinary dialect of Manobo. Archaeologist Robert L. Carneiro of New York City says that the Tasaday stone axes are blatant fakes. Anthropologist Thomas Headland of Dallas says that rain forests 4000 feet above sea level cannot provide enough edible roots to sustain human life. Anthropologist Gerald Berreman of U. C. Berkeley points out that the Tasaday caves are devoid of "middens," garbage scraps found at any genuine human dwelling place.

By 1991 Elizalde was back in the Philippines. Harcourt continues to sell *The Gentle Tasaday* as if it were true, and *National Geographic* makes no retraction at all.

### Primitive Christian Paradise

If it wasn't stone-age simplicity in Mindanao that provided paradise on earth, it was Christianity in Northern Luzon.

As soon as Isabel Chapman became a Christian in 1981, she heard God's call to the Philippines. In England she had been an ordinary insurance agent who smoked and drank too much, but within four months she found herself trudging through leech-infested rice paddies into mountain regions occupied by headhunting tribes. As she told it in her popular 1984 Hodder and Stoughton book *Arise and Reap*, she journeyed right into areas where no other missionaries, nor any white person, had ever dared to venture.

At last she reached the home of the Bute Bute tribe, who hacked off people's heads to mark all significant events such as weddings. Like the Tasaday, these people were almost naked and had no metal tools. The men labored all day in rice paddies for the tribe's scant, mushy, tasteless gray food. The people were covered with tattoos carved into their skin with blunt, dirty instruments; and many of these tattoos were oozing pus or caked with scabs. The few teeth left in their mouths were brown and rotten. Their hair was crawling with lice, and their eyes were blotched with yellow matter and dirt. They had huge goiters under their chins. The ground was too parched and hard in the dry season to sustain any plants, and so the tribe lived mainly on rice and coffee. Every female past puberty was pregnant as well as suckling a young child, and they were so fertile in filth and poverty that they had up to ten children trailing behind them.

The second night she was there, Isabel preached in English and a traveling companion translated. When the village knelt in repentance, their physical ailments were all healed and they began to speak in tongues. The next day they began to build a bamboo church, and the chief decided to go away for three years of Bible College.

Their goal accomplished, Isabel and her companions walked along jungle paths to the nearby village of Lewan, which was already Christian. Brightly colored birds darted through lush green foliage, and clusters of ripe bananas, mangoes, and all kinds of exotic fruit hung low for the taking. An occasional monkey would swing lithely through the trees and chatter at the travelers. A tremendous sense of the peace of God reigned there.

> The beauty of His holiness hung in the rich foliage of the trees and breathed through the golden twilight air. A second Garden of Eden it seemed, and I found refreshment and rest during our days of ministry there.

209

Evening was the time I loved best. As the last fingers of sunlight trailed scarlet threads on the distant mountain tops, and dusk drew itself like a veil across the face of the earth, I would make my way to a spring which cascaded down the mountainside and was channeled along a piece of hollowed bamboo to burst in a shower of cool silver drops over a glittering pool. Here this earthly paradise produced a spectacle more lovely than all imagining, for hosts of fireflies would gather in the shades of twilight and illuminate the pool with a thousand glowing lights, settling on the trees and transforming the scene into a Christmas picture.

Although Isabel's story may be true in spirit and her motives may be pure, the story has improved a bit with the telling. The area that she visited in 1981 had already attracted an abundance of missionaries and white men; the Bute Bute were not stone-age people; and they did not practice ritual headhunting. It seems that the spectacular 1981 conversion and physical healing of an entire village was never noticed by trained missionaries stationed in the area. If the contrast between the Bute Bute wasteland and the nearby Garden of Eden is true, why didn't the malnourished Bute Bute folk walk down the trail and eat some delicious fruit? Isabel tells a dramatic story, but one wonders what a British film crew will find if they go to make a documentary of her paradise. It may be somewhat like the Senoi dreamers and the gentle Tasaday all over again.

We all need hope; therefore people like illusions. But Georges Bernanos urges us to live without illusions: "In order to be prepared to hope in what does not deceive, we must first lose hope in everything that deceives."

## Paradise in Oregon

If it wasn't Christianity in Northern Luzon that provided paradise on earth, it was God's revelation in Oregon. At least that was the conviction of my friends who had once been missionaries in the Philippines and were now entering a prophet's inner circle.

The English wit Sydney Smith said, "What a mystery is the folly and stupidity of the good!" Perhaps that is because good people have so much heart, and as French wit La Rochefoucauld said, "The mind is always the dupe of the heart."

Invitations to paradise on earth are dangerous bait. They snag the heart, especially if they offer us a hope of paradise for our children.

In about 1970 an obviously wealthy psychologist set out to empower evangelical Christians and Mormons in Oregon, California, and Utah. His name shall be Stanley Matrel in this account. The Doctor, as he was called, claimed to have a "rare Ph.D. degree from the Ohio State University in Economics, Marketing, Real Estate, Social and Counseling Psychology." He said he had "taught under the University of Chicago and the Oregon State of Higher Education." His "Dynamic Life" seminars attracted clean-living middle-class couples who were in life's ordinary middle-age doldrums—feeling a bit bogged down by stress or the general state of the world. The Doctor had a cure for everything. He was a Bible-quoting Barry Minkow.

His plan was revealed in "sensational seminars" and "tremendous tapes." Followers moved along from a $200 introductory seminar to a series of $300 Dynamics seminars and a set of thirty taped talks that eventually sold for $995. Such pre-inflation investment was modest in light of the fact that the Doctor was God's first prophet since St. Paul, destined to become the most important man in America—either President or above the President. God had revealed to the Doctor that Christ would not return for 2,000 years; thus the Doctor's followers and their descendants would be materially blessed for twenty centuries. His explicit instructions would provide them all with radiant health, magnificent wealth, and rapturous marriages. A few dozen of these Christian families were selected to leave everything behind and live together in an earthly paradise, the Doctor's lake-side ranch in Oregon. He started a school for their children, who could all grow up to be healthy, happy Christian millionaires.

The Doctor's logo included a Christian dove and an American eagle. He didn't sell the Eiffel Tower, but he did sell partnerships in real estate syndication, cruises, lithographs, tax-avoidance advice, mail-order jewelry up to $43,500 per piece, rules of nutrition, the answer to addictions, $5,000 annual memberships in his club, and a $495 set of tapes on creative salesmanship.

Of the latter, he said, "Our success in sales depends on our ability to psychologically convince a person to the point of his believing and accepting our idea, which may have been a complete contrast to his previous beliefs. He knew that in his bones.

In his popular women's seminars the Doctor smoothly convinced wives that they had been displeasing God and cheating their husbands by wearing short hair and failing to perform symbolic sex acts that the Doctor described. Women also had to wear V-shaped necklines, not round ones, and had to match the color of their lipstick to their most private parts. Hundreds and hundreds of listeners were first disconcerted, then mesmerized. Many of them returned repeatedly to advanced seminars to learn more of God's strict new rules for right living.

I felt uneasy when my friends packed up their five young children and left triumphantly for the paradise, and I urged them to be careful. They were licensed professionals who worked for a world-famous missionary agency based in Southern California, and the Doctor needed their expertise. After several months, they admitted that life on the Doctor's ranch was not yet what had been promised; God had told the Doctor to begin by chastening his flock in order to thoroughly discipline their spirits. Unquestioning obedience and sacrifice were needed because "whom the Lord loveth, he chasteneth." Two years later, they were still being chastened. They didn't admit it even then, but they had put themselves into the hands of a sociopath.

The Doctor was in trouble for fraud, tax evasion, and severe beatings of his youngest child, whose mother was his sister-in-law; but like many confidence artists, he was too slippery for our cumbersome legal system. He bewildered his flock by cutting them off from old friends, putting them on a fasting diet for days at a time, fondling my friend in bed to test her obedience, forcing people to appear nude for humility's sake, running up huge bills on a member's credit card, permanently failing to pay workers their salaries, splitting up couples against their will, and sending at least one couple's children to an outpost thousands of miles away. He and his top leaders seriously discussed capturing a certain member who ran away and locking him up for the rest of his life. At first most of his flock was too devoted and trusting to resist, and eventually too traumatized to resist. Like the people who followed Jim Jones to Guyana, they were robbed of their autonomy.

One day the Doctor told two little boys to carefully poison weeds for several hours. They got tired and sloppy and did a poor job. This gave the Doctor an excuse for special group discipline. He called everyone together and ordered the father of the two boys to strip and kneel down before him with the boys watching. He prepared a large stick. Then he supervised from his Arabian stallion while every person was forced to take a turn beating the father. Light blows were not allowed; the Doctor wrote down scores for the strength of the blows. When the man's back was raw and bleeding, he was forced to go to the stallion and kiss the Doctor's feet.

Eventually the members were so destitute financially that the commune fell apart, and some of them sued the Doctor for defrauding them. Their lawyer showed me the documents and told me that they didn't have much chance of collecting from this confidence artist. The last I heard of Dr. Matrel, he had fled from Oregon law enforcement and had taken a swank Wilshire Boulevard address. I happened to mention him to a neighborhood friend of mine as an example of a white-collar criminal on the loose. To my surprise, she answered, "I know about Dr. Matrel from TV and his ads in the *Los Angeles Times*. I don't believe he could really be a crook. In fact, if I had some extra money I would invest it with him." She is a bright, talented, ambitious woman.

There is a little fable about the fact that charlatans are so convincing. Two goddesses named Truth and Falsehood went swimming. Falsehood got out first and put on Truth's clothes. Truth refused to wear Falsehood's clothing, so she had to go home naked.

# HOLY HOAXES

*Of all villainy there is none more base than that of the hypo-crite, who, at the moment he is most false, takes care to appear the most virtuous.*

—Cicero

Just as Judas is the name for all traitors, so Tartuffe is the name for all religious hypocrites. Dr. Matrel is nothing new; he is Tartuffe all over again. People like that are always with us.

Unfortunately, most church people haven't seen the wise and witty French comedy *Tartuffe* by Molière, although it has been tickling audiences for over 300 years. It is as up to date as male midlife crisis and the latest televangelist scandal, and as moral as the Bible.

## The Paragon of Purity

In Richard Wilbur's easy English translation of *Tartuffe*, one of Tartuffe's devoted followers says at the opening:

> *He's a fine man, and should be listened to.*
> *I will not hear him mocked by fools like you.*

A young woman named Dorine answers saucily:

> *You see him as a saint. I'm far less awed;*
> *In fact, I see right through him. He's a fraud.*

The rest of the play shows how the buffoonish Tartuffe fleeces a gullible family man named Orgon while trying to seduce Orgon's pretty young wife—who detests him. The entire family sees through Tartuffe's angelic act except for Orgon and his mother, who are both infatuated with him. Orgon not only gives Tartuffe financial support, but all his loyalty and affection as well. He thinks Tartuffe is a para-gon of purity, and he is flattered to have such a saint in residence.

In vain, Orgon's kindly Christian brother-in-law asks him if he is so dazed by Tartuffe's hocus-pocus that he can't even see straight.

Charlatans exploit our love of Heaven, but those whose hearts are truly pure and lowly don't make a show of sanctity. Orgon can't stand to hear such sensible advice, because he is determined that Tartuffe is a spiritual genius.

Orgon has a young-adult son and daughter from his first marriage. He wants to have Tartuffe in his family, and so he decides to force his daughter to marry Tartuffe in spite of the fact that she loves someone else. Tartuffe is willing to marry Orgon's daughter in order to have more access to the woman he lusts after—Orgon's wife.

In a fit of middle-aged vanity, Orgon disowns his faithful son in favor of the new son he wants instead—Tartuffe. Then he signs his whole estate over to Tartuffe, who dutifully accepts the gift although he doesn't want it. Tartuffe explains that although he despises worldly wealth, he will take it and use it for Heaven's glory and mankind's benefit, lest it should fall into wicked hands that would use it for sin and crime.

Once Tartuffe holds title to all of Orgon's property, Orgon overhears Tartuffe trying to seduce his wife. Then Tartuffe evicts Orgon from his own home and arranges to have him thrown into jail; but because this is a comedy instead of a tragedy, Tartuffe ends up in jail instead, and everything is set right.

The church officials of France were so corrupt and arrogant that they were openly enraged at Molière when *Tartuffe* came out. They pretended that his satire was an insult to true religion, and they had it banned. Even when the play was legal, they once got the police to burst in and stop it. Molière pointed out to the King that powerful wrongdoers often tolerate sober criticism, which they easily ignore; but they can't tolerate satire. Religious hypocrites are willing to be cruel, but they are not willing to be ridiculed. Public laughter is the best way to combat them.

### The Rogue Rabbi

Dr. Matrel was a Tartuffe who founded a commune, destroyed marriages, and abused entire families. Jim Jones was a Tartuffe who did all that and finally poisoned his broken-spirited followers with cyanide-laced Kool-Aid. Compared to those two, the Tartuffe named Michael Esses was almost benign. Even so, he left behind a trail of waste, betrayal, and spiritual hurt.

Born to Arabic-speaking Jewish immigrants in about 1923, Michael Esses had to wear earlocks (curls in front of his ears), and received a strict Jewish education. He interrupted his rabbinical training by enlisting in the Air Corps the day after Pearl Harbor, and he was discharged over three years later as an officer. He received his doctorate in Hebrew Letters and was ordained a rabbi on June 30, 1950, in New York City.

Michael ended up in Anaheim, California, with a young family and a thriving drapery business. One night in 1965, Jesus appeared to him, reached out his nail-pierced hands, and said, "Michael, Michael, why do you hate me?" From that night on he was an active Christian teacher, the only converted rabbi active in American Christendom. He quickly became a ruling elder in the local Presbyterian church; and in 1968 he transferred to what became Melodyland Christian Center across the street from Disneyland.

Famous guest speakers at Melodyland included Pat Robertson, Pat Boone, Ruth Carter Stapleton, Dennis Bennett, Nora Lam, Oral Roberts, Jim Bakker, Maria Von Trapp, Corrie ten Boom, Hal Lindsey, and many others. Michael was a popular teacher there; in August 1970 he was ordained by Pastor Ralph Wilkerson and joined the staff as a full-time minister. He was a counselor to such world leaders as Reagan, Carter, Nixon, and Begin. He once spent a week with Sadat at his palace in Aswan. Logos publishers brought out his autobiography titled *Michael, Michael, Why Do You Hate Me?* subtitled *A Rabbi Meets His Messiah*. He became a popular speaker at churches and conferences across the country. Then in 1979 he dropped out of sight.

In 1983 Betty Esses wrote her second book about her husband, Michael Esses, titled *Survivor of a Tarnished Ministry* and subtitled *The True Story of Michael and Betty Esses*. It's a harrowing tale.

Max (Michael) Esses never wore earlocks, because he did not come from a Hasidic family. He was a high-school dropout who joined the army a year after Pearl Harbor and was discharged six months later. He soon married, had four children, and moved to California to go into business. He was an atheist with no rabbinical training. He deserted his original family in 1951 and met eighteen-year-old Betty Neal in Portland, Oregon. When she tried to break off the romance, he persuaded her to elope to Canada. She learned before long that he was a bigamist and that he had affairs behind her back from the start, but she stayed with him. He was an extremely energetic and changeable man who could turn on immense charm when he chose to do so.

One night in 1965 Betty informed Michael that she was finally going to divorce him because of his brazen adulteries; but the next morning he announced that he had met Jesus during the night. (He later told a friend what Betty suspected—that he had made that up.) She was glad that their life started to revolve around church activities, but she soon found that his filthy language, bizarre behavior, and sexual affairs were not over. She was shocked the first time she heard him introduced in church as an ex-rabbi, and she saw no evidence that he ever met world leaders; but she didn't dare to object publicly. She gave in to pressure and wrote her husband's fake autobiography *Michael, Michael, Why Do You Hate Me?* She knew that all of his degrees were bogus.

In spite of the fact that Michael Esses' ministry was a tangle of cynical lies, people flocked to him. As the English author Samuel Butler observed at the turn of the century, hypocrisy and promotion can cause churches to grow as well as sincerity and sacrifice. Similarly, people who have chickens know that artificial nest eggs will encourage hens as well as real ones.

> *So round white stones will serve, they say,*
> *As well as eggs to make hens lay.*

The church hens laid plenty of eggs for Michael Esses. He came up with endless ways to get people to donate directly to him to supplement his church salary, and behind the scenes he squandered a small fortune. He loved to buy expensive jewelry. He showed bank employees his safe deposit boxes full of cash and gold. His closets and drawers were loaded with an endless array of extravagant suits, shirts, shoes, and ties—many never worn even once.

Betty claims in her book that near the end of their marriage Michael removed over $600,000 of personal assets to Mexico to evade California community property laws. He managed to wangle an extra $8,000 loan from Melodyland. In October 1979 he left with his latest lover, a young woman who was pregnant with his child. As soon as he left, Michael opened several new charge accounts and charged $20,000 worth of purchases to Betty.

At last report, Michael was preaching in New Mexico and had never once contacted any of the several children he left behind with his previous wives, although some of them longed for a word from him. Betty's book begins, "How do I admit my part in the pretense, the sham, the out-right lies . . .? My prayer is . . . to protect the innocent sheep who sit in thousands of pews every Sunday and are so easily fleeced." She concludes, "Michael and hundreds of Christian leaders like him succeed in their deceit because Christians let them." She urges honest church people to stop indulging dishonest leaders with denial, cover-up, and compromise.

## Christianity Rediscovered

Not all religious malarkey comes from the fringes of evangelicalism or the Pentecostal tradition, by any means. Dr. Jacob Needleman, who seems to have a lot in common with Carlos Castaneda, is a much-published philosophy professor at California State University at San Francisco. He wrote *Lost Christianity: A Journey of Rediscovery* in the 1970s—in purplish prose, on a Rockefeller Foundation fellowship. It was published in 1980 by Harper & Row, first in hardcover and later in a handsome softcover. It was widely reviewed and widely praised.

Dr. Needleman explains that he was sought out by (unnamed) Western religious leaders who were unable to understand what they were looking for in Christianity, which is a faith lost in the dust of the centuries. Needleman sought to answer the question "What does the Church really want?"

Needleman found three mentors who gave him his answer. First, he found part of his answer in the "firm, black, alive" eyes of the leader of the Russian Church in Western Europe. This man's message was "to become open."

In an airport in Bankok, Needleman met a mysterious middle-Eastern monk of unknown origin, unknown name, and unknown church; a wandering holy man with occult interests. A year later a mystery package somehow came to Needleman in the mail from Egypt. Inside was over 1000 pages of manuscript by this holy man, with news that he was dead. There was no way to tell who had sent the package or how he had got Needleman's name and address. Needleman discovered to his surprise that he was mentioned in the manuscript, and the manuscript was a work of philosophical genius. (Frankly, the quotations from it sound like Needleman, not like a work of genius.)

Third, Needleman met an unorthodox Roman Catholic priest named Father Vincent who no longer thought of himself as a Christian. He had just returned from twenty years with a tribe in Africa, where the word for sexual abstinence is a prefix that means "holy-power-of-the-second-birth." No name is given for the language, the tribe, or the African country. The tribe hunted lions and rhinos in the jungle, which seems like a clue that the country is fantasy land. During an emergency once, Father Vincent and three other priests experienced miraculous peace while transporting a dozen loads of screaming people downstream in a badly broken boat in a raging torrent. The priests had never handled even an unbroken boat before. After every magically successful trip, they carried the broken boat up the trail to fill it with more perfectly healthy people and risk the flood again. It does not seem to occur to Needleman that real men would have simply walked downhill once instead of riding downriver in a broken boat twelve times and then carrying the boat back uphill twelve times.

In the end, Needleman discovered that the "missing link" in Christianity is refined religious sensibility or soul energy. "It is no longer simply a question of whether this manuscript is accurate or not, right or not, authentic or not. It is myself that is in question, my own sense of what I am, what I need to know in order to begin living."

In 1991 Jacob Needleman published a similar book titled *Money and the Meaning of Life* (Doubleday). While writing it, he discovered that money was invented to link the material world to God. We have lost touch with the original spiritual component of money, and our job is to rediscover it. The high point in this book is the moment he describes when one of his appreciative college students gave him a mahogany box filled with half a million dollars in gold. "The radiance of the gold blazed into my brain and a powerful bolt of electricity snaked down the length of my torso, igniting everything in its path, especially in the region of the solar plexus and genitals."

Once again Jacob Needleman was taken seriously by distinguished reviewers who seemed to be asleep at the switch.

### Sensation Sellers

In the 1970s Dr. Matrel portrayed himself as the first prophet since St. Paul, Michael Esses portrayed himself as America's only

Christian rabbi, and Jacob Needleman portrayed himself as the rediscoverer of Christianity. Sergei Kourdakov, author of *The Persecutor*, portrayed himself as a Christian convert from the Soviet secret police; John Todd, author of *Spellbound* and *Angel of Light* portrayed himself as a convert from the Illuminati; and Betty Maltz, author of *My Glinpse of Eternity*, portrayed herself as a person who had died, gone to heaven, and returned to life on earth. That is also the decade when comedian-evangelist Mike Warnke burst on the scene as America's leading ex-Satanist.

As a hard-drinking, heavy-set freshman at California's San Bernardino Community College in the fall of 1965, Warnke catapulted into drugs, sex, and Satanism. He was soon reduced to a 110-pound speed freak with three bullet holes in his legs and scabs all over his face from shooting up crystal. He handled $50,000 in one drug transaction alone. In late 1965 he marched with Martin Luther King in Alabama, then dropped out of college, met Satanic leader Anton LeVey in San Francisco, and even visited Charles Manson in the desert. As a Satanic high priest in early 1966, he had 1,500 followers and led some of them in acts of rape. He had two full-time love slaves in his apartment, wore bizarre clothes, sported hip-length bleached-white hair, and painted his six-inch fingernails black. After almost dying from a heroin overdose in May 1966, Warnke joined the Navy and spent six months in a blur of drugs, violence, and heroism in Vietnam. Later, he earned two bachelor's degrees, two master's degrees, and a doctorate from Antioch University. Now a converted Christian, Warnke and his Warnke Ministries Center in Kentucky has handled 50,000 counseling calls and letters a month.

In 1992 *Cornerstone* magazine's investigative journalists concluded that all the above information is false. Before he entered the Navy in 1966, Warnke was an unremarkable Roman Catholic with short dark hair. Martin Luther King didn't march when Warnke was in college, and Charles Manson was in prison then, not in the desert. According to his old friends, Warnke was noted for his tall tales, acting ability, and far-fetched pranks. All the extravagant wealth, fame, moral degradation, and sexual adventures in Mike Warnke's life, according to these investigators, are imaginary, although Warnke has achieved considerable wealth and fame in later life as an evangelist on the rock concert circuit.

In 1972 Warnke got off to a modest start as co-designer of a garish trailer called a "Witchmobile," in which he displayed occult materials such as voodoo oil for San Diego evangelist Morris Cerullo. At that time, according to his detractors, Warnke invented a spellbinding Satanic past for himself that went along with the Witchmobile. Early in 1973 he published his mostly fictitious life story titled *The Satan Seller*, which has reportedly sold 3 million copies, followed by other books and over a million records. He has appeared on various TV shows, including *Larry King Live, The Oprah Winfrey Show, 20/20*, and *The 700 Club*, and in 1986 alone he received over $1,000,000 in love offerings in addition to all his other income. June 29, 1988, was declared "Mike Warnke Day" by the governor of Tennessee.

### Reports from Underground

It seems that 1988 was a good year for fake ex-Satanists. That is when Laurel Wilson published *Satan's Underground* (Harvest House) under her pen name Lauren Stratford. In it she describes in graphic detail her lifetime of child abuse, rape, child pornography, incest, teen pregnancies, sex slavery, prostitution, murder of her babies, sadomasochism, bestiality, Satan worship, fiendish torture—and eventual healing with the help of Hal Lindsey's sister-in-law, Joanna Michaelson. *Satan's Underground* sold 145,000 copies and launched Laurel Wilson into a full-time counseling ministry. She followed it with a second book, *I Know You're Hurting*.

"Lauren Stratford" was an only child growing up in the clutches of a diabolically perverted mother and incestuous father. But in real life Laurel Wilson had an attentive older sister named Willow who vouches for their sheltered Christian upbringing. Laurel entered Seattle Pacific College briefly in 1959, and the school soon recommended that she get psychiatric care; later she graduated from the University of Redlands and taught music. Although "Lauren" had been sexually ravaged since childhood and had given birth to three babies by her early twenties, the man who wed Laurel Wilson when she was twenty-four bears witness that she was a virgin before their brief marriage. No one has ever seen her pregnant. She says that Frank Cole Wilson, her biological father, was a Satanist and pornographer who died in 1983; but in fact Frank Cole Wilson, her adoptive father, was a Christian medical doctor who died in 1965.

221

At the end of 1989 *Cornerstone* investigators published an article exposing Laurel Wilson's Satanic abuse for what it was: a hoax. In the course of her real life, Laurel Wilson has at times faked blindness; claimed to be abused by an evil stepmother, although she had no stepmother; claimed to be a lesbian lover of Virginia McMartin, the famous preschool owner, and faked a rare disease. Friends and relatives from her past bore witness that Laurel Wilson is a chronic victim impersonator. Even after her publisher reluctantly discontinued her books, her ministry associates continued to promote her. In 1991 her new publisher, Pelican Books, advertised *Satan's Underground* as factual in *Publishers Weekly* and featured it at the international Frankfurt Book Fair.

If Laurel Wilson is a chronic victim impersonator, Troy Lawrence is a chronic convert. In 1990 he tried to launch an organization named Ex-New Agers for Jesus and published *The Secret Message of the Zodiac*, which tells how astrology bears witness to Christ. In 1991 he published *New Age Messiah Identified* (Harrison House), which tells about his growing up in the occult and his conversion to evangelical Christianity in 1984. Lawrence reveals the secret identity of the Tara Center's New Age messiah called Lord Maitreya. His book was a hit; it immediately sold 50,000 copies in Christian bookstores.

It happens that in 1989 an author named Darrick Evenson published a popular Mormon book, *The Gainsayers: A Converted Anti-Mormon Responds to Critics of the LDS Church*. Evenson converted to Mormonism in 1978 and served as a Mormon missionary in California in 1983 and 1984. In March 1991 he spoke at a Mormon temple in Arizona, calling Christian evangelists fools. The next day, Troy Lawrence spoke at a Baptist church in Arizona, denouncing the New Age movement. The two men are the same man.

Troy Lawrence is the evangelical pen name of Mormon Darrick Evenson. He sometimes explains to evangelicals that he poses as a Mormon as part of his plan to undermine Mormonism in the future, and to Mormons he sometimes says he is tricking evangelicals. He has also produced a booklet and tapes promoting Masonic beliefs, and says he might also join Jehovah's Witnesses.

### Invisible Evil

Lauren Wilson and Darrick Evenson appear to be delusional

although the people who publish and promote them seem sane. In *People of the Lie,* M. Scott Peck notes that some people are abnormally deceptive and destructive, and he attempts to distinguish those who are mentally ill from those who are truly fiendish. Most mentally ill people are not evil, but all truly evil people are mentally ill as well as evil. The reason that spiritually evil people are often found in churches and other respectable institutions is not that churches breed liars; it is that churches attract liars. Many evil people go to churches for protective covering, for an aura of godliness.

Peck notices that evil people do not appear to suffer deeply. (That is noticeably true of Mark Hofmann, the Utah forger, and Dr. Dale of Indiana.) They do not admit any weakness or imperfection in themselves, and so they appear to themselves to be always on top of things and in command.

> Their appearance of competence was just that: an appearance. A pretense. Rather than being in command of themselves, it was their narcissism that was in command, always demanding, whipping them into maintaining their pretense of health and wholeness. . . . What possesses them, drives them? Basically, it is fear. They are terrified that the pretense will break down and they will be exposed to the world and to themselves. They are continually frightened that they will come face-to-face with their own evil.

In July of 1992, the Washington State Department of Health explained why it was revoking the license of Christian psychologist John G. Finch: "guilty of unethical practice of psychology; repeated acts of immorality and misconduct; acts of moral turpitude, dishonesty or corruption; incompetence, negligence, or malpractice; promotion for personal gain; abuse and sexual contact with clients; exploitation of trust and dependence of clients; sexual exploitation of clients; and failure to terminate clinical relationships with clients when it was clear the clients were not benefiting from therapy."

Some of Dr. Finch's victims complaind that their reports about him had been discounted, hushed up, and ignored. A few had filed charges against him in 1982 , and eleven new complaints were filed in 1990. In 1991 Dr. Finch paid $300,000 to a woman who charged that he had tricked her into having sexual intercourse with him for over twenty years while charging her for it as therapy. (She had met him at a Bible conference and trusted him implicitly because he was a "very important Christian.")

Dr. Finch's unusual prestige sprang from honors accorded him at Fuller Theological Seminary's School of Psychology since its founding in the early 1960s in Pasadena, California. (John Finch was a good friend of the Weyerhaeuser timber family, who donated $1 million to found the school.) The psychology building bore his name, an annual symposium bore his name, and he held a special niche as distinguished visiting professor. Psychology students occasionally journeted to Puget Sound for a couple of weeks of intensive therapy alone with Dr. Finch in an isolated cabin.

All that ended in 1992. A seminary task force interviewed over fifty people and reported a pattern of emotionally abusive and antagonistic behavior by Dr. Finch against faculty, staff, students and clients. Dr. Finch's name was expunged at Fuller Seminary. He had unsuccessfully tried to avert this comedown by announcing in an open letter to the seminary that "in the abyss" (of 1991) God had reached him in a new way, making his work much more effective. He invited everyone to register for his first "Christian Journey Inward" conference.

In that letter Dr. Finch congratulated himself that God's grace had transcended his "psychologism" and had caused the Spirit to "extentiate" his own "Christian Psychology" through the fruit of the Spirit, making him more richly equipped to do God's will. He referred to that as the purpose behind his "persecution." Grace was unusually "easy and quick" for Dr. Finch, he explained, due to "vast spiritual resources" he had accumulated over the years.

John Milton wrote about hypocrisy in *Paradise Lost*:

> *For neither man nor angel can discern*
> *Hypocrisy, the only evil that walks*
> *Invisible, except to God alone.*

There is a New Orleans Creole saying about that: "When the Devil goes to mass, he hides his tail." And the American humorist Josh Billings once remarked thoughtfully, "If the world despises a hypocrite, what must they think of one in heaven?"

No one can blame the Bible for failing to warn us about hypocrites in the church. For example, near the end of the Sermon on the Mount, Jesus warned about ferocious wolves in sheep's clothing

(Matthew 7:15–20). Dietrich Bonhoeffer wrote about the meaning of that in *The Cost of Discipleship*.

> The disciples of Jesus must not fondly imagine that they can simply run away from the world and huddle together in a little band. False prophets will rise up among them, and amid the ensuing confusion they will feel more isolated than ever. There is someone standing by my side, who looks just like a member of the Church. He is a prophet and a preacher. He looks like a Christian, he talks and acts like one. But dark powers are mysteriously at work; it was these who sent him into our midst. Inwardly he is a ravening wolf: his words are lies and his works are full of deceit.

Bonhoeffer says that there is no need to be distrustful or to go prying into the hearts of others. Jesus tells us that the bad tree will eventually bring forth bad fruit. Sooner or later we shall find out where a man stands, we shall be able to sift the good from the bad, and we will know the difference between appearance and reality.

> *Wickedness is always easier than virtue, for it takes the short cut to everything.*
>
> —Samuel Johnson

# Part IV:
# THE SLIPPERY SLOPE—
# FRAUD SQUADS IN ACTION

# CHAPTER 7
# DOING BATTLE WITH DECEPTION

*For a lie always harms another; if not some other particular man, still it harms mankind generally.*

—Immanuel Kant

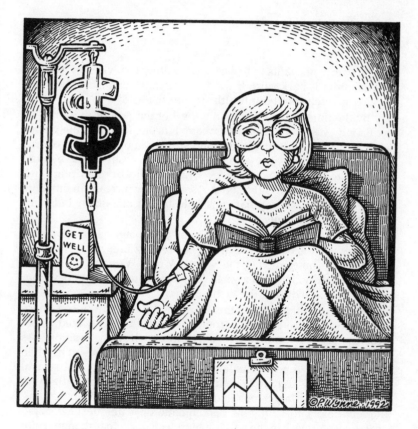

Look out, hoaxers; here come the consumer advocates and general fake-finders. Look out, innocent bystanders; some "vigilantes for virtue" are peddling paranoia. Meanwhile, most brave whistle-blowers don't get medals; they get dishonorable discharges instead.

# COUNTERING COUNTERFEITERS

*The only thing necessary for the triumph of evil is for good men to do nothing.*

—Edmund Burke

Almost everyone wants to be healthy, wealthy, and wise; but the traditional order is backward. If we were wiser, we would not be bamboozled so often about our health and our finances.

By the time of the Civil War, a third of the American money in circulation was counterfeit. Abraham Lincoln founded the Secret Service to combat counterfeiters, and since then our federal government has waged a fairly successful but very costly battle against counterfeiters of cash. Now, however, high-quality offset printing and color copiers have brought about a spectacular increase in amateur counterfeiting. (One popular trick is to bleach one-dollar bills and reprint them as $20 bills.)

The circulation of counterfeit money sabotages a country economically. That is why Hitler attempted to blitz England with counterfeit pound notes during the Second World War, and the United States reportedly dropped a small fortune in counterfeit money from the sky into Laos during the Vietnam war.

Canada, Britain, and other countries have introduced innovations to frustrate today's currency forgers; but the United States Treasury has been strangely reluctant to depart from tradition. (As composer Kurt Adler said once, "Tradition is what you resort to when you don't have time or money to do it right.") There are several ingenious proposals that would make it easier for ordinary citizens to spot forged bills: larger portraits, special colored ink combinations, different colors for different denominations, a unique new paper weave, a watermark in the paper, a high-tech patch that changes color when tilted, and (if possible) implanted holograms. Any of these innovations would discourage currency forgers by making their task more difficult.

It seems, however, that counterfeiters rise to almost any challenge. When Visa and MasterCard introduced holograms on their cards in 1985, they immediately cut their fraud losses by 60 percent. But by the time they had replaced millions of cards around the world, forgers had learned to copy their holograms. International crooks and credit-card companies are engaged in an endless contest, and the world capital of card counterfeiting is Hong Kong.

Since 1986 the identification-document counterfeiting industry has also boomed, annually producing tens of thousands of fake birth certificates, green cards, pink slips, and Social Security cards. Buyers usually get what they pay for: genuine low-price fake documents. In 1992 federal Immigration and Naturalization Service agents finally launched a crackdown on this business.

Most Americans realize that someone might be showing them forged documents or trying to slip them counterfeit money or counterfeit Rolex watches; but few realize that they might be buying counterfeit auto parts. In 1990 alone, the FBI confiscated $50 million in bogus auto parts in raids in fifteen states. Some of these parts carried the General Motors label and came in what looked like General Motors boxes. Among many other items, the FBI seized safety-glass that shatters, oil filters made out of cans stuffed with rags, and brake linings made of compressed cardboard. Needless to say, the bogus parts look genuine, and many of them are dangerous. About $3 billion worth are sold in the United States annually.

Unfortunately, there is no coordinated federal response to most kinds of fraud. Some authorities say that fully one half of investment opportunities in the United States today are counterfeit. Americans are individually bilked out of a total of $80 billion per year, not counting the trillions that Americans have lost in recent years to the big-time confidence artists who loot our nation's future. Fraud is always with us, but in the 1980s it was allowed to run rampant in our major financial institutions: the savings-and-loan industry, the insurance industry, and the banking industry.

Most people would prefer not to think about how much the crimes of the Bank of Credit and Commerce International alone have cost the world. That bank, commonly known as BCCI, is appropriately nicknamed the Bank of Crooks and Criminals International. Such fiscal horrors are enough to make an old-fashioned person want a dose of old-fashioned nerve tonic.

**231**

## Sugar Pills

Bogus medicines like nerve tonics have always been on the market. From about 1850 to 1940, medicine men like Professor Popple and Nevada Ned Oliver, with troupes of vaudeville-type entertainers such as Healy's Liver Pad Concert Company and the Big Sensation Medicine Company, criss-crossed our country dispensing ballyhoo and cure-alls such as Hamlin's Wizard Oil, King of Pain, Vigor of Life, Herbs of Joy, Hostetter's Celebrated Stomach Bitters, and Kickapoo Indian Salve—purportedly made from buffalo tallow.

These companies put on plays and other free shows, sometimes featuring stand-up comics, orchestras, singers, dancers, magicians, strong men, fire-eaters, and ventriloquists. Fraudulent Indian medicine shows became the most popular of all because Americans longed (then as now) for natural herbal medications from cultures wiser than our own. Obliging entrepreneurs provided an array of concoctions, ranging from helpful to harmful; those that worked best were the cough syrups, liniments, and laxatives.

Princess Lotus Blossom was originally a Midwestern farm girl named Violet McNeal, but she became the Queen of Medicine Shows by posing as a Chinese maiden. She sold Tiger Fat (the Orient's most miraculous medicine), and Vital Sparks for men (which could restore virility to eunuchs). In reality, she made Vital Sparks by slightly moistening little black candies called buckshot and rolling them in bitter aloe powder, then pouring them into boxes. She priced Vital Sparks at $5 per box, but she gave a box free to anyone who bought a small tin of Tiger Fat for one dollar.

She made the Tiger Fat by melting petroleum jelly in a bucket, then stirring in a bit of camphor, menthol, eucalyptus, turpentine, wintergreen, and paraffin. Each tin of Tiger Fat cost her about seven cents, sold for a dollar, and purportedly cured everything from ringworm to rheumatism. (In our day a major cosmetic company has been selling jars of pink-tinted petroleum jelly under a fancy name for about ten dollars; few purchasers seem to notice that they have bought inexpensive, old-fashioned petroleum jelly.)

When Lotus Blossom lost her youth, she called herself Madame V. Pasteur and sold V. Pasteur's Herbs. She mixed an array of ordinary wholesale herbal powders in her hotel bathtub, then packaged them. During her act she would call an onlooker forward and check him for nasal inflammation by having him blow through a glass tube into a clear container of water. She explained that an inflammation would turn the water cloudy. (In fact, the water turned cloudy because it was really lime water, and carbon dioxide makes lime water cloudy.) Then she poured a solution of her herbs into the cloudy water, and it was instantly clear. (What she really poured in was vinegar, and vinegar clears limewater.) People who wanted their bodies to be quickly cleared of inflammation eagerly bought V. Pasteur's Herbs at a dollar a box. Violet McNeal told the story of her medicine show career in her 1947 biography *Four White Horses and a Brass Band.*

Brother Jonathan always came into town as an elegant gentleman with a gold-headed ebony cane, first befriending the mayor, praising local doctors, and buying things from merchants. He quoted the Bible and Shakespeare, and mentioned his alleged friendships with President Grover Cleveland and other celebrities. In his lectures he explained, "I come to you as one who bears the Balm of Gilead out of Judea. . . . My medicine encircles the world. . . . Children cry for it. . . . The Giver of Life!" In fact, his Balm of Gilead was mainly water, Epsom Salts, and powdered rhubarb; but he put on a magnificent show.

## Bitter Medicine

Although many medicine men were more or less ethical, others were blatant crooks. Worse yet, in the days before aspirin and vitamins, the main ingredient in many medicines was opium, alcohol, or cocaine. So it was that early in this century reformers rightly set out to remedy the situation; in 1907 the Pure Food and Drug Act went into effect. As the authority of the Food and Drug Administration increased, most Americans assumed that their medications were safe and pure. But the gap of almost 2,000 percent between the cost of a legitimate antibiotic and its counterfeit has caused a new epidemic: counterfeit pharmaceuticals.

According to a 1990 exposé in *Newsweek,* between 1981 and 1984 over a million bogus birth-control pills were smuggled into the United States through Panama. In 1987 an American pharmacist named Javid Naghdi spent $21,185 producing 1,201 bottles of Naprosyn, which he unloaded into the medicine market for $192,680 by claiming that he was overstocked. The pills looked perfect, and they went to dealers and drugstores from Texas to Washington; but they were mainly aspirin. Fortunately, a California pharmacist noticed that they smelled wrong, and Naghdi was caught. He jumped bail, fled to London, and continued his scam. He was caught there offering to sell nine million bottles of fake Tagamet, Naprosyn, and Anspor. He is reportedly considered the most dangerous prescription-drug counterfeiter known to the FDA, and he presently resides in the penitentiary in Atlanta.

Forged drugs look like the real thing and come in the right packaging; some are chemically correct, some are half-strength, and others are totally phony. In Europe, patients have received millions of doses of counterfeit heart medication, many of them half-strength. In Nigeria it is estimated that more than a quarter of pharmacy drugs are fake; one batch of antibiotic capsules contained nothing but perfumed talcum powder. In 1988 in Mexico 15,000 name-brand burn remedies were contaminated with sawdust, coffee, and dirt.

The sprawling pharmaceutical business is all too easily penetrated by criminals. In one case the raw ingredients of fake Zantax probably came from Turkey; the tablets were pressed and packaged in Greece; they were brokered by a pharmaceutical firm in Switzerland; and they were distributed by a firm in Amsterdam. Although drug counterfeiters pop up everywhere, Italy is the source of a large percentage of the fake drugs that plague poor countries. Multinational drug companies reportedly spend millions battling the pirates; but when they are successful they settle cases out of court and have the records sealed because they don't want the public to know about the problem. They assure inquirers that the problem is minimal, but the World Health Organization's director of drug management says the situation is completely out of hand.

As if fake medicines are not bad enough, according to the article "Pretenders" by Edward Dolnick (*Health*, July/August 1992), in 1986 the U.S. House of Representatives subcommittee on health and long-term care estimated that one in fifty American doctors are unlicensed and only posing as physicians.

Even when doctors and drugs are genuine, the circumstances of drug testing and approval by the FDA can be frightening when they come to light. For example, over half the insomniacs in the largest study behind the 1982 approval of Halcion were enrolled, treated, and examined by Dr. William C. Franklin of Houston—a known fabricator of medical studies. The Upjohn Company underreported Halcion's side effects such as paranoia and memory loss, and also assured the FDA that the notorious Dr. Franklin's role in their testing was negligible; in 1992 *Newsweek* finally uncovered the truth about Franklin's significant role. By then some Upjohn stockholders were suing the company for misrepresentation, four countries had banned Halcion, and three others had lowered the approved dosage. Perhaps some insomniacs would have been better off taking forged Halcion made out of aspirin instead of the real thing.

## Blood Money

Just as medicines are a valuable international commodity handled by brokerage firms, so the buying and selling of blood in the United States has become a multibillion-dollar industry that operates out of sight, with almost no government regulation. In 1989 the *Philadelphia Inquirer* published an investigation that revealed how the public is hoodwinked into thinking that donated blood goes to local people at the lowest possible cost. In fact, donated blood is apt to change hands repeatedly and sell for what the market will bear.

As a case in point, in 1988 the residents of Appleton, Wisconsin, were falsely warned that their local blood bank was dangerously low, and they responded generously. In reality, half the blood collected in Appleton was already slated to be sold at profit to a blood bank in Lexington, Kentucky. Lexington raised the price and sold half the blood from Appleton to a blood bank in Fort Lauderdale, Florida. Fort Lauderdale sold all this blood at a higher price yet to four hospitals in New York City. The Appleton blood had made a 2,777 mile journey on speculation and was finally sold for $120 a pint to hospital patients in Manhattan. (Prices vary widely; sometimes a unit of donated blood costs a patient $300.)

Most Western nations have a system that guarantees a safe, adequate supply of blood to every part of the country at fair prices, but in the United States blood can be traded for profit like stocks. Every year, blood banks shift blood unnecessarily all over the country, increasing the cost, expanding profits by $50 million, and weakening safety controls in the process. America's "non-profit" blood banks reportedly generate at least $1 billion a year in revenue; some of their officers earn extremely high salaries, supplemented by expensive company cars and other benefits. (In 1992, public outrage about similar extravagance in the United Way charity forced its high-flying national director to resign.) Aaron Kellner, retired president of the New York Blood Center, admitted about the blood business, "People are being fooled now. They don't know. It's unethical."

As early as 1975, the distinguished authors Robert and Suzanne Massie published *Journey*, warning the public about the heartless and haphazard blood industry that they had coped with for eighteen years while they battled to keep their hemophiliac son alive. The book was a spellbinder, but it seemed to sink without a ripple. Fourteen years later, the ambitious *Philadelphia Inquirer* exposé seemed to sink quietly also. The ear of the general public is far more alert to juicy gossip than to serious calls for reform. Ralph Nader, the nation's most famous whistle-blower, gets more respect than attention.

In 1990 a congressional report charged that there is scientific misconduct at some of the universities that receive Public Health Service funds. The scientists who receive federal grants can have a financial interest in the drug they are testing. In one case, at least thirteen of the researchers paid to test a heart drug owned stock or stock options in the company that made the drug. According to the report, the National Institutes of Health ignores conflicts of interest of the scientists who received federal grants, and universities retaliate against whistle-blowers in their midst.

## Chronic Fiction Infection

Deceptions about health, illness, reproduction, and aging are as pervasive as the common cold and sometimes as relentless as cancer.

On Valentine's Day in 1986 the *Stamford Advocate* published an article about a study supposedly showing that mature single women have practically no chance of getting married because of a shortage of bachelors. *Newsweek* featured the story on its cover and stated that after a certain age women are more likely to be killed by a terrorist than to get married. Sociologists saw that the statistics were wrong, but their protests were generally ignored; the scary marriage-study hoax was repeated for years in books and magazines.

In 1986 another odd thing happened. Dr. Charles Bluestone of the University of Pittsburgh submitted an article to the *New England Journal of Medicine* reporting that amoxacillin was effective for the middle-ear infections that are extremely common to children. A month later, Dr. Erdem Cantekin submitted an article; his analysis of the same federally funded research showed that amoxicillin did not work for middle-ear infections. The *New England Journal of Medicine* published Bluestone's study and suppressed Cantekin's; for trying to speak up, whistle-blower Cantekin was fired from his job. In 1991 Cantekin's five-year-old charge finally became news, along with the fact that Bluestone had received $260,000 in honorariums from interested drug companies, and his research center had received $3.5 million in grants from those companies. In the meantime, for good or ill, amoxicillin has been used on hundreds of thousands of children by doctors who believed that its efficacy for ear infections is unchallenged.

Medical fictions range from potentially tragic to grimly comic. In 1991 a patient named Stuart Nisbet complained in the *Los Angeles Times* that he had been in a Burbank hospital from 9:00 A.M. to 5:00 P.M. one day for minor surgery, and had received one dry turkey sandwich with a small carton of orange juice for lunch. When he examined his itemized hospital bill later, he saw that the "food service" had cost $299. He naïvely told his surgeon about this overcharge, and the surgeon laughed. Itemized hospital bills are a standing joke, because they are routinely used for "shifting costs," a form of "creative bookkeeping." That is now standard operating procedure in more ways than one.

What may be the world's most bizarre medical fraud came to light at the same time as the Bluestone affair and the $299 turkey sandwich. Dr. Cecil B. Jacobson, once a geneticist at George Washington University in Virginia, was guilty of tricking patients at his fertility clinic. He falsely convinced some women that they were pregnant and had miscarriages; worse yet, he impregnated at least eleven women (possibly up to seventy-five) with his own sperm instead of using a carefully controlled donor program as he claimed.

In February 1992, just when Dr. Jacobson went to court, *Health* magazine reprinted a different kind of miscarriage story. Wilma Dole of Fort Lauderdale, Florida, wrote to the *New York Times* from her hospital bed; she had used the newspaper's recipe for chicken, which called for one-fourth cup (rather than one-fourth teaspoon) of freshly ground pepper. Mrs. Dole, who was seven months pregnant at the time, started to eat the chicken with her husband and his new boss.

The chicken was so hot that all three rushed toward the water faucet, the table tipped over, the boss accidentally knocked Mrs. Dole unconscious, and in the confusion Mr. Dole assaulted him. Mrs. Dole was hurt and had a miscarriage; Mr. Dole lost his job and went to jail. Mrs. Dole said, "I am writing you to say that I think the recipe is too hot."

The distraught *New York Times* recipe writer may have feared a lawsuit. She called directory assistance, the fire department, and two hospitals, in vain; none of them had heard of Wilma Dole. Then she called the police, who informed her that William Doyle, a writer, publisher, and well-known practical joker, resided at Wilma's return address. When she called him, he admitted, "I'm Wilma." He hadn't been gullible enough to believe her recipe, but she had been gullible enough to believe his tall tale about the recipe.

Another prenatal catastrophe appeared in print at the same time, in the February 1992 issue of *Campus Life* magazine. In an autobiographical article titled "Someone to Love Me," author Anne Williman told about her college boyfriend, Judd, who had physical defects. His left hand had a thumb but no fingers, and his left arm was scarred by a long birthmark. On his right hand two fingers ended at the first joint, and his right leg was missing. These defects had all been caused by the umbilical cord being wrapped around him in several places before he was born. Anne, a strict, conservative Christian with a fatal disease, loved Judd in spite of his drinking, lying, breaking the college rules, and ruining her academic record. Judd had even smuggled drugs into the United States from Canada. Anne eventually broke off the romance because Judd did not seem deeply in love with her.

As far-fetched as this entire account seems, one part is clearly impossible: no baby can lose fingers and a leg because of a tangled umbilical cord. When asked about this medical mumbo-jumbo, a *Campus Life* editor explained that the story was purchased a few years earlier by a past editor who believed it. If the present staff had thought it was fiction, they would have marked it fiction so their readers wouldn't be misled. Furthermore, *Campus Life* editors try to make sure that even their fiction is accurate and dependable; but none of the magazine's bright, talented workers had noticed that the "true story" was biologically impossible. The editor's response to a reader who called in about it was "Thanks for being a watchdog!"

# MISCONSTRUING THE SIMPLE TRUTH

*Everything should be made as simple as possible, but not simpler.*

—Albert Einstein

As C. S. Lewis pointed out, watchdogs tend to wag their tails at familiar people who have done them no kindness, and they tend to bark at strangers who have done them no harm. So it is that human watchdogs sometimes sleep through deception and raise a ruckus over utter innocence.

For example, watchdogs decided that the brilliant Scottish explorer James Bruce, Lord of Kinnaird (1731–94), had to be lying about his years of exploration in Ethiopia. His richly detailed five-volume masterpiece, *Travels to Discover the Source of the Nile,* was an instant best-seller; but it soon turned him into a laughing-stock because to the educated it seemed too far-fetched. He portrayed himself as too brave, Ethiopia as too harsh, and Ethiopians as too barbaric. (Noble savages and primitive paradise were in fashion then.) After Bruce's death, others ventured to Ethiopia and found to their surprise that all his claims rang true, and there were witnesses in Ethiopia who remembered him well. As a television character used to say when her indignation suddenly evaporated, "Never mind. . . ."

In 1897 a Jewish man named Moses Shapira, who had converted to Christianity and changed his name to William Benedict, offered to sell the Berlin Museum fifteen strips of parchment scrolls that a bedouin had found in a cave on the eastern shore of the Dead Sea. The scrolls included a ninth-century B.C. version of the entire book of Deuteronomy. When the Berlin Museum declined, Shapira offered the scrolls to the British Museum for £1 million. Two strips of the scrolls were put on display there, and the *London Times* explained their importance; but a French archaeologist convinced museum scholars that the strips were a fraud. Shapira took his scrolls away to Rotterdam and committed suicide, and no one ever saw the scrolls again. In the light of the Qumran Dead Sea Scrolls which surfaced about fifty years later, some modern scholars think that perhaps Shapira's scrolls were genuine after all.

Healthy skepticism is a virtue, but negativism is not. Those who enjoy attacking medical quackery are sometimes the greatest quacks of all: petty tyrants who persecute good doctors or outlaw helpful remedies. History is full of examples. For example, citrus fruit, which had long saved British sailors (nicknamed "limeys" because of the limes they ate) from scurvy, was banned from ships by British authorities who scorned the custom; thanks to the removal of their folk remedy, thousands of sailors became severely ill, and some died of scurvy before citrus fruit was used on board again.

A similar story has been taking place in the United States today. Tens of thousands who suffer extreme nausea from cancer chemotherapy, extreme weight loss from AIDS, extreme spasticity from multiple sclerosis, and extreme loss of vision from glaucoma, are denied the one medicine of last resort that can help them: marijuana (leaves and flowers of the hemp plant). According to my pharmacist, it was a legitimate medicine until 1937; then it was outlawed. I am such an anti-smoking fanatic that I think tobacco should be outlawed, and I am appalled by our nation's addiction to alcohol and illegal drugs; but I think that prescription marijuana should be available again to those who critically need it. In 1988 a Drug Enforcement Administration judge named Francis Young declared marijuana to be "one of the safest therapeutic substances known to man." It would be "unreasoning, arbitrary and capricious for DEA to continue to stand between those sufferers and the benefit of this substance." Countless doctors and patients agree, and even the Food and Drug Administration agrees. In 1992 the White House Office of Drug Control Policy accused the Public Health Service chief of an "intolerable lack of compassion" if he continues to withhold this medicine from federally approved patients.

Nevertheless, the Public Health Service refused to budge or to say why. (It told sufferers to take costly and ineffective THS pills instead, which is like Marie Antionette saying of people who were starving, "let them eat cake." There is a rumor that the timber industry is behind this ban because of the fact that hemp is a hardy inexpensive crop and produces better paper than wood pulp.) Even studies that could analyze the effectiveness of marijuana are blocked

240

by the fact that it is listed as a Schedule I drug like LSD and heroin; in contrast, cocaine is listed as a less dangerous Schedule II drug and is prescribed by doctors. Unfortunately, cocaine can't help victims of advanced cancer, AIDS, multiple sclerosis, and glaucoma.

In a similar way, countless twentieth-century incest victims have been denied comfort and help because Sigmund Freud abruptly decided to deny the truth of incest. According to Freud, incest victims dream up their traumas for neurotic reasons; but it now seems that he dreamed up that theory for professional advancement. Mislabeling clients, like mislabeling products, is a shortcut to success.

Therapeutic failure is the main product of highly touted treatments for homosexuality. In spite of bright promises and high hopes, it is increasingly evident that psychotherapy is unable to transform anyone's strong homosexual orientation into a heterosexual orientation. Furthermore, according to Evangelicals Concerned, high-profile ex-gay ministries are often led by people who do not prove to be ex-gay in the long run after all, and a few prominent ex-gay counselors are known to have compromised the very clients who came to them for reorientation.

In a world of human frailty, professional jealousy, bad judgment, and hidden agendas, who will protect us from our protectors? In Johnstown, East Texas, in 1992 a health worker announced falsely that 6 of the high school's 197 students had tested HIV positive. Now we not only need people to warn about AIDS; we also need people to warn about people who warn about AIDS. Which authorities can we trust? A century ago, Scottish physicist Lord Kelvin (1824–1907), president of the Royal Society of London, warned that the x-ray was a hoax. Sometimes the world seems overrun with debunkers run amok.

## Wild-eyed Warnings

Through human history, exciting rumors about deceptions tend to turn into witch hunts and purges; the world is full of demagogues disguised as reformers, sowing discord in the name of correction. Many would-be leaders in both secular politics and religious politics seize success by adding fiction to fact to create their own faction. Sensationalism seems to sell almost anything, as Hitler knew well. Shocking news travels fast, and it also tends to stick fast.

Fashions in fear change like fashions in clothes. By 1945 someone concocted the rumor that the Japanese named one of their towns USA so they could legally sell products marked "made in USA." (That rumor was at work again forty years later.) By 1955 the ogre was the Soviet Union rather than Japan; many people came to believe the rumor that President Eisenhower was a card-carrying Communist.

It was during this great Communist scare that a few members of Santa Ana Community Church decided that the word *community* had been foisted on them as part of the Russian plot to take over the United States from within. About thirty years later, Christian fundamentalists in the same area decided that Westin South Coast Plaza Hotel at 686 (close to 666) Anton Street, Costa Mesa, was a shrine for followers of Satanist Anton Levay. As real as the dangers of Communism used to be, and as real as the dangers of Satanism still are, both threats inspire a great deal of foolishness and outright fraud.

One of the most popular rumors about Satanism is the idea that Proctor and Gamble's logo, thirteen stars between the horns of a crescent moon, is a Satanic symbol. (That rumor was allegedly fanned by a couple who sold competing Amway products.) Authors turn out books warning that everything from rainbows to the study of personality types are a cover for the occult. Dire warnings usually sell; and the more sinister they are, the better they sell.

Ever since 1974, when a couple of men filed an unsuccessful petition against education channels being used for religion, people have believed words falsely attributed to atheist Madalyn Murray O'Hair: "If this petition is successful, we can stop all religious broadcasting in America." In spite of the fact that O'Hair wasn't involved and the petition had failed, by 1983 the FCC received almost sixteen million pieces of mail protesting "the O'Hair petition." Millions of dollars and untold time and energy have been squandered on this quixotic campaign to save religious broadcasting. Such conspicuous waste must inspire ambitious souls to try to harness this kind of naïve public fervor for practical purposes.

"There is a Trojan horse inside the evangelical camp. A new battle has broken out, and the enemy is on the inside, not the outside. In fact, the enemy has secretly placed dynamite at the evangelical foundation which supports the whole superstructure of Christian truth." This was the opening salvo of *The Battle for the Resurrection* by Norman L. Geisler of Liberty University. What was the dangerous deception this time? An extremely slight difference of opinion among conservative Christians concerning the manner in which the human body is transformed in the resurrection.

## Thunderbolts

Non-Christians cash in on sensationalism also. In 1992 a new book titled *The Dead Sea Scrolls Deception* promised book buyers that the scrolls would "demolish the entire edifice of Christian teaching and belief," but a wicked deception has been at work. The "real" reason the scrolls were kept away from scholars for forty years after their discovery, the author was a secret Roman Catholic plot to delay the inevitable collapse of Christianity. According to this theory, the scrolls will prove Christianity false, and the sooner the better.

Meanwhile, the sober *Financial Times* of London trumpeted in 1991, "a mysterious scrap of papyrus published in an obscure American journal may transform our knowledge of early Christianity." The distinguished scholar and writer Dr. Robin Lane Fox began breathlessly, "A thunderbolt may be about to strike early Christian history. We have a new candidate for the title of the earliest surviving text of sayings ascribed to Jesus, including one never before recorded. It was written, perhaps, between 100 and 125, in a language which historians had not expected, and its reappearance is a mystery which stretches from Oxford to America." He concluded that if the document is genuine, it is further evidence that the Gospels do not contain the real words of Jesus.

Those who analyze the Robin Fox article find to their surprise that no one has seen any more than a mere photocopy of a hand-drawn sketch of the ancient papyrus document; and no one has seen the journal in which the sketch was allegedly published. The photocopy was sent to scholars at Oxford by someone whose Montana return address proved false, and who gave his name as Battson D. Sealing—"bats on the ceiling." (This was not an April Fool article.) Although there is no Battson D. Sealing, there is a real, respected Robin Lane Fox; and he may or may not be very gullible. Literary prankster A. N. Wilson twitted Fox about all this in the *Spectator*, but chose to leave what is probably someone's private joke a public mystery.

Robin Lane Fox is an atheist at Oxford. In contrast, Charles Dodgson (better known as Lewis Carroll) was a Christian at Oxford. In 1865 he published *Alice's Adventures in Wonderland*. But in 1983 a mysterious committee of twelve anonymous Americans calling themselves the "Continental Historical Society" launched what they call "the greatest literary controversy of all time," claiming that Carroll was a hoaxer and Queen Victoria was the true author. In their brief book, *Queen Victoria's Alice in Wonderland*, Lewis Carroll is revealed to be the Knave (bogus author) who stole the tarts (Victoria's writing) in *Alice in Wonderland* (the first of Victoria's two tarts). The Red Queen stands for Christ. Furthermore, the White Queen's fat curls in John Tenniel's illustrations were planned to look like *carrots* made of *hair*, in order to show that Victoria was the *heir* to *karats* (diamonds). Victoria's secret adultery with the King of France, which produced a secret love-child, will be revealed in the yet-unpublished sequel, *Queen Victoria's Through the Looking Glass*, according to the Society.

Lewis Carroll experts calmly pooh-pooh all this as mock-scholarship, and there is a rumor in academia that it is a spoof by a past editor of the prestigious literary journal *Kenyon Review*. Nevertheless, *Queen Victoria's Alice* is soberly listed in reference guides and has been featured in the *Washington Post* and the *Los Angeles Times*. Its cover is graced by a glowing commendation from the chairman of the Humanities faculty at Sarah Lawrence College. The book's San Francisco promoter touts it as a college literature textbook, and the English departments of two Texas colleges have actually made it required reading, according to the Society.

As if dynamite from a Trojan horse, an impending thunderbolt from a scrap of papyrus, and the greatest literary controversy of all time were not enough, Christianity's favorite twentieth-century author is said to be a witch. John Todd, a convert from occultism to Christianity, excited his followers in the 1970s by exposing C. S. Lewis's dark secret; Lewis was a warlock. Although Todd turned out to be a fake convert, his claim about Lewis survived. According to the *Times Educational Supplement* in London, at the end of 1991 a Canadian professor of education named David Booth was forced to serve as a defense witness in a California court case against a school district that used *Impressions*, the reading anthology he had edited. Parents who were allegedly spurred on by Christian Educators Association International, Citizens for Excellence in Education, Traditional Values

Coalition, and Focus on the Family, charged that selections in Booth's anthology such as C. S. Lewis's Christian classic *The Lion, the Witch and the Wardrobe* were teaching religion: specifically, Wicken (witchcraft) or Satanism.

David Booth in turn warned British readers and radio listeners that Americans have never before heard of using literature to teach reading (he has not heard of *McGuffey's Readers*, evidently), and that American fundamentalists don't believe in reading any fiction. Some people enjoy being alarmed about brainy British authors, and others enjoy being alarmed about brainless American fundamentalists.

(Fundamentalists are not the only ones to spread wild warnings about good books. Some black activists have tried to get Mark Twain's *Huckleberry Finn* removed from schools because they think it has white racism hidden within it. In reality, of course, Huckleberry Finn is a powerful attack upon white racism, just as *The Lion, the Witch and the Wardrobe* is a powerful attack upon Satanism.)

## Inside Dope

Although occultists and fundamentalists may be the most fashionable people to fear in contemporary society, there are always Jews and Roman Catholics. The oath of the Knights of Columbus is frightening. As early as 1913 a special committee of Congress announced that it was a fake, but it was still being circulated when John F. Kennedy made his bid for the presidency in 1960. It says,

> I do promise and declare that I will, when opportunity presents, make and wage relentless war, secretly and openly, against all heretics, Protestants and Masons, as I am directed to do, to extirpate them from the face of the whole earth; and that I will spare neither age, sex, nor condition, and that I will hang, burn, waste, boil, flay, strangle, and bury alive those infamous heretics; rip up the stomachs and wombs of their women, and crush their infants' heads against the walls in order to annihilate their execrable race. . . .

Since 1934, people who like to stir up fear of Roman Catholics and Jews have been quoting Benjamin Franklin. That is when the "Benjamin Franklin Prophecy" first appeared in William Dudley

Pelley's pro-Nazi sheet *Liberation* in North Carolina. Pelley said he found the following passages from Franklin in the Constitutional Convention diary of Charles Cotesworth Pinckney (but there is no such document).

> In whatever country Jews have settled in any great numbers, they have lowered the moral tone, depreciated the commercial integrity, have segregated themselves, and have not been assimilated, have sneered at and tried to undermine the Christian religion, have built up a state within a state, and have, when opposed, tried to strangle that country to death financially. If you do not exclude them from the United States, in the constitution, in less than 200 years they will dominate and devour the land and change our form of government.
>
> I fully agree with Gen. Washington that we must safeguard this young nation, as yet in its swaddling clothes, from the insidious influence and impenetration of the Roman Catholic Church which pauperizes and degrades all countries and people over whom it holds sway.

George Washington's warning about Jews is also oft-quoted:

> They work more effectively against us than the enemy's armies. They are a hundred times more dangerous to our liberties and the great cause we are engaged in. It is much to be lamented that each state, long ago has not hunted them down as pests to society and the greatest enemies we have to the happiness of America—the Jews.

In reality, this is an altered and edited version of Washington's words about speculators in currency, *not* words about Jews.

"Lincoln's Warning" still passes as a message from Abraham Lincoln, but it didn't exist until a bitter ex-priest published it in his 1886 book *Fifty Years in the Church of Rome*. Lincoln is falsely quoted as saying,

> I do not pretend to be a prophet. But though not a prophet, I see a very dark cloud on our horizon. And that dark cloud is coming from Rome. It is filled with tears of blood. It will rise and increase, till its flank will be torn by a

flash of lightning, followed by a fearful peal of thunder. Then a cyclone such as the world has never seen, will pass over this country, spreading ruin and desolation from north to south. After it is over, there will be long days of peace and prosperity: for Popery with its Jesuits and merciless Inquisition, will have been forever swept away from our country. Neither I nor you, but our children, will see these things.

The most successful alarmist forgery of all is probably *The Protocols of the Learned Elders of Zion,* which claims to report an 1887 meeting of Jewish leaders and Freemasons who were planning to undermine Christianity and rule the world. It first appeared in Russia in 1905, gradually attracting attention. (Henry Ford believed in it at one time.) *Protocols* says things like, "The goyim are a flock of sheep, and we are their wolves. And you know what happens when the wolves get hold of the flock?" In 1921 the *London Times* exposed the work as a forgery created by a Russian attorney named Sergis Nilus, and that spoiled its reputation among informed people but did not end its usefulness. Hitler made use of it, and it is reportedly used today in some countries of the Middle East. Gullible readers still think that they are getting special inside information from behind the scenes.

People who believe in *Protocols* are apt to also believe that the Holocaust never happened, that it was an elaborate hoax. Thus a small but ardent band of whistle-blowers is forever trying to set the record straight about the "Holocaust hoax," and outraged witnesses to the Holocaust are forever trying to set the record straight about the no-Holocaust hoaxers.

Disinformation tricks and false warnings are nothing new; these everlasting forms of manipulative deception make up a large part of human culture, starting with events in ancient folktales and ending with events in the latest political campaign.

# COURTING DISILLUSIONMENT

*I am strongly in favor of common sense, common honesty, and common decency. This makes me forever ineligible for any public office.*

—H. L. Mencken

In the clamor of soundbites, fake information, and false alarms that make up much of public discourse today, most individual tellers of hard truths don't get heard. When they blow whistles, no one listens. Timidity, credulity, or indifference cause the press to ignore most cases of fraud and deception, especially if the story is complicated; and the religious press seems dedicated to keeping things as placid as possible. Investigative journalism is a rare and beautiful thing in our day, and it seems to get more rare and beautiful all the time.

Because watchdogs for the public interest often end up serving as lapdogs for those in power instead, it is frustrating for ordinary citizens to try to work within the system. Sometimes the main function of review boards seems to be burying complaints.

Months after an abused client of a "Christian" psychologist in Pasadena submitted a detailed fraud report to the California Medical Board in 1984, the board replied that it would not investigate because the psychologist had denied the accusations by telephone. Like a cult leader, this psychologist lied about her credentials, her career, her fees, and the services she would render. She pretended to be a medical authority, gave dangerously wrong advice about chronic diseases, prescribed bourbon for stress, made nightmarish psychiatric diagnoses of normal people, and lied about clients to their families and friends. She pressured various female clients to become her employees or to live in her stately home, and sometimes took openly sadistic pleasure in other people's suffering. Her wealth and self-promotion attracted a constant stream of new clients, and distraught ex-clients could find no way to warn others.

In Tustin, California, a multi-millionaire gynecologist sexually molested and abused women for thirty years; but when he was reported, he simply denied the accusations (like the Pasadena psychologist) and continued. At the end of 1991, the Medical Board finally initiated proceedings against him for five of his alleged misdeeds; and when a newspaper happened to report that fact, over 160 victims came forth with horror stories from the past. Embarrassed by the outcry, the board rushed to shut down his practice. After that, the Department of Consumer Affairs tried in vain to force improvements upon the lax and allegedly dishonest board; and in October 1992 the governor finally forced its executive director to resign in disgrace.

In the meantime, I learned to my horror that the notorious Tustin doctor was the same one who had been taking a friend of mine out to fancy restaurants a couple of years earlier. He wanted to marry her, but she declined. Then he gave her a free injection of her usual migraine-headache medication, and she almost died. (She had been getting these from her own doctor for years with no bad reactions.) Whatever the dangerous injectin was, she feels lucky to be alive, no thanks to the Medical Board.

Like public agencies, our creaking courts often have an Alice-in-Wonderland quality. Courts tend to rely upon plea-bargain fantasies that bear as much relation to reality as our whimsical hospital bills; and even when there is no plea-bargaining, outcomes are sometimes bizarre. At the 1989 sentencing of the first two executives caught by Operation Ill Wind, a federal investigation of Pentagon procurement fraud, U.S. District Judge Richard Williams of Virginia expressed disgust that such fraud is allowed. He could have sentenced the men to forty years and twenty years in prison; but instead he sentenced them to six months and three months in a halfway house.

For Orange County fraud prosecutor Joe D'Agostino, his most disappointing case was that of former Costa Mesa attorney James Pichette. It all started in 1987, when Pichette was first arrested for stealing from a client. He was released on bail, and in the next two years he was arrested twice more for similar offenses. In 1990 Pichette pleaded guilty to seventeen counts of theft and faced up to ten years in prison; but the judge put him on probation and delayed sentencing over a year to enable Pichette to pay his debts.

249

Pichette didn't pay his debts, so the judge sent him to jail for a year at the beginning of 1992; but the jail was overcrowded, and probation officers sent Pichette home with an electronic bracelet that would make him easy to find. Thus he held a job in a mortgage brokerage firm and went on living with his family in an upscale house with a pool and Jacuzzi, a fact which made his fraud victims furious. His elderly landlord was furious also, because month after month the Pichettes never paid their $2,300 rent, and the landlord had to launch a court battle to try to evict them. He claimed that when he came to repair the pool, the Pichette family lounged nearby and watched him. This was five years after Pichette's first arrest for fraud.

One of the saddest facts about our judicial system is its phenomenal slowness and inefficiency. Some people lose their cases simply because they die before they get their day in court. In any case, justice delayed is justice denied.

There is a new phenomenon in modern legal suits; both sides usually hire from one to several "expert witnesses" to give related evidence. These experts generally earn from $600 to $5,000 per day, and although most of them do this in their spare time, thousands have made a full-time profession of it. There are over eight thousand subjects in the Forensic Services Directory, with a list of experts for each of them. Obviously, forensic experts cannot all be as expert in their fields and as unbiased as they are supposed to be, or they would not so frequently contradict each other.

The first of many cases that have hinged upon the testimony of handwriting experts was the so-called "Trial of the Century," in which a handwriting expert suddenly reversed himself about who wrote the ransom note in the kidnapping of twenty-month-old Charles A. Lindbergh, Jr., in 1932. That trial has recently come to look more and more like a fraud; careful assessment of the evidence seems to indicate that the real baby-killer had fled to Germany with the money, and an innocent man, Richard Hauptmann, was executed in his place. What few people realize is that professional handwriting experts have no credentials, no screening, no standards of competence, and a very poor track record for accuracy. Although some of them may be brilliant, anyone can call himself a handwriting expert—and it seems that anyone does.

These are the kinds of things that people are up against when they seek justice in court, and honest lawyers say so in advance.

DOING BATTLE WITH DECEPTION

## Integrity International

Much of the Bible is a hoarse shout about injustice, and injustice is the reward of most whistle-blowers who try to expose fraud. They often lose their careers, reputations, homes, friends, and health. "I was so naïve that I thought the system worked," one of them said. "That if you reported something to your superior, it would be taken care of. Not only was it not taken care of, but I was taken care of." That is because the common institutional reaction to "people who act out of conscience" is not gratitude, but fury.

In her book *Thomas Chatterton*, Louise J. Kaplan sums up the situation: "As usually happens in the unravelling of an imposturous deed, the one who blows the whistle becomes the villain and somehow begins to look like a paranoid maniac, an envious libeler, a cruel and insensitive betrayer."

At congressional hearings in 1989, the National Academy of Science reported that accusers often suffer ostracism and career damage even if their complaints are judged valid and helpful. The associate dean for academic affairs at the University of San Diego testified, "The customary response [to academic fraud] has been to cover up or ignore misconduct. . . ." Paul Scatena, a professor at City University of New York, added, "The superior will almost always win over the lower person. Graduate students are very, very vulnerable. This is a generalization, but it's about as true as it gets: you cannot do this type of thing in your own institution and survive. If you do have a career left afterwards, it will be elsewhere. It's going to be hell."

Donald Soeken is a clinical psychologist at St. Elizabeth's Hospital in Washington, D.C., and his wife is a statistician for the University of Maryland. They made a survey of 233 whistle-blowers and found that the average person in their study was a religious family man in his forties, with a strong conscience and high moral values. After blowing the whistle on fraud, ninety percent of them were fired or demoted, twenty-six percent had to seek psychiatric or physical care, fifteen percent suffered divorce, ten percent attempted suicide, and eight percent went bankrupt. In spite of all this, only sixteen percent said that they would not blow the whistle again.

Dr. Soeken strongly warns people everywhere to put self-protection first and to blow the whistle anonymously, but his personal ministry in life is to help wounded whistle-blowers recover from their traumas. He has named a large farmhouse in West Virginia the Whistle Stop, a retreat center where he helps "people who act out of conscience" to regain their self-esteem by showing them that they are not alone and not crazy. He sometimes testifies in court for them. He has started an assistance group called Integrity International.

## Paying the Price

In 1979, Professor Robert Sprague of the University of Illinois hired a young psychologist named Stephen Breuning to do research on a grant from the National Institutes of Mental Health. Breuning was paid a total of $11,352 to determine the side effects of some tranquilizers used on violent retarded children, by examining forty-five patients every six months for two years. At the end of the study, Breuning turned in dramatic statistics; but Dr. Sprague noticed that Breuning had not been in the area during that period and had left no assistants to do the examinations.

Sprague notified the NIMH in a six-page letter, and Breuning discreetly resigned; but there was no admission in medical journals that Breuning's published statistics were fabricated. Sprague kept pressuring the NIMH until in 1987 it announced the fraud publicly, and in 1988 Breuning pled guilty in court. He had to repay the money he had taken under false pretenses, and the University of Pittsburgh had to repay the $163,000 it had received for phantom equipment and hired help for Breuning's nonexistent work.

After sixteen years of generous grants from the NIMH, Sprague's next renewal application was first denied, then cut down by eighty percent. He said that if he had been a graduate student or untenured researcher instead of a tenured professor, he would have been "crushed," his career ruined. That is the price of integrity.

Biologist Mansour Samadpour illustrated Sprague's point in 1988, when he was completing his doctorate at the College of Ocean and Fishery Sciences at the University of Washington. He read fabricated data in a recent master's thesis about food toxins and reported it repeatedly to Jack Matches, the professor in charge. When that did no good, his complaint found its way to the dean, who instructed Matches to have the thesis corrected by its author, who was then working on a doctorate. Only sham corrections were made, however.

In 1990 Samadpour accepted a promising job with the Food and Drug Administration, only to have the offer canceled a month later because Matches notified the agency that Samadpour was a trouble-maker. At that point, Samadpour's lawyer complained to the university about retaliation, and an academic investigation began. The university committee found that the thesis in question did not meet minimum standards; neither Matches nor his student understood the key experimental technique in it, there were no laboratory notes, and the student couldn't even recall what his diluting agent had been. But things barely changed. As of 1991, the uncorrectable master's thesis stood firm; its author continued up the academic ladder; Matches went on teaching; and Samadpour realized that he would probably have to change fields in order to have a research career.

In 1992 one of the biggest scientific scams of all was revealed in the book *Teller's War: The Top-Secret Story Behind the Star Wars Deception*. It told how some of our leading nuclear-weapons scientists, led by Edward Teller, intentionally misrepresented the success of research on x-ray lasers and the feasibility of other infeasible weapons, in order to acquire massive funding. Roy Woodruff, a senior researcher at Lawrence Livermore Laboratory, tried through the mid-1980s to warn senior policy-makers that the x-ray lasers were a hoax; but he was opposed, banished to a remote corner of the lab, and finally forced out completely. In 1992 a Pentagon scientist named Aldric Saucier was fired on Valentine's Day after complaining about waste, fraud, and mismanagement in the Star Wars program. But Saucier, who said, "I think it's a duty of a government employee to make sure the taxpayer dollar is well-spent," filed a complaint with Civil Service officials under the Whistle-blowers' Protection Act. He was rehired, but he lost his security clearance.

## The Straight and Narrow

Walter Stewart and Dr. Ned Feder, scientists at the National Institutes of Health in Maryland, have played significant roles in exposing six major cases of scientific misconduct so far—including the case of Nobel prize winner David Baltimore, who is no longer president of Rockefeller University. In spite of the fact that their whistle-blowing had already angered many fellow scientists, they went to work in 1991 to invent a combination of computer programs that they call a "plagiarism machine." This machine detects brief passages that are identical. It can check two documents for sections of word-by-word copying, and it can also check one document against thousands of other articles and books in the same field of study. It is a plagiarizer's worst dream come true.

Within a year of starting work on their machine, Stewart and Feder had already done thousands of comparisons and had discovered a half-dozen cases of what appears to be plagiarism. They say that they are surprised at how individualistic human sentences are: there is extremely little coincidental duplication of even the briefest phrases. Although people who plagiarize usually do so from obscure sources and dead authors, there are glaring exceptions. Stewart and Feder were soon called on to testify at a court case involving a manual of plastic surgery that contains dozens of passages copied directly from a leading plastic-surgery textbook.

Perhaps the happiest case of contemporary whistle-blowing is the one that culminated in 1991. Paul Biddle was a Vietnam veteran who became a certified public accountant and a successful business advisor, then a government auditor. He ended up working for the Office of Naval Research at Stanford University, where he discovered that in ten years $150 to $200 million in federal funds for research had been diverted into frills such as flowers, yachting expenses, a Lake Tahoe retreat, receptions, and luxurious home furnishings. His concern was brushed aside by both Stanford and the Navy, and so he finally got the attention of Representative John Dingell, chairman of the House committee that was supposed to supervise such funding.

Biddle's careful work and Dingell's zeal led to reform at Stanford and at thirteen other universities that were also misusing research funds, including Yale, Dartmouth, the University of Pittsburgh, and Rutgers. Instead of getting fired like many whistle-blowers, Biddle received one of the Navy's highest civilian rewards for meritorious service. He said, "I think probably God is looking for a lot of little people to get America back on the straight and narrow."

> *As scarce as truth is, the supply has always been in excess of the demand.*
>
> —Josh Billings

# CHAPTER 8
# DAMNED, DUPED, OR DELIVERED?

*God regards pure hands, not full.*
—Latin Proverb

Are we willing to sell our souls for the pleasure and power that lies can bring? Have we become unwitting pawns and puppets of deceivers? How to be wise as serpents and harmless as doves, and how to end the ultimate deception.

# HARD-HEARTED CYNICS
## WHO DEVALUE LOVE

*What is a cynic? A man who knows the price of everything
and the value of nothing.*

—Oscar Wilde

Cynics aim to do well rather than to do good. Their Golden Rule is
"Do unto others before they do unto you." It is called the Golden
Rule, they say, because whoever has the gold gets to make the rules.
They know that cheaters often prosper, and good guys finish last.
"Don't call a man a fool," the cynic advises. "Borrow from him. . . ."

When someone asked Willie Sutton why he robbed banks, he
reportedly answered, "That's where the money is." (Smarter people
are different from armed robbers in that they find safer ways to steal.)
In contrast to Willie Sutton's kind of cynical common sense, the wisdom that springs from love is uncommon sense; we have many
names for it, including ethics, goodness, altruism, and honesty.

Since the beginning, human history has been a never-ending
dance of cheaters and cheated. A medieval merchant dampens his
spices to make them heavier, and a California physician files a fortune
in phony auto-insurance claims for imaginary accident victims. The
methods, fashions, stakes, and laws change from one culture to
another, but the basic pattern stays the same: a drama of duplicity.

### Doublespeak and SLOP

Deceptive communication is not a criminal offense, but it is a
kind of murder of the mind. Clear words are honest words, and dou-
ble-dealers prefer double-talk. In fact, people in advertising and public relations jobs are often paid handsome salaries—far more than
preachers and teachers—to befog and befuddle the public.

In 1974, a United States air attaché in Cambodia told reporters,
"You always write it's bombing, bombing, bombing! It's not

bombing! It's air support!" That is when the National Council of Teachers of English started giving its annual Doublespeak Awards for ridiculous euphemisms and verbal deception. There is never any shortage.

Since then the National Transportation Safety Board invented the term "controlled flights into terrain" to replace *plane crashes*. And the Pentagon invented the term "permanent pre-hostility" for *peace*.

In 1991 the Defense Department had a new substitute for the old word *bombing*: "servicing the target." It also substituted "force packages" for *warplanes*. That was also the year of "soft targets" and "hard targets" instead of *people* and *buildings*. There were many honorable mentions in 1991. In Japan, the term "hair-disadvantaged" was being used instead of *bald*. A middle school in Fall City, Washington, was using the term "behavior transition corridors" instead of *hallways*. Some analysts were referring to "meaningful downturn in aggregate output" instead of *recession*. And Senator Ted Stevens of Alaska coined the term "pay-equalization concept" for the senators voting themselves a $23,200 annual *pay raise*.

In 1992 honors went to "high-velocity, multi-purpose air-circulator" for *electric fan*, "unique retail biosphere" for *farmers' market*, "wastewater conveyance facility" for *sewage plant*, "monitored retrievable storage site" for *nuclear fuel dump*, and "immediate permanent incapacitation" for *death*.

The cynicism at the core of Doublespeak is also at the core of sloppy journalism. Norman Bradburn, director of the National Opinion Research Center at the University of Chicago, is especially concerned about the popularity of call-in polls, which are taken seriously by much of the public although they are no more accurate than gossip. Bradburn calls them SLOP surveys, to stand for Self-selected Listener Opinion Polls. At their best, SLOP surveys only reflect opinions of a particular audience; but they can't even be trusted that far.

In 1990, *USA Today* asked callers to use a special 1-900 number to vote for one of two statements: "Donald Trump symbolizes what made America a great country" or "Donald Trump symbolizes the things that are wrong with this country." The tally showed that 81 percent of the 6,406 respondents chose the first statement and only 19 percent chose the second. The resulting *USA Today* headline burbled, "You like him! You really like him! Despite the hype, Trump's a hero to many." But sleuthing uncovered the fact that 72 percent of the favorable calls (well over half of all the calls that came in) came from a certain insurance company building. They were fake calls set up electronically by one person.

Bradburn is resigned to the fact that radio SLOP surveys are here to stay. "Who's going to give up a good show just for the truth?"

## The Pinocchio Syndrome

"Who is going to give up anything just for the truth?" one wonders. According to the 1991 national opinion survey that became the book *The Day America Told the Truth*, 91 percent of Americans lie regularly at work and at home; 86 percent of those surveyed lie regularly to their parents; 75 percent lie regularly to their friends; 69 percent lie regularly to their lovers; and 61 percent lie regularly to their bosses. Almost half say they regularly call in sick when they are well. (Needless to say, people who lie this much might have lied on the survey.)

According to a survey by the Josephson Institute for the Advancement of Ethics, 75 percent of high school students and 50 percent of college students admit to cheating on exams. At Pasadena High School, when one of Jonathan Schorr's pupils got caught cheating on a test, he argued that he deserved full credit for the answers he got right without cheating. Another of Schorr's pupils began a term paper by describing the violent murder of the man he was writing about; when Schorr pointed out that the man had died peacefully of natural causes, the pupil replied, "It's a simulation!"

According to a 1991 Roper survey, nearly one-third of the respondents think it is all right to understate the number of miles they drive each year in order to lower their insurance premiums. The same number think it is all right to inflate one's past salary when applying for a new job. Over one-fourth think it is all right to lie about present debts when applying for a bank loan, and just under one-fourth think it is all right to pad the claim after an accident. One-seventh think it is all right to lie when applying for auto insurance, and the same number think it is all right to lie to an insurance company about the value of a car that was stolen. Over one-tenth think it is all right to stay out of work and to get unneeded medical treatment in order to collect more money after an accident.

When a man says that he is "basically honest," someone has noted, he means that he is honest if it doesn't cost him anything.

"Give me a man who will do a day's work for a day's pay, who will refuse bribes, who will not make up his facts, and who has learned his job." That was C. S. Lewis back in 1943, denouncing the modern idea that there are no true, permanent values and that people can invent new kinds of morality. "Out of this apparently innocent idea," Lewis warned, "comes a disease that will certainly end our species (and, in my view, damn our souls) if it is not crushed." Fifty years later, the disease has not been crushed.

Faking facts, cheating on tests, copying other people's research papers, lying on resumés, lying to get elected to public office, lying to stay in office—Ben Bradlee, longtime editor of the *Washington Post*, laments the increase in lying today: "I'm not talking about exaggerating, misrepresenting, misspeaking. I'm talking about the real McCoy. . . . It seems to me that lying has reached epidemic proportions in recent years and that we've all become immunized to it. Lying has become just another tool for making deals, for selling beer, or war, soap, or candidates."

## The White-Lie House

Bradlee considers the past thirty years of presidential lies alarming and gives a few examples. Richard M. Nixon assured Americans that we were not bombing Cambodia (a neutral country) in 1969, but we were in process of dropping 110,000 tons of bombs there in 3,630 B-52 raids. John F. Kennedy assured the public that he did not have Addison's disease, but in fact he did.

Lyndon B. Johnson claimed that his great-great-grandfather died at the Alamo, and when his biographer asked him about it, he interrupted her. "Goddam it, why must all those journalists be such sticklers for detail? . . . The fact is that my great-great-grandfather died at the battle of San Jacinto, not the Alamo. When I said the Alamo, it was just a slip of the tongue. Anyway, the point is that the battle of San Jacinto was far more important to Texas history than the Alamo." (But Johnson's great-great-grandfather was not at the Alamo or San Jacinto; he traded real estate and died at home in bed.)

Jimmy Carter was an honest man who campaigned with the promise "I'll never lie to you." (A Georgia associate complained, "We'll lose the liar vote.") But Carter urged voters, "Please write. . . .

259

I open every letter myself, and read them all," and the letters were forwarded unopened to his workers in Atlanta.

Ronald Reagan used to claim that during World War II he served overseas as a Signal Corps photographer, and he filmed the horrors of the Nazi death camps. But he never left the United States during World War II and didn't see the Nazi death camps.

George Bush announced his nomination of Clarence Thomas to the Supreme Court with a memorable claim: "The fact that he is black and a minority has nothing to do with the sense that he is the best qualified at this time." (Bradlee comments, "I don't know anyone in America who believes this statement to be true. . . .")

Clarence Thomas himself appeared to be less than candid when he subsequently claimed under oath that he had never once discussed the Roe vs. Wade issue with anyone. If false, this claim amounted to out-and-out perjury; yet Thomas was promptly appointed to the Supreme Court with this possible perjury unexplained and unexplored. More disturbing yet, there was not any explanation about why the far-fetched claim was unexplained. Perhaps American journalists are so cynical now that they take it for granted that an incoming Supreme Court Justice fibs about himself under oath.

Lily Tomlin once said, "No matter how cynical I get, I can't keep up."

### I Cannot Tell a Lie

In the May 5, 1986 issue of *Newsweek*, columnist Meg Greenfield analyzed the combined cynicism and gullibility of American journalists. In the first place, everyone who deals with ordinary officials in Washington knows that there is a vast gulf between what most of them say for the record and what they say privately. Furthermore, the political history of our time has been a series of titillating scandals and sad surprises in high places, showing that people from Vice-President Spiro Agnew to United Nations Secretary General Kurt Waldheim were not what they said they were. (Morality-loving Agnew took envelopes of payoff cash in the vice-presidential office, and humanity-loving Waldheim went to great lengths to cover up his past activities as a Nazi officer.)

According to ethics expert Michael Josephson, we have had more scandals since 1985 than in the previous five decades put together. Meg Greenfield's complaint about her own profession is that each new Washington scandal seems to make journalists more cynical about everything in general, but no more perceptive about things in particular. That is why reporters tend to disbelieve or harass honest people while overlooking major lies and frauds until they hit the fan. Greenfield believes the press should be tougher, more focused, and less trusting of the all-is-well bulletins that they are handed from on high. Our country needs better watchdogs.

Four years after her piece on cynicism, Greenfield cast light upon Washington's favorite sport: the blame game. Although political candidates act eager to shoulder responsibility for the country's security and well-being, once they are elected most of them are obsessively preoccupied with convincing the public that they are not responsible for much at all; others are. This leads to whining, blustering, finger-pointing, and deception. Since most people instinctively realize that being grown up means accepting responsibility, it is no wonder that they don't respect politicians. Although voters may childishly elect politicians who tell them comforting half-truths, they want their office-holders to act grown up.

Ironically, Greenfield says, Parson Weems' pious old story about little George Washington and the cherry tree is a kind of founding document of our politics; telling the truth and taking responsibility for your conduct was what schoolchildren used to learn first about our Founding President. Parson Weems was on to something crucial: in Greenfield's words, "Refusing to take responsibility for one's own actions is a low-grade form of lying."

## What Is a Lie?

Low-grade forms of lying, like low-grade fevers, can be dangerous because they are not taken seriously. We lie with silence, suggestion, or implication as well as with words; we also lie with objects, gestures, positions, and tones of voice. When the Bible says that Satan is the father of lies, it seems to mean all kinds of intentional deceptions, unspoken as well as spoken.

Truly unintentional errors are not lies, and most people would also exclude good-spirited joking and good-spirited teaching. (In both cases, occasional deception is only temporary.) The lies in magic acts and tricky games are not real lies if it is understood at the outset that deception is part of the agenda. The same is true of tricks used to resist criminals, such as hiding valuables inside a fake book on the bookshelf or leaving a light and a radio on to give the impression that someone is home when the house is empty. Most people reason that there is no prohibition against deception in out-and-out war, and some feel that way about international diplomacy as well. Deception is a necessary part of self-protection from burglars of all kinds.

Likewise, standard pleasantries are not real lies; when one says politely "I'm fine, thank you" or "Delighted to meet you," factuality is not an issue. When an atheist says good-bye, he does not mean literally "God be with you," and when a host says, "Es su casa [this house is yours]," he means merely that your visit is welcome, if that. Countless kind customs like these make it sound as if people are healthier, wealthier, handsomer, happier, and in more agreement than they really are. "Putting a good face on things" and "keeping up appearances" are usually matters of courtesy or cheer. For example, the custom of women not wearing wristwatches with evening gowns came from pretending to be in a leisure class not bound by time constraints. (Today some people carry cellular phones just to give the impression that they are as busy as they wish they were.)

In contrast to innocent deceptions, the "mental reservation" lie, a type which many children invent on their own, is a very real lie. Oddly enough, some religious legalists have recommended it; they reason that since God hears all our words, not just those spoken aloud, God will not count our deception as a lie if we secretly think the right words. Thus George Washington could have told his father, "I cannot tell a lie; I did not cut down your cherry tree . . ." and it would have been true because under his breath little George added "last week." This is actually more dishonest than ordinary lying, and it deceives the liar even more than it deceives his listener. It deceives the liar about his own dishonesty, about God's gullibility, and about the nature of truth. It is an exercise in self-deception, much like crossing your fingers behind your back. Crossing your fingers is just the opposite of crossing your heart.

# SOFT-HEADED SUCKERS
# WHO DEVALUE TRUTH

*Each believes easily what he fears and what he desires.*

—Jean de la Fontaine

Snow White is a symbol of gullibility; she bit into a poison apple from the wicked queen because it looked perfectly good. After she eventually revived from her coma, one can safely assume that Snow White was more responsible and didn't bite into any more poison apples. Fairy tales and history are full of cautionary tales like this, but deception comes in so many tempting forms that most of us have been tricked over and over.

Many will admit that they have been stung, but others can't admit it, even to themselves. My competent widowed aunt was suddenly befriended by a charming young couple who loved her lifetime home and furnishings so much that she sold it all to them for about half its worth, in spite of her daughters' frenzied protests. Then she moved into a little apartment next door to her lovely old house and watched while the new owners immediately sold it for its real value and disappeared. "Nothing wrong with that" was my aunt's attitude. The psychological term for this kind of reaction is *denial.*

We are seduced by fear and flattery, and we embrace comfortable illusions. Many of us are putty in the hands of people who seem to be paragons of kindness. That is why ghoulish gypsters sometimes go to cemeteries to meet lonely widows and romance them out of their money. Certain unscrupulous televangelists promise physical healing to donors, even to dead donors. Scientology promises psychological perfection and the secrets of the universe to those who pay their way through its many levels of enlightenment.

Trade schools promise jobs and success to people who long for careers as barbers, bartenders, broadcasters, chauffeurs, computer operators, construction workers, mechanics, or security guards. "I don't think there is one industry as permeated with fraud and misrepresentation as the trade-school industry. The situation is a catastrophe," said Ronald A. Reiter, a California deputy attorney general. Although many trade schools are reputable, others prey on the needy and naïve, who then default on government grants and loans. All too often, the schools' owners end up with millions, the students end up on welfare, and the taxpayers end up with the bill.

In addition to phony trade schools, home-improvement fraud, rent skimming, charity scams, and bogus business opportunities that range from chinchilla breeding to vending machines, the gullible public regularly falls for religious swindles. In the second half of the 1980s more than 15,000 Americans lost over $450 million to a variety of "born-again" and "church-connected" confidence artists who used Bible verses and messages from God to promote investment scams. That's not counting the untold fortune donated to bogus ministries and corrupt charities.

## Noble Lies

It is not only crooks who deceive. Many people practice deception with benign motives, both inside and outside the church. They tell "useful lies" to cause others to believe or do what is good for them. They believe that the end justifies the means.

When philosophy professor Loyal D. Rue spoke at a 1991 symposium of the American Association for the Advancement of Science, he said we need a modern fake religion. Rue assumes that life is dark and meaningless, but that people should be shielded from that knowledge so they will behave well. "It remains for the artists, the poets, the novelists, the musicians, the filmmakers, the tricksters and the masters of illusion to winch us toward our salvation by seducing us into an embrace with a noble lie. . . . It must be a lie that inspires us to give up selfish interests in the service of noble ideals."

In his book *Magic*, Earle J. Coleman expressed the same idea. Although stage magic is a matter of tricks and technical skill, as he admits, he says it provides the audience with a much-needed sense of wonder and belief in the miraculous. "Magic Art in the Grand Style should make men aware of something beyond mere natural appearances, by throwing a rainbow bridge across the abyss separating natural and spiritual consciousness." Coleman evidently believes that ordinary magician's tricks approximate the supernatural.

264

Sometimes such tricks have been used in the church. In 1389 a vial of the clotted blood of St. Januarius surfaced in Naples, Italy, over 1,000 years after his death. The blood liquefies three times a year, and many Italians take this as a great miracle. But in the October 1991 issue of *Nature,* scientists announced that they had duplicated the miraculous blood by mixing chalk with hydrated iron chloride and sprinkling it with salt water; when their mixture was gently shaken, it liquefied. Medieval alchemists could have made this kind of "blood" in 1389. A church spokesman in Naples said that people are welcome to believe in the saint's blood or not, as they see fit. "The main thing is that if it helps somebody to come closer to God, all well and good."

Well and good. In the early 1500s some Dominican priests in Bern, Switzerland, bedecked the face of a statue of the Virgin Mary with drops of varnish to make it appear that she miraculously wept. They also inserted a speaking tube in order to speak through her on special occasions.

## Well and Good?

In 1514 a description of Jesus Christ was published in Venice, Italy, supposedly written by Publius Lentelus, a Roman Procurator of Judea. It was a literary forgery, but it was widely accepted as true. Many thousands in our day have heard this description intoned in a darkened chapel at Knotts Berry Farm, while a ghostly blonde portrait of Jesus was gradually revealed.

> He is a tall man, well shaped and of an amiable and reverend aspect; his hair is of a color that can hardly be matched, falling into graceful curls . . . parted on the crown of his head, running as a stream to the front after the fashion of the Nazarites; his forehead high, large and imposing; his cheeks without spot or wrinkle, beautiful with a lovely red; his nose and mouth formed with exquisite symmetry; his beard, and of a color suitable to his hair, reaching below his chin and parted in the middle like a fork; his eyes bright blue, clear and serene. . . . No man has seen him laugh.

Tourists in Southern California not only enjoy the bogus description of Jesus at Knotts Berry Farm but also enjoy swallows from the

Holy Land that have allegedly been returning to Mission San Juan Capistrano at 7:00 a.m. on St. Joseph's Day, March 19, since the founding of the mission in 1776. (The swallows allegedly fly three times around the original site of the mission, then arrive at its present site.)

Father John O'Sullivan, a mission priest, said he and an old mission Indian named Acu observed the miracle in 1921. The story was first reported in a local newspaper in 1924. O'Sullivan elaborated in a book in 1930 and then started promoting the swallows on the radio. The story soon caught on nationally as an annual newspaper feature, and in 1939 the song "When the Swallows Come Back to Capistrano" sold three million records.

The public likes charming legends. No matter that the swallows come to California from Argentina, not from the Holy Land. And no matter that they come irregularly, to a widespread area. Early arrivers have been explained away as scouts, and those that settle far from the mission have been explained as lost. Happy tourists often mistake the mission's resident pigeons for swallows. As a past mayor of Capistrano once explained, "If it's the nineteenth of March and it flies, it's a swallow."

Some Protestants love any heartwarming stories that seem to authenticate the Bible, whether they are true or not. One of these had it that Charles Darwin renounced evolution on his deathbed, another that Noah's ark has been found at last, and another that the New Jerusalem has been sighted moving this direction in space. Other Protestants have spread the rumor that scientists are keeping secret the discovery of a black hole over the North Pole—because that's where Heaven is located.

Some people insist that the word "true" applies to anything they like, and Americans like stories that affirm their own political as well as religious sentiments. One defender of Oliver Stone's inaccurate historical films reasoned in print this way: "Everyone has his own reality and perception of 'truth.' No one else can fully understand our individual personal reality; therefore, no one else can say our reality is true, or not true."

Actor Kevin Costner said that Stone's film *JFK* "has an emotional truth"; and Stone himself said it "speaks an inner truth." As columnist John Leo commented, "emotional truth" and "inner truth" are terms for fiction. "What I think Stone and his actor are saying here is that it doesn't much matter whether this is literally true or not, so long as it steers culture where we want it to go . . ."

Americans also love stories that authenticate their social sentiments. When news broke in 1991 that the author of the best-selling "Book of the Year," *The Education of Little Tree,* was a vicious, gun-toting white Klansman named Asa instead of a gentle, self-taught Cherokee, the professor who exposed the hoax got calls all day from people who were heartbroken. "People are going to feel betrayed, and they shouldn't blame themselves," he said. "They were betrayed."

Asa's widow first called the news "these diabolical charges," and Asa's agent blamed it on "a family mix-up." But as proof piled up, the widow switched to "it just did not occur to me that you didn't know," and the agent insisted lamely, "To me, it was an honest life." One *Little Tree* fan defended the imposture this way: "I don't see it as a hoax or cheating—if he could actually write a book this beautiful, it actually existed in his mind." (In other words, likable fiction is as true as facts.)

Rennard Strickland, author of the book's glowing introduction, took a similar stand. He said that Carter's identity "does not surprise me or cause great concern. [*Little Tree*] is not the work of a bigot." Another *Little Tree* fan responded more honestly, "It's slightly sickening. . . . You wanted [the book] to be true because it was so sweet and it left you feeling hopeful."

Many frauds are sweet and leave us feeling hopeful. But in the end they are slightly sickening.

# SOFT-HEARTED, HARD-HEADED
# LOVERS OF TRUTH

*A prudent question is one-half of wisdom.*

—Francis Bacon

Which is better—to stay blissfully unaware of the deceptions that riddle our world, or to be cynically aware of them and to stop caring? Charles Spurgeon's advice applies here: "Of two evils, choose neither." We are not supposed to be self-protectively naïve or self-protectively cynical. Christ warned his disciples to be wise as serpents and harmless as doves (Matthew 10:16); and this means to be shrewdly aware, yet personally innocent. Well-informed innocence is the way of ethical wisdom.

Fannie Hurst was a novelist, not a theologian, but she had it right when she said, "It takes a clever man to turn cynic, and a wise man to be clever enough not to."

One of the costs of being wise in this way is that sometimes it obligates a person to act like the Good Samaritan in Jesus' parable. The Samaritan stopped to help someone who was battered, instead of passing by on the other side of the road like the travelers who either refused to see the need or else saw it and hardened their hearts. One can't defend truth every time it is battered, any more than one can die in every ditch; but Christ's disciples are often called upon to defend the truth at one point or another.

Loyalty to truth calls for hard facts, hard thinking, and hard decisions. Unfortunately, there is no national clearing house to monitor scam reports, nor are there any registries that list known frauds, imposters, and perjuries. Therefore Good Samaritans for truth are usually on their own, individually lighting small, flickering candles in what Vernon C. Grounds calls "a world dark with duplicity."

## Centurion Ministries

James McCloskey is a Good Samaritan. He grew up in a well-to-do Presbyterian family in Philadelphia. He dropped out of church, graduated from Bucknell University, served in the Navy in Japan and Vietnam, and eventually became a successful consultant to Japanese firms that were doing business in the United States. Still a bachelor in his thirties, he began attending church again, and the sermons there drove him into the Bible. "As I'm reading the New Testament," he recalls, "I'm really starting to feel that Christ was speaking to me."

In 1979, when he was thirty-seven, he resigned from his excellent job, rented out his house, and drove his Lincoln Continental to Princeton Seminary and moved in. In 1980 he was serving as a student chaplain at Trenton State Prison two days a week. A prisoner who was serving his sixth year of a life sentence for murder convinced McCloskey that he had been falsely convicted. McCloskey started investigating. It took him two-and-a-half years to do it, but his investigation finally set that man free.

By then McCloskey had written his senior thesis about radical discipleship. He described past Christian leaders who "separated themselves from one life and blindly began another at the beckoning of Christ. Their work was both risky and revolutionary. Their personal inner knowledge of God and His Truth led them to challenge existing unjust structures, orders, and systems. It led them to witness against and try to amend, reform, or eradicate terrible injustices."

McCloskey felt God's call to a unique new kind of ministry. Recalling the centurion at the foot of the cross who said of Jesus, "Beyond all doubt, this man was innocent" (Luke 23:47, *New English Bible*), he named his project Centurion Ministries. (*Newsweek* calls McCloskey "The Divine Detective.") He took an office in the basement of a building across the street from Princeton University and was soon getting hundreds of requests from destitute life-sentence prisoners every year. He could only accept a handful of these cases. He charged nothing. In the spring of 1992 he freed his eleventh and twelfth prisoners, Clarence Chance and Benny Powell, who had been in prison for seventeen years for a murder they didn't commit.

Clarence Chance first got McCloskey's attention in about 1987 with a letter that said:

> I've written numbers, numbers, and NUMBERS of letters like the one I am going to write you now. I've written to newspapers, *60 Minutes*, NAACP, law firms, senators, *20/20*,

Phil Donahue, magazines, the FBI, Jesse Jackson and other organizations trying to arrest someone's interest in my case, with hopes of getting them involved to the point of conducting a thorough investigation that would turn up crucial evidence to set me free.

I couldn't have killed this guy. . . .

I was incarcerated in the custody of the L.A. County Sheriff's dept., IN JAIL!!! when this crime happened!

In McCloskey's opinion, about 10 percent of the accused who go to jury trial are wrongly convicted. Some common reasons for this are incorrect eyewitness identification, coerced testimony, bogus jailhouse confessions, incompetent defense attorneys, police errors, corruption, and overlooked evidence. In the case of Clarence Chance, it seems that all of these factors played a part.

Chance's attorney said of McCloskey, "He's as close to a saint as any human being I've ever met." One of the men he freed earlier said, "When I describe Mr. McCloskey, I always say the dictionary don't have words to describe how good is that man." A leading Philadelphia defense attorney said of him, "He investigates like no one I've ever met, and I've come into contact with top-flight police investigators, federal investigators, and private investigators. He's single-minded in his dedication, not taken in by a sob story, and wedded to one thing—the truth."

Across the Atlantic, a retired Church of Scotland minister named A. Q. Morton developed a *cusum* chart form of computerized stylometric analysis to determine who really wrote what. Morton analyzed the alleged confession of Tommy McCressen, who had already served over a year in Old Bailey for his part in the £26,000 armed robbery of a post office. Morton found that the confession that had led to McCressen's conviction was not by McCressen; it was made up of sentences by one of the detective constables who handled the case. Thanks to this new evidence, the English Court of Appeal reversed McCressen's conviction in 1991, and he was a free man.

No doubt some law enforcement officers have intentionally framed innocent people as an act of cruelty, just as others have intentionally framed guilty people as a shortcut to justice. Is it ever right to lie for a good cause?

## From Tyndale to Twain

Mark Twain was only half joking when he said, "One ought always to lie, when one can do good by it." John Wesley absolutely disagreed: "I would not tell one lie to save the souls of all the world." St. Augustine taught that no Christian should ever tell a lie; although some lies are far worse than others, and he found it hard to condemn anyone who lied to save a life, all lies are wrong. This is because Satan is the great deceiver, the father of lies; Jesus is the way, the truth, and the life. According to Augustine, "One never errs more safely than when one errs by too much loving the truth."

Eleven-hundred years after St. Augustine, a Christian named Augustine Packington deceived the Bishop of London for the sake of truth; Packington was a London merchant who was a secret friend of William Tyndale. The Bishop was angry because Tyndale had translated the New Testament into English and had smuggled thousands of copies into England from Belgium. Packington told the Bishop that he knew who some of Tyndale's distributors were, and that he could buy up all the unsold copies for the Bishop to destroy. This delighted the Bishop, and it delighted Tyndale even more. With Packington's help, the Bishop bought and burned the Bibles; and Tyndale used the much-needed money to bring out a larger, better edition. England soon received Tyndale's improved Bible, thanks to the fact that Packington had tricked the Bishop. Tyndale was later caught and executed, but his Bible spread through England and eventually became the basis for the King James or Authorized Version.

Dietrich Bonhoeffer, a German pastor and theologian who was killed by the Nazis, taught that being truthful before God sometimes justifies lying to human beings. He gave the example of a boy whose teacher asked him in front of the class whether it was true that his father came home drunk at night. (There are no right answers to some wrong questions.) The boy answered "no" in order to protect his parents. Although the answer was literally untrue, Bonhoeffer believed it was more true in God's sight than a "yes" would have been; the boy was answering to the best of his ability the teacher's underlying question about where his loyalty lay. He did not lie about that. His first loyalty was to his family, not his school.

Needless to say, this kind of reasoning requires immense wisdom and integrity. Bonhoeffer almost seemed to praise lying.

Mark Twain had to give a humorous after-dinner speech in praise of lying once, and he included a sober idea: "Lying is universal—we all do it; we all must do it. Therefore, the wise thing is for us diligently to train ourselves to lie thoughtfully, judiciously; to lie with a good object, and not an evil one; to lie for others' advantage, and not our own; to lie healingly, charitably, humanely, not cruelly, hurtfully, maliciously . . ."

Changing gears, he continued, "to lie gracefully and graciously, not awkwardly and clumsily; to lie firmly, frankly, squarely, with head erect, not haltingly, tortuously, with pusillanimous mien, as being ashamed of our high calling. Then shall we be rid of the rank and pestilent truth that is rotting the land; then shall we be great and good and beautiful, and worthy dwellers in a land where even benign Nature habitually lies, except when she promises execrable weather. . . ."

"Joking aside," he continued, "I think there is much need of wise examination into what sorts of lies are best and wholesomest to be indulged, seeing we must all lie and do all lie, and what sorts it may be best to avoid. . . ." Twain was in a way more honest than the scrupulous Christian who used to momentarily step just outside his office door at a signal from his secretary, so she could say to an unwelcome caller, "He's not in his office." Twain would have considered that maneuver little different from the "mental reservations" lie.

## The Truth about Self-deception

Mark Twain also said, "When a person cannot deceive himself the chances are against his being able to deceive other people." It seems that fraudulence, gullibility, and self-deception are closely related. And the greatest of these is self-deception. As eighteenth-century economist Adam Smith put it, "Self-deceit, this fatal weakness of mankind, is the source of half the disorders of life."

Cornelius Plantinga, Jr., of Calvin Theological Seminary, uses what went on in England in the 1930s as a vivid example of self-deception. In those days, the few people who warned about Nazi aggression were commonly considered hysterical alarmists. Winston Churchill sounded the alarm year after year, but few others in England could bear to think that Germany was in the hands of dangerous criminals. Still reeling from World War I, people clung to the idea that they were safe from the threat of another war, and they acted accordingly. "Fifty years later, we know some of the cost of that self-deception."

As Plantinga reminds us, self-deception goes back to Adam and Eve. They were dupes of the serpent, and dupes of themselves. They hoodwinked themselves into thinking that they could outsmart God.

"Off it goes, down the ages—the history of self-deception in a cast of thousands. Aaron cannot imagine how the golden calf popped right into existence. David is indignant that a rich man should seize a poor man's lamb. Peter is outraged at the suggestion that he is capable of denying our Lord." All three were no doubt sincere—sincerely self-deluded.

Albert Einstein reportedly remarked once to psychotherapist Fritz Perls that two things are infinite: the universe and human stupidity. Perls corrected him: stupidity is not so widespread as playing stupid. He meant that we choose to be gullible about ourselves because it is easier and more comfortable than being wise.

Like Aaron, David, and Peter, we would like to think we are more faithful, more benevolent, or more courageous than we really are. We like to sustain ourselves with a delicious sense of adequacy.

It is human to want to feel both good and safe. We needed that feeling as babies, and our parents should have given it to us. But it seems to me that in order to keep on feeling good and safe, humans often make themselves very bad and unsafe. Most destructive and self-destructive behavior is just a shortcut to feeling good and safe; and as C. S. Lewis said, shortcuts often lead to very dangerous places.

M. Scott Peck points out in *People of the Lie* that truly evil people almost always appear to feel calm, in control, and on top of things. "What possesses them?" Peck asks; and he answers "fear." They are hounded by such chronic fear of their own evil that life has become a gigantic pretense.

In order to deny their imperfection, truly evil people avoid self-examination. They prefer to walk in spiritual darkness rather than light. They never admit that they are sinful and frightened.

The rest of us have milder forms of that same disorder. Therefore, we need to examine ourselves fairly often to confess our sins and imperfections, checking ourselves for the telltale whitewash that makes us feel good and safe when we are not. Plantinga claims that phrases like the following signal a probable need for confession: "I'm only human," "Everybody does it," "I was provoked," "I did what I had to do," "I did this for your own good," "Nobody is hurt by what I do," "I was only following orders," and "Nobody's perfect."

A little of this regular self-examination is essential, but C. S. Lewis warned that very much of it is wrong. We should look at our sins no longer than it takes to recognize them and repent, because concentrating upon either our faults or our improvements means concentrating upon ourselves. The less of that, the better. In heaven, he says, we will each be like a room full of God and our fellow creatures, not a room full of self; yet we will be more genuinely ourselves there than ever before. I think we will overflow with the heavenly goodness and safety that we were born desiring.

In the meantime, although our capacity for self-deception is almost fathomless, as Plantinga says, so is God's capacity for forgiveness and healing.

> *If we claim to be without sin, we deceive ourselves and the truth is not in us.*
>
> — I John 1:8

> *If we confess our sins, he is faithful and just and will forgive us our sins and purify us from all unrighteousness.*
>
> —I John 1:9

> *For him who confesses, shams are over and realities have begun.*
>
> —William James

# A HOAXER'S EPILOGUE

Early in 1992 I went on an impromptu spoofing binge. I had an old friend named Steve in England who somehow decided that my published charges about certain literary and document forgeries were insincere. The fact that I have a history of successful forgery detection meant nothing, in his opinion. For over three years he hounded me to admit in print that he was right and my forgery charges were wrong. He insisted that he could easily recognize a forgery if he ever saw one.

Exasperated, I finally forged a loony letter to Steve from a world-famous forger I had often told him about—Mark Hofmann, who was in Utah State Prison for murder. In the return address I used an old euphemism for a state prison—Utah State Technical College. "Mark Hofmann" assured Steve that Kathryn Lindskoog was ignorant about forgeries and that Germany's famous forged Hitler diaries are genuine. "Hofmann" included as "proof" a sample of forged Hitler handwriting, claiming that it was genuine. (I had photocopied that forged Hitler handwriting from the *Los Angeles Times*.) To my dismay, Steve not only believed the Hofmann letter, but he published the whole thing in his literary journal, "genuine" Hitler handwriting and all. Steve warned me in a triumphant February 20 letter that with Hofmann on his side he was tempted to sue my publisher.

Steve kept adding to the letter, and so it did not arrive until mid-March, shortly before April Fool's Day. Therefore, instead of simply explaining that I had forged Hofmann's letter as a satire, I sent a second one contradicting part of the first one. The second letter bore the actual return address of Utah State Prison and concluded with a wink and a nudge: "I probably won't write again during the current term because I won't have any free time." By this time, other readers of Steve's journal had convinced him that Hofmann was a convicted forger, as I had claimed all along; but Steve was undaunted. He told me that Hofmann's guilt proved Hofmann's expertise.

Next Steve received from someone anonymous a Xerox copy of a *Los Angeles Times* article by consumer-advocate Ralph Nader, stating that Hofmann was right and I was wrong. (With one of the fonts on

275

my personal computer I imitated *Los Angeles Times* print; then I fit the fake article into part of a real newspaper page and Xeroxed it there. It was easy.) A few days later I sent Steve a Xerox of the *Times* letters column with an intriguing letter from an imaginary Florence Jacobsen of Glendora, California, in response to Nader's article. This was whimsical play.

Before long Steve received four more Xeroxed letters from the *Los Angeles Times*, a couple of Xeroxed magazine items, and pleasant personal letters from several strangers including Clifford Irving, the famous Howard Hughes forger, and Konrad Kujau, Germany's famous Hitler forger. (I had repeatedly told Steve about Irving and Kujau.) This is what "Kujau" told Steve:

> It has been my recent pleasure to receive a copy of your Journal No. 77 from a concerned reader, and now I want to object to a statement there about forgery and related matters. Like your colleague J. Sawyer, I am a Professional Graphologist as well as an artist, and I challenge your contributor K. Lindskog [sic] to prove her claim that any members of our profession were in error. Those who make forgery charges must be held to account and not allowed to circulate innuendoes and false implications about matters with which they are essentially unacquainted or uninformed. Although Americans may think that the matter is one of frivolity, the matter is a serious one in Europe. "Durch Schaden wird man klug." (One learns painfully to avoid Error.)
>
> I have not examined the [questioned] manuscript, but I would like to do so although as a Lutheran I prefer to read ... books in German. I can assure you that an unfounded assumption of forgery is actionable under German Law. The courts will not look kindly upon published statements, for which I am certain that you are not responsible if you do not agree with them in your Journal, and most particularly if you make a point of disavowing them. Historical Documents cannot be allowed to be attacked by the whim of uninformed outsiders.

276

Steve also got a preposterous April 10 letter on heavy white stationery from a nonexistent Oregon attorney named Bates, calling his bluff:

> I have been retained temporarily by Multnomah Press of Portland, Oregon, to ascertain the current state of preliminary procedures for action as described in your February 20, 1992, letter to Kathryn Lindskoog of Orange, California. That letter, which is now formally registered in the Office of Fraud and Libel Jurisprudence in the State of Oregon, has served legal notice (under aegis of the Informal Complaints Act of 1979) that you are now launching a libel suit against Multnomah Press. Your attorney will be billed for the standard $20 filing fee.
>
> In the aforementioned letter of February 20, 1992, you describe your plan to call upon either J. Sawyer or Mr. Hofmann as witnesses for the prosecution. You also express your intention to withdraw these witnesses and your entire suit if attorneys of Multnomah Press agree to compensate you adequately for alleged damages. (You did not specify the "whacking" amount.) Because of the Statute of Limitations and the strong possibility of a countersuit, it is essential that all concerned parties promptly expedite negotiations in order to avoid a possible $1,500 fine for frivolous litigation under Statute 110–B114.
>
> Please provide brief answers to the following questions as soon as possible:
>
> 1. Are you prepared to prove in court that [a work in question] was not forged?
>
> . . .
>
> 5. What do you consider an adequate settlement in this case?
>
> Please submit also at your convenience your attorney's name and address and the status of his preliminary preparations as of April 30, 1992.

I figured that Steve would follow his usual course and consult his friendly neighbor who was a retired attorney, or else he would write to the imaginary Bates; either way, he would find out that Bates was a fake, and I was the only possible source. All in all, I secretly sent

Steve a flurry of fourteen forgeries in April, full of clues that the series was a joke. I thought he would have to catch on fast.

But he didn't show anyone the attorney's letter and didn't answer it. Instead, he notified me that he hadn't really intended to sue. In the meantime, he was so excited about Florence Jacobsen that he sent her revelations on to the *Guardian*, one of the best newspapers in England, for a feature. Because the spoof was out of hand, on May 11, I sent a confession, an apology, and a list of the fourteen forgeries to both Steve and the *Guardian*. Unfortunately, the *Guardian*'s May 26 article about my confession didn't make it very clear that the forgeries were only a spoof, and Steve's August journal hinted broadly that they were an alarming exhibition of American lawlessness.

In his August journal, Steve printed photocopies of his bogus letters from Konrad Kujau and Attorney Bates with the warning "Forged" superimposed beside them nine times in large black letters. But in the letters section of the same journal, he published a photocopy of a letter from a frequent correspondent of his without any such warning. I had made the original look very convincing, and he must have dismissed my May confession that I forged it. The high point of my brief career as a forger came when the purported author of that forged letter, the actual aunt of C. S. Lewis's two stepsons, read Steve's August journal and wrote to me to complain about my previous foolish hoax without realizing that her own letter to Steve was forged.

Thus I learned that although it is surprisingly easy to toss off silly forgeries, it is hard to avoid doing accidental harm with them and absolutely impossible to overestimate human gullibility.

# Appendix:
# Biblical Wisdom about Deception

From beginning to end, the Bible is full of specific stories about the users of deceit. Genesis alone has all of these: the snake lying to Eve, Cain pretending that he didn't know what happened to Abel, Sarah denying to an angel that she laughed behind the tent door, Abraham claiming that Sarah was his sister, Jacob tricking his father and cheating his brother, Jacob tricked into marrying the wrong woman, Laban and Jacob both deceiving each other, Rachel tricking Laban, Dinah's brothers slaying the family of the man who wanted to marry her, Jacob's sons deceiving him about Joseph's death, Potiphar's wife pretending that Joseph assaulted her, Tamar tricking her father-in-law into getting her pregnant, and Joseph making it look as if Banjamin had stolen a special silver cup.

The entire Old Testament is full of tricks, illusion, and self-deception—from the fatal first trick in the Garden of Eden (in Genesis 3) to the willful public ignorance that grieved the prophets: "These are rebellious people, deceitful children, children unwilling to listen to the Lord's instruction. They say to the seers, 'See no more visions!' and to the prophets, 'Give us no more visions of what is right! Tell us pleasant things, prophesy illusions.'" (Isaiah 30:9–10)

The New Testament is also full of tricks, illusion, and self-deception—from the wise men tricking Herod (in Matthew 2) to John's final warning at the close of Revelation: "Outside are the dogs . . . everyone who loves and practices falsehood. . . . I warn everyone who hears the words of the prophecy of this book: If anyone adds anything to them [forgery], God will add to him the plagues described in this book. And if anyone takes words away from this book of prophecy [dishonest editing], God will take away from him his share in the tree of life and in the holy city, which are described in this book. He who testifies to these things says, 'Yes, I am coming soon.' Amen. Come, Lord Jesus. The grace of the Lord Jesus be with God's people. Amen." (Revelation 22:14–21)

In addition to the Bible's array of stories about truth and falsehood in action, and the overarching theme that truth will triumph, the Bible offers memorable words about deception. Here are examples from the middle of Proverbs 20:

Many a man claims to have unfailing love, but a faithful man who can find? (v. 6)

Differing [false] weights and differing [false] measures—the Lord detests them both. (v. 10)

Even a child is known by his actions, by whether his conduct is pure and right. (v. 11)

"It's no good, it's no good!" says the buyer; then off he goes and boasts about his purchase. (v. 14)

Food gained by fraud taste sweet to man, but he ends up with a mouth full of gravel. (v. 17)

The following list of Bible passages about deception is far from complete, but it can be used for a helpful survey.

**Genesis**
3:13
21:23
27:12
27:35–36
29:25
31:7
31:20–35
34:13
37:31
44:1–13

**Exodus**
5:9
8:8–29
20:16

22:9
23:1–8

**Leviticus**
6:2–4
19:11
19:16
19:35–36
25:17

**Numbers**
13:32
14:36
25:18

**Deuteronomy**
5:20

19:16–20
22:13–19
24:14–15
25:13–16

**Joshua**
7:11
9:4–23

**Judges**
16:4–19

**1 Samuel**
19:11–17
21:13
28:8–12

**2 Samuel**
3:25
13:5–13
19:27

**1 Kings**
13:18
14:2–5
20:38–40
22:20–22
22:29–30

**2 Kings**
10:19
18:29–32

**Nehemiah**
6:1–4

**Esther**
2:20

**Job**
6:28–30
12:16
13:4–5
15:35
31:4–6
36:18

**Psalms**
5:6–9
7:14
10:7
12:1–2
26:4
32:2
43:1
52:2–4
55:11
58:3
62:4
64:2–4
101:4–7
119:118
120:2
140:11

**Proverbs**
6:13–14
8:7–8
11:1
12:5
12:17–20
14:17

19:1
20:8–17
23:1–3
26:24–28
28:10

**Ecclesiastes**
5:5–6

**Isaiah**
9:14–16
28:15
30:10–13
33:15–16
36:14
37:10
59:3–4

**Jeremiah**
3:10
4:10
6:13
7:4, 8
9:3–5
17:9–10
20:7–10
27:10–14
29:8–9
29:30–31
37:9
49:16

**Lamentations**
2:14

**Ezekiel**
18:12
22:29

**Daniel**
8:23–25
11:21–25

**Hosea**
7:3
10:2
11:12
12:7

**Amos**
8:5

**Obadiah**
3
7

**Micah**
2:11
3:5
6:12

**Zephania**
3:13

**Zechariah**
8:17
10:4
13:2–4

**Malachi**
3:5

**Matthew**
2:16
15:19
24:4–5
24:11
24:24
27:64
28:12–13

**Mark**
12:15
14:56

**Luke**
19:8
20:20
21:8

**Acts**
13:10
23:13–15
27:30–32

**Romans**
1:29
3:13
7:11
16:18

**1 Corinthians**
5:9–11

**2 Corinthians**
4:2
11:3
11:13
11:26
12:16

**Galatians**
1:6

**281**

2:4
6:3–7

**Ephesians**
4:14
4:22–25
5:6
6:11

**Colossians**
2:3–7

**1 Thessalonians**
2:3

**2 Thessalonians**
2:3
2:9–10

**1 Timothy**
1:10
4:2

**2 Timothy**
3:12–13

**Titus**
1:10

**Hebrews**
3:13

**James**
1:16–17
1:22
1:26

**2 Peter**
2:1–3
3:15–16

**1 John**
1:8
2:26
3:7–10

**2 John**
7

**Revelation**
2:20
12:9
13:14
18:23
19:20
20:3–10

What does the Bible say about the power of deception today?

*Destructive forces are at work in the city;*
*threats and lies never leave its streets.*

Psalm 55:11

*The heart is deceitful above all things*
*and beyond cure*
*Who can understand it?*
*"I the Lord search the heart*
*and examine the mind,*
*to reward a man according to his conduct,*
*according to what his deeds deserve."*

Jeremiah 17:9–10

*To God belong wisdom and power;*
*counsel and understanding are his...*
*To him belong strength and victory;*
*both deceived and deceiver are his.*

Job:12:13, 16

# Recommended Reading

*Anastasia: The Riddle of Anna Anderson* by Peter Kurth (Boston: Little Brown, 1986). The story of the woman who claimed to be Anastasia, daughter of Czar Nicholas and Czarina Alexandra of Russia.

*Archaeological Fakes* by Adolph Rieth, translated from the German by Diana Imber (New York: Praeger, 1967). Everything from shrunken heads to golden cups; from cave paintings to a Dutch history document that dates back to the flood.

*The Balloon Craze in France, 1783–1799: A Study in Popular Science* by James Martin Hunn (Vanderbilt University Ph.D. dissertation, 1982, available from University Microfilms International). A bizarre bit of European history and some peculiar hoaxes that fooled Paris.

*Betrayers of the Truth* by William Broad and Nicholas Wade (New York: Simon and Schuster, 1982). Cases of scientific fraud spanning 2,000 years, and today's scientists who "lie, cheat, and steal and who either embellish, fabricate, fudge, trim, cook, or otherwise finagle their data to further their careers, their power, or their views."

*The Book of Lies* by M. Hirsch Goldberg (New York: William Morrow, 1990). A rollicking collection of all kinds of deceptions that are part of our history and our daily lives.

*The Book of Rotters* by Alan Bold and Robert Giddings (Edinburgh: Mainstream Publishing, 1985). The stories of over seventy dastardly villains, including some eminent forgers, plagiarists, and swindlers.

*The C. S. Lewis Hoax* by Kathryn Lindskoog (Portland: Multnomah Press, 1988). The biographical fakery and literary forgery dominating Lewis affairs since his death in 1963.

*The Case of the Midwife Toad* by Arthur Koestler (New York: Random House, 1972). Koestler's exploration of a scientific hoax and its significance.

*The Catalog of Lost Books* by Tad Tuleja (New York: Fawcett, 1989). A collection of arcane titles and authors of nonexistent great books such as *Cacophony of the Spheres* (1651) by Guy-Marine Ratatouille, useful for intellectual fakery.

# RECOMMENDED READING

*The Compleat Practical Joker* by H. Allen Smith (New York: William Morrow, 1980). A survey of famous and infamous practical jokes by the self-appointed High Commissioner of Practical Jokery.

*Counterfeiter: The Story of a Master Forger* by Charles Black and Michael Horsnell (New York: St. Martin's Press, 1989). The career of a talented crook who invented better ways of forging British and American currency in the 1970s.

*Darwin on Trial* by Philip E. Johnson (Washington, D.C.: Regnery/Gateway, 1991). A secular cross-examination of the ideology of Darwinism, designed to expose its intellectual fraudulence.

*Doublespeak* by William Lutz (New York: Harper & Row, 1989). The funny and frightening use of language to deceive rather than to inform.

*The Education of Little Tree* by Forrest Carter (Albuquerque: University of New Mexico Press, 1986). Tender autobiography of a Cherokee orphan boy, first published in 1976 and chosen as Book of the Year by American Booksellers Association in 1991. Revealed in 1976 and again in 1991 as a fraud invented by notorious white Ku Klux Klansman Asa Carter.

*Facts & Fallacies* by Reader's Digest (Pleasantville, N.Y.: Reader's Digest Association, 1988). A large illustrated collection of strange and unusual information, including the stories of several major forgeries and deceptions.

*Faking It in America: Barry Minkow and the Great ZZZZ Best Scam* by Joe Domanick (Chicago: Contemporary Books, 1989). How a zany California teenager became a fake carpet-cleaning tycoon, then bilked investors out of millions.

*False Prophets: Fraud and Error in Science and Medicine* by Alexander Kohn (New York: Basil Blackwell, 1986). Plagiarism, forgery, suppression of the truth, "massaged" data, and phantom experiments punctuating the history of science.

*Fake? The Art of Deception* by Mark Jones, ed. (Berkeley: University of California, 1990). Forgeries in politics, religion, and science through the centuries. This large, lively, richly illustrated book by nearly 100 contributors is the result of a special exhibit at the British Museum.

*Flim-Flam! Psychics, ESP, Unicorns and Other Delusions* by James Randi (Buffalo: Prometheus Books, 1982). A rollicking exposé of false claims that range from psychic surgery to the Bermuda Triangle, from levitation to pyramidology.

*Forgers and Critics: Creativity and Duplicity in Western Scholarship* by Anthony Grafton (Princeton, N.J.: Princeton University Press, 1990). A scholarly overview and analysis of over 2,500 years of serious forgery and detection in Western civilization.

## RECOMMENDED READING

*Forgers and Forgeries* by W. G. Constable (New York: Harry N. Abrams, 1954). An excellent 23-page booklet from the "Art Treasures of the World" series, analyzing the sources and qualities of forgeries, with many examples.

*The Further Adventures of Sherlock Holmes* by Richard Lancelyn Green (New York: Penguin Books, 1985). A collection of Sherlock Holmes stories written by various authors after the death of Arthur Conan Doyle, including a bold literary hoax.

*A Gathering of Saints* by Robert Lindsey (New York: Simon and Schuster, 1988). The story of Mark Hofmann's forged historical documents and the Utah murders that resulted. This book is an exciting way to learn about the complexities of document authentication.

*The Great American Hoax* by Alan Abel (New York: Trident Press, 1966). The story of the "Society for Indecency of Naked Animals," shows how easy it was for a professional comic to hoax much of the U.S. and England about the need to defend morality by putting clothes on animals.

*Great Crimes* by H. R. F. Keating (Stamford, Conn.: Longmeadow Press, 1991). Illustrated descriptions of almost 50 famous crimes, including frauds.

*The Great Eskimo Vocabulary Hoax* by Laura Martin and Geoffrey K. Pullum (Chicago: Univ. of Chicago Press, 1991). The development of the contemporary academic myth that Eskimos have many words for snow.

*Great Exploration Hoaxes* by David Roberts (San Francisco: Sierra Club Books, 1982). Ten famous explorations spanning 450 years that have turned out to be false. The author includes among others Cabot, Hennepin, Cook, Peary, and Byrd.

*Great Hoaxes and Famous Imposters* by Carlson Wade (Middle Village, N.Y.: Jonathan David Publishers, 1976). Amazing tales of twenty hoaxers in a light, popular style.

*Hermit of Peking: The Hidden Life of Sir Edmund Backhouse* by Hugh Trevor-Roper (New York: Penguin, 1976). Shocking facts about an invincible criminal and pornographer who was highly honored by the University of Oxford.

*Hoaxes* by Curtis D. MacDougall (New York: Dover, 1958). An updated classic first published in 1940, "a compendium of accounts of how forgers, swindlers, imposters and other hoaxers have thrived on human gullibility through many centuries."

*How To Lie with Statistics* by Darrell Huff (New York: Norton, 1954). How to avoid being duped by impressive but deceptive statistical nonsense.

*Impostors in the Temple* by Martin Anderson (New York: Simon & Schuster, 1992). A complaint about American universities, including behind-the-scenes price-fixing, misuse of government research funds, and athletic abuse.

*Inventing Reality: The Politics of the Mass Media* by Michael Parenti (New York: St. Martin's Press, 1986). A critique of today's misleading news, entertainment, and advertising from the point of view of the political left.

*Journey* by Robert and Suzzanne Massie (New York: Knopf, 1975). The inspiring story of a family that struggles successfully against hemophelia, but struggles unsuccessfully against "helpers" who endanger hemopheliacs for their own gain.

*Legends, Lies, and Cherished Myths of American History* by Richard Shenkman (New York: William Morrow, 1988). A quick survey of hundreds of misconceptions about the heritage of the United States.

*Lies, Deception and Truth* by Ann E. Weiss (Boston: Houghton Mifflin, 1988). How trickery operates in both nature and human affairs, with conflicting ideas about how to honor truth in practice. Brevity, clarity, and simplicity turn this complex material into easy reading.

*The Life and Death of Rochester Sneath: A Youthful Frivolity* by Humphry Berkeley (London: Davis-Poynter Ltd. 1974). The actual correspondence between Berkeley and the distinguished victims of his whimsical 1948 hoax.

*Lying: Moral Choice in Public and Private Life* by Sissela Bok (New York: Pantheon, 1978). A sober, scholarly survey of historically significant definitions, analyses, condemnations, and justifications of lying.

*Magic: A Reference Guide* by Earle J. Coleman (New York: Greenwood Press, 1987). The history, psychology, and techniques of magical trickery, with many sources.

*Making People Disappear: An Amazing Chronicle of Photographic Deception* by Alain Jaubert (New York: Permagon-Brassey, 1989). Photographic propaganda and the specific techniques that totalitarian regimes have used to produce faked photos.

*Media Hoaxes* by Fred Fedler (Ames: Iowa State Univ. Press, 1989). The history of media hoaxes, emphasizing journalism.

*Medicine Show: Conning People and Making Them Like It* by Mary Calhoun (New York: Harper & Row, 1976). A brief and easy overview of the marvelous traveling frauds who entertained and sold fake medicine across the United States until World War II.

*The Myth of Neurosis: Overcoming the Illness Excuse* by Garth Wood (New York: Harper & Row, 1986). How an uneasy conscience is vastly different from genuine psychological illness, and why the best cure is hardship, duty, love, and sacrifice.

# RECOMMENDED READING

*One Fairy Story Too Many* by John Ellis (Chicago: Univ. of Chicago Press, 1985). How the Brothers Grimm faked their collection of German fairy tales for political reasons, and how repeated proofs of the sloppy hoax have all been ignored.

*Outrage: The Story Behind the Tawana Brawley Hoax* by Robert McFadden, et. al. (New York: Bantam, 1990). The sordid facts about a notorious 1987 abduction and rape that never happened, and the political charlatans behind it.

*The Oxford Book of Villains* by John Mortimer (New York: Oxford Univ. Press, 1992). A famous detective novelist's collection of infamous crooks, criminals, con-men, and traitors from fact and fiction.

*People of the Lie* by M. Scott Peck (New York: Simon and Schuster, 1983). A psychiatrist's analysis of the reality and deceptiveness of evil in people who are secretly cruel.

*The Pleasures of Deception* by Norman Moss (New York: Reader's Digest, 1977). An especially delightful survey of all kinds of astonishing hoaxes and their perpetrators, with perceptive reflections.

*The Predatory Society: Deception in the American Marketplace* by Paul Blumberg (New York: Oxford Univ. Press, 1989). A sociologist's survey of how customers are cheated, based largely upon reports from workers in all kinds of businesses.

*The Scholar Adventurers* by Richard D. Altick (New York: Macmillan, 1960). A rogues' gallery of fascinating fakers in literature, science, and other fields of academic endeavor.

*Signs of the Times: Deconstruction and the Fall of Paul de Man* by David Lehman (New York: Poseidon, 1991). An exposé of the moral bankruptcy of a fashionable literary philosophy and its originators.

*Stealing into Print: Fraud, Plagiarism and Misconduct in Scientific Publishing* by Marcel C. LaFollette (Berkeley: University of California Press, 1992). A stunning survey of past and present sins in scholarly publishing, from a knowledgeable science editor.

*Stolen Words: Forays into the Origins and Ravages of Plagiarism* by Thomas Mallon (New York: Houghton Mifflin, 1989). An outrageous and amusing look at literary crime, with a variety of examples, past and present.

*The Technological Bluff* by Jacques Ellul, translated by Jorce Main Hanks (Grand Rapids: Eerdmans, 1990). Ellul's warning that people are easily seduced into thinking that powerful new equipment can solve all our problems, when in fact advanced technology is fragile and much of what it produces serves no useful purpose.

*They Never Said It: A Book of Fake Quotes, Misquotes, and Misleading Attributions* by Paul F. Boller and John George (New York: Oxford Univ. Press, 1989). Hundreds of popular quotations that are attributed to wrong sources.

*Teaching Science in a Climate of Controversy* by the Committee for Integrity in Science Education (Ipswich, Mass.: American Scientific Affiliation, 1989). An overview of scientific evidence about human origins for high school teachers, to help to avoid omissions, overstatements, and distortions.

*This Solemn Mockery: The Art of Literary Forgery* by John Whitehead (London: Arlington Books, 1973). An overview of Chatterton, Ireland, Psalmanazar, Major Byron, MacPherson, Wise, and other major forgers, plus speculation about the identity of the author of the works of Shakespeare.

*Thomas Chatterton: The Family Romance of the Imposter-Poet* by Louise J. Kaplan (New York: Atheneum, 1988). A brilliant hoaxer who committed suicide at 17, considered from a psychoanalytic point of view.

*The Unreality Industry: The Deliberate Manufacturing of Falsehood and What It Is Doing to Our Lives* by Ian I. Mitroff and Warren Bennis (New York: Birch Lane Press, 1989). The media's increasing pseudo-reality, which works like a mind-altering drug and lulls the public into "collective dumbness."

*The Vanishing Hitchhiker: American Urban Legends and Their Meaning* by Jan Harold Brunvand (New York: W. W. Norton, 1981); *The Mexican Pet: More "New" Urban Legends and Some Favorites* (1986); *Curses, Broiled Again: The Hottest Urban Legends Going* (1989). Three collections of popular false rumors from a student of American folklore.

*Why Kids Lie: How Parents Can Encourage Truthfulness* by Paul Ekman (New York: Scribner's, 1989). Unexciting, down-to-earth observations about ordinary family life.

*You Must Be Dreaming* by Barbara Noel and Kathryn Watterson (New York: Poseidon Press, 1992). The shocking revelation of how one of the world's most respected psychiatrists intentionally deceived, drugged, and defiled trustful female patients.